Revision WorkBook

Tort

Fourth edition edited by

Dr E D Pitchfork BSc, PhD, CChem, FRSC,
Cert, Ed (F & HE), Barrister-at-Law

HLT Publications

HLT PUBLICATIONS
200 Greyhound Road, London W14 9RY

First Edition 1990
Reprinted 1991
Second Edition 1992
Reprinted 1992
Reprinted 1993
Third Edition 1994
Fourth Edition 1995

ISBN 1 0 7510 0607 6

British Library Cataloguing-in-Publication.

A CIP Catalogue record for this book is available from the British Library.

Printed and bound in Great Britain by
Hartnolls Limited, Bodmin, Cornwall

CONTENTS

ACKNOWLEDGEMENT

Some questions used are taken or adapted from past University of London LLB (External) Degree examination papers and our thanks are extended to the University of London for their kind permission to use and publish the questions.

Caveat

The answers given are not approved or sanctioned by the University of London and are entirely our responsibility.

They are not intended as 'Model Answers', but rather as Suggested Solutions.

The answers have two fundamental purposes, namely:

a) To provide a detailed example of a suggested solution to an examination question, and

b) To assist students with their research into the subject and to further their understanding and appreciation of the subject of Laws.

INTRODUCTION

This Revision WorkBook has been designed specifically for those studying tort to undergraduate level. Its coverage is not confined to any one syllabus, but embraces all the major contract topics to be found in university or college examinations.

However, since it is anticipated that many students will be intending to sit the University of London LLB external examinations, the questions used are primarily from past tort papers from that course.

Each chapter contains in its first few pages, brief notes explaining the scope and overall content of the topic covered in that chapter. There follows, in each case, a list of key points which will assist the student in studying and memorising essential material with which the student should be familiar in order to fully understand the topic. Recent cases and statutes will be noted as necessary. However, on the assumption that the student will already possess a textbook/casebook, case law has been kept to the bare minimum for the sake of simplicity.

Additionally in each chapter there will be a question analysis which will list and compare past examination questions on similar topics in tort papers. Students are reminded that in order to derive maximum benefit from this WorkBook, they should possess a set of past examination papers issued by University of London for this subject. The purpose of such a question analysis is to give an appreciation of the potential range of questions possible, and some idea of variations in wording, different formats in questions and alternative modes of combining different issues in one question.

Each chapter will end with, usually, three or four typical examination questions, together with skeleton answers and suggested solutions. Wherever possible, the questions are drawn from recent University of London external tort papers. However it is inevitable that, in compiling a list of questions by topic order rather than chronologically, not only do the same questions crop up over and over again in different guises, but there are gaps where questions have never been set at all. Where a topic has never been covered in an examination question, a specimen question will have been written as an example, together with skeleton answer and suggested solution.

Undoubtedly, the main feature of this Revision WorkBook is the inclusion of as many past examination questions as possible. While the use of past questions as a revision aid is certainly not new, it is hoped that the combination of actual past questions from the University of London LLB external course and specially written questions, where there are gaps in examination coverage, will be of assistance to students in achieving a thorough and systematic revision of the subject.

Careful use of the Revision WorkBook should enhance the student's understanding of tort and, hopefully, enable him to deal with as wide a range of subject matter as anyone might find in a tort examination, while at the same time allowing him to practise examination techniques while working through the book.

In this revised 1995 edition the final chapter contains the complete June 1994 University of London LLB (External) Law of Tort question paper, followed by suggested solutions to each question. Thus the student will have the opportunity to review a recent examination paper in its entirety, and can, if desired, use this chapter as a mock examination – referring to the suggested solutions only after first having attempted the questions.

HOW TO STUDY TORT

The law of tort, covering as it does the legal duties that one person owes to another, is an inherently fascinating area. In particular, the cases that a student comes across can be readily understood and appreciated from a factual point of view as they concern (relatively speaking) day-to-day situations. However, a problem immediately arises of the sheer volume of information and data that is contained in a textbook of tort law. A factor which contributes to this volume is that tort is basically a case law subject, ie it is a subject in which the general principles and detailed rules have been laid down by judgments of the courts over a period of years, often in a rather haphazard manner due to accidents of litigation. It is, therefore, vital that the student extracts (with the help of his lectures and textbooks!) the general principles from this mass of cases. This is by no means an easy task, and many rules in tort have exceptions, but without a framework of clear principles in which to place cases which illustrate the workings of the principles and their limitations, understanding and progress will be difficult.

In addition to the judge-made law, tort has a number of statutes which have extended, refined and often changed the common law, such as the Animals Act 1971, the Occupiers' Liability Acts of 1957 and 1984 and the Consumer Protection Act 1987. These and other relevant statutes must clearly form part of the data bank from which the student erects his framework of principles of the law of tort.

Yet another problem awaits the student of the law of tort, namely that certain areas of the law are still being developed by the courts, and whilst in law generally it is advisable to keep up to date, in certain areas of tort is is absolutely essential. Thus in recent years the courts have restated and/or refined the law as regards duty of care in negligence, liability for causing economic loss and nervous shock and the economic torts, such that a student who does not keep up to date may not merely be relying on old law but on wrong law.

To summarise, the student of the law of tort needs to have a good grasp of the principles of tort law as laid down by the cases and statutes. In addition, a good knowledge of case law is required to explain and illustrate the working of these principles in practical situations. Fortunately, both these requirements can be satisfied by a study of one set of materials, but the student should be particularly careful not to fall into the trap of memorising lists of cases with no clear understanding of the ratio decidendi therein.

Finally the student should, wherever possible, study the original sources, ie the original cases and statutes. However learned or illustrious a textbook author is, the textbook is essentially a secondhand version of the facts. Given the amount of material in the tort syllabus, this is a counsel of perfection, but it is well worth following whenever time permits. In particular, when a student encounters difficulties, a reading of the original authorities will often make not only the point being checked clear, but several others.

REVISION AND EXAMINATION TECHNIQUE

Whole books have been written on how to study and this brief note makes no pretence at being an infallible guide. In any case, skill in revision and examination techniques is an art best acquired by actual practice.

The more you study, the more you devise your own short cuts for efficient preparation for exams. Unfortunately, it is only when you actually sit the examination that you can see whether your particular method of revision is successful. If it is not, it is an expensive and frustrating way to find out.

While it is true that examination techniques are best learned actually sitting examinations, it is not necessary to wait until the real thing. 'Mock' examinations, tackled under realistic conditions, can be very helpful. Revision aids like this WorkBook, not only give some idea of potential questions and possible solutions, but can be used most efficiently by the student as a form of examination rehearsal. For example, select a question and, without looking at the skeleton answer, write out your own. Compare it with the skeleton answer in the WorkBook and if you appear to be working along the right lines, then proceed to write a full solution – preferably under simulated examination conditions. Once you have completed your own solution you can see how it tallies with that given in the WorkBook.

Or, if you have time, tackle a full quota of four or five questions at once – as a mock examination.

Remember, none of the solutions given is represented as the 'only' solution, nor need the exact sequence be the same – the main aim is to give you guidance as to a possible way of tackling the question and as to presentation of your answer.

The short list of do's and don'ts below attempts to set out some suggestions which it is hoped most students will find of practical use in planning their revision and tackling examinations.

Do's

i) Do plan ahead and make your plans increasingly detailed as you approach the examination date.

    Allocate enough time for each topic to be studied, bearing in mind the time actually available to you before the exams.

ii) Do exercise constant self-discipline, especially if studying at home.

iii) Do, during your course of study, especially once revision starts, constantly test yourself orally and in writing.

iv) Do keep up-to-date. While examiners do not require familiarity with changes in the law during the three months prior to the examination, it obviously creates a good impression to show you are acquainted with any recent changes. Sources that you might look at in order to be up to date include: leading journals such as Modern Law Review, Law Quarterly Review and New Law Journal;

cumulative indices to law reports such as the All England Law Reports, and such sources as the Law Society's 'Gazette' and the Legal Executive 'Journal'.

v) Do familiarise yourself with past examination papers, and try at least one 'mock examination' well before the date of the real thing.

vi) Do read the instructions at the examination carefully. While any last minute changes are unlikely – such as the introduction of a compulsory question – it has been known to happen.

vii) Do read the questions carefully. Analyse problem questions – work out what the examiner wants. PLAN YOUR ANSWER before you start to write.

viii)Do note mark allocations (if any) on the question paper. It is pointless to spend an excessive amount of time in producing a perfect answer to a part of a problem that carries only a tiny percentage of the marks.

Don'ts

i) Don't finish the syllabus too early – constant revision of the same topic leads to stagnation – but DON'T leave revision so late that you have to 'cram'.

If you *are* the sort of person who works better to a deadline – make it a realistic one!

ii) Don't try to learn by rote. In particular, don't try to reproduce model answers by heart. Learn to express the basic concepts in your own words.

iii) Don't answer the question you expect to see! By all means 'problem-spot' before examinations by going over old exam papers but make sure that what the examiner is asking for really does match what you are preparing to write about.

iv) DON'T PANIC!

TABLE OF CASES

TABLE OF STATUTES

READING LIST

Textbooks are very much a matter of personal choice, but it is essential to use regularly a book which deals with the law in sufficient depth and detail to satisfy the examiner.

Essential reading

PITCHFORK   *Tort Textbook*, HLT Publications (1995)

WINFIELD & JOLOWICZ   *On Tort*, Sweet & Maxwell (1994, 14th ed)

SALMOND & HEUSTON   *Law of Tort*, Sweet & Maxwell (1992, 20th ed)

Additional reading

JONES   *Textbook on Torts*, Blackstone Press (1993, 4th ed)

WEIR   *A Casebook on Tort*, Sweet & Maxwell (1992, 7th ed)

HEPPLE & MATTHEWS   *Tort: Cases & Materials*, Butterworth (1991, 4th ed)

MARKESINIS & DEAKIN   *Tort Law*, Oxford University Press (1994, 3rd ed)

BRAZIER   *Street on Torts*, Butterworth (1993, 9th ed)

1 INTRODUCTION AND LIABILITY

1.1 Introduction

A tort is a civil wrong which is not solely a breach of contract or a breach of trust, and which gives rise to civil proceedings to enforce a right.

The law of tort is concerned with the legal duties that individuals owe to each other and with the legal rights that the law will protect.

1.2 Key points

a) *Liability*

A tort is some act by the defendant which, without just cause or excuse, causes some form of 'harm' to the plaintiff. 'Harm' is used here in a legal sense and two concepts must be examined.

   i) Damnum sine injuria

       ie damage without wrong. There are many kinds of harm of which the law takes no account, and so any damage suffered is damage without wrong, eg invasion of privacy, competition between traders. *Bradford Corporation* v *Pickles* [1895] AC 587 is the leading case where although damage was caused to the plaintiff it was caused only by the defendant exercising his legal rights and was therefore not actionable.

   ii) Injuria sine damne

       ie wrong without damage. Here behaviour is actionable even though no damage has been caused. There are two kinds of tort; those which are actionable only on proof that actual damage resulted, eg negligence, and those which are actionable per se, eg trespass to land, libel which are actionable even though no actual damage follows.

b) *Malice*

Malice in the sense of an improper motive is relevant to certain torts only, eg malicious falsehood, nuisance in certain situations and some defences to defamation. But as a general rule motive is irrelevant in that a good motive is no justification for an illegal act and a bad motive does not make a legal act wrongful. See *Bradford Corporation* v *Pickles* (above) where the motive for the defendant's lawful actions was to coerce the plaintiff into buying the defendant's land at the defendant's price.

1.3 Analysis of questions

Obviously students must be aware of which torts are actionable per se and which require proof of actual damage. Although questions are rarely set on this distinction, if this basic knowledge is not known it is difficult to see how a pass grade could be obtained. Occasionally a question is set on malice or intention in the law of tort generally.

1.4 Questions

QUESTION ONE

'The general rule is that, if conduct is presumptively unlawful, a good motive will not exonerate the defendant, and that, if conduct is lawful apart from motive, a bad motive will not make him liable.' (Winfield and Jolowicz).

Discuss this statement. Should the law of tort attach more importance to the defendant's motives?

University of London LLB Examination
(for External Students) Law of Tort June 1990 Q2

Suggested Solution

Perhaps the best known case on lawful conduct not being made unlawful by a bad motive is *Bradford Corporation* v *Pickles* [1895] AC 587, where the defendant was held not liable for intentionally intercepting water flowing through his land via undefined channels. The defendant's motive in doing this was to coerce the plaintiff into buying the defendant's land at the defendant's price, and it was held that as his act was lawful his motive could not make it unlawful. This was re-emphasised by the House of Lords a few years later in *Allen* v *Flood* [1898] AC 1. *Chapman* v *Honig* [1963] 2 QB 502, where a landlord maliciously served a notice to quit on a tenant, and *Wyld* v *Silver* [1963] 1 QB 169, where persons exercised a long-defunct right to hold a fair solely to prevent the erection of buildings for which planning permission had been granted, are more modern examples.

Clearly, however, there are some areas of the law of tort where motive is relevant. Thus malice will have to be shown in malicious prosecution or malicious falsehood, and in defamation the presence of malice will destroy the defence of fair comment or qualified privilege.

Another area in which motive is relevant is nuisance. While malice is by no means an essential ingredient of this tort, the presence of malice may mean that an interference is deemed unreasonable, as in *Hollywood Silver Fox Farm* v *Emmett* [1936] 2 KB 468 where the defendant was held to have committed a nuisance when he acted maliciously, and it seems clear that in the absence of malice no nuisance would have been found. *Christie* v *Davey* [1893] 1 Ch 316 is a similar example of malice being taken into account.

Finally, it is in the area of economic torts that motive may be relevant. Thus in *Mogul Steamship* v *McGregor, Gow & Co* [1892] AC 25, it was held that the motive of the defendant was irrelevant and a cause of action would only arise where the defendant's action was unlawful. A few years later in *Allen* v *Flood* [1898] AC 1 the

House of Lords reached a similar conclusion. However, in *Quinn* v *Leatham* [1901] AC 495 the House of Lords held that a tort had been committed where the defendants acted lawfully but with a malicious motive. The anomalous finding in *Quinn* has been confined to cases of conspiracy to injure. Motive is relevant to this tort which can be carried out (inter alia) by the doing of a lawful act by unlawful means by two or more persons: *Mulcahy* v *R* (1868) LR 3 HL 306, 317. This leads to the strange conclusion that if an individual carried out the acts they would be lawful, ie the motive would be irrelevant, but if carried out by more than one person the acts would become actionable because of the motive, as in *Huntley* v *Thornton* [1957] 1 WLR 321 where the reason for denying the plaintiff employment was to uphold the dignity of certain union officials. By contrast in *Crofter Hand Woven Harris Tweed* v *Veitch* [1942] AC 435, where the defendants' motive was to protect their members' interests, it was held no action would lie.

In the tort of inducing a breach of contract, the relevant defences were summarised in *Edwin Hill* v *First National Finance Corporation* [1989] 1 WLR 225; [1989] 3 All ER 801. It was stated that absence of malice was irrelevant: *South Wales Miners' Federation* v *Glamorgan Coal* [1905] AC 239, but that a moral duty to induce a breach of contract, as in *Brimelow* v *Casson* [1924] 1 Ch 302 was a defence, so again motive may be relevant.

Lastly, in the tort of interference with trade by unlawful means, it was held in *Lonrho* v *Fayed* [1991] 3 All ER 303 that an essential ingredient of this tort was an intent to harm the plaintiff where lawful means are used or to direct the unlawful act against the plaintiff, so again motive is relevant here.

Thus it can be seen that while traditionally the law has disregarded motive, there are some important exceptions to this rule in both nuisance and defamation and in the relatively new and still developing area of economic torts the courts seem more ready to pay attention to the defendant's motives.

The difficulty of attaching more importance to the defendant's motives is that often the criterion used in fixing liability is objective, rather than subjective, as well as the difficulty of ascertaining the defendant's motive, especially as unreasonable behaviour does not necessarily prove the existence of malice. As public law (eg planning law) controls a person's freedom to act in detriment to the interests of the community, and the law of tort regulates behaviour between individuals, it might seem an unwarranted infringement on personal liberty to delve into a person's motives and make lawful acts unlawful. Even greater problems could arise if unlawful acts were to be made lawful because of a good motive; eg an employer removes a guard from dangerous machinery to enable the employee to work faster and obtain higher wages – the employee is injured and would not have been if the guard had been kept in place. Should the employer's good motive exonerate him? On the other hand why should a malicious defendant be able to rely on a defence of justification in defamation? The reliance on motive would also tend to create uncertainty as regards the liability of a particular defendant.

Overall, therefore, it is submitted that a case has not been made out for attaching more importance in tort to the defendant's motives.

QUESTION TWO

Discuss the proposition that the law of tort attaches too little significance to motive or purpose as a basis of liability.

University of London LLB Examination
(for External Students) Law of Tort June 1993 Q5

Skeleton Solution

Definition of terms – the general rule as to motive – exceptions: nuisance; defamation – discussion.

Suggested Solution

The law of torts may be seen as a number of specific rules prohibiting certain kinds of harmful behaviour, such as negligence, trespass or defamation. Depending upon one's viewpoint, there may be a fundamental general principle underlying these rules that it is wrongful to cause harm to others. In *Mogul Steamship Co Ltd v McGregor, Gow & Sons* [1892] AC 25, Bowen LJ said that whenever someone intentionally caused harm without lawful justification or excuse, liability should follow. That was not the case at the time and nor is it that straightforward today. In truth, the mental element will often play a small part in establishing liability in tort.

One has to consider carefully the terms. By motive or purpose, one means the ulterior reason behind the act, which frequently will be malice. This is not the same as intention, which is the mental element immediately behind the particular act. To take an example: A sees B, a child, shoplifting so he slaps B across the face. This is a trespass to B's person. A's intention was to strike him. However, his motive or purpose may have been to punish him. Without the intention, this would not have amounted to a battery; the motive is no defence. Of course, there will be a grey area where the terms merge. The word 'purpose' perhaps connotes a longer-term intention and is sometimes used synonymously with intention. However, what we are concerned with in this question is how important is the underlying reason in tort.

One can say immediately that the presence of a malicious motive will not generally make an otherwise lawful act actionable (*Allen v Flood* [1898] AC 1), nor will it exonerate the defendant who has acted unlawfully. One can further state that, with some exceptions, the defendant's motive will generally be irrelevant. In negligence, for example, my ulterior reason for driving negligently so as to cause an accident will count for nothing.

One exception is private nuisance. A spiteful motive – in other words, malice – can make interference with a person's use and enjoyment of land unreasonable and therefore an actionable nuisance. In *Christie v Davey* [1893] 1 Ch 316, the defendant was held liable for deliberately and maliciously banging on a party wall to annoy the plaintiff, a teacher of music. Again, in *Hollywood Silver Fox Farm Ltd v Emmett* [1936] 2 KB 468, a defendant who deliberately caused guns to be fired near the plaintiff's boundary in order to scare his foxes during breeding time was held liable. Both of these activities might not have amounted to a nuisance in the absence of malice.

Another exception is defamation, where the defence of qualified privilege can be defeated by proving malice, as can the defence of fair comment. Malice in the former may mean not only an improper purpose but a lack of belief in the truth of the statement subject to the qualified privilege. In the latter, malice refers to an evil motive, as in *Thomas* v *Bradbury, Agnew & Co Ltd* [1906] 2 KB 627, where a book reviewer's demeanour in the witness box showed personal hostility to the plaintiff.

There are certain torts which depend upon proof of intention – such as conspiracy, inducing breach of contract, intimidation – but it remains the case that motive as an element is the exception. In which case, should it have greater significance? To take negligence again: the imposition of a duty is largely based upon objective criteria and the foresight of the reasonable man. Whether or not one can say there is a general duty of care following cases such as *Murphy* v *Brentwood District Council* [1991] 1 AC 398 is questionable, nevertheless there is a large body of case law which establishes the parameters of negligence and any extension of that duty is by analogy. Motive is incompatible with recognition of that duty. As a defence, it would allow the plaintiff to say that, although he was negligent, his motives were such as to override this liability. However, one can argue that a person is no less negligent and the damage is not reduced merely by the fact that the defendant had a positive motive or purpose.

One is considering motive as a positive factor here. As a negative factor, there is more scope for saying that it should have greater significance. While it is unlikely that existing torts will change to include it, motive may have an important role in developing torts. The tort of harassment was recognised by the Court of Appeal in *Khorasandjian* v *Bush* [1993] 3 WLR 476 and this is an area where motive or purpose may prove to be an important element. Similarly, if a tort of privacy is established, the motive of the tortfeasor may well be significant.

It is difficult to say whether there is too little significance attached to motive, although undoubtedly it has little relevance in many areas. If tort is made up of various rules prohibiting certain types of behaviour, then the motive of the tortfeasor in behaving in that way is inevitably of relatively little importance.

2 PARTIES AND TYPES OF LIABILITY

2.1 Introduction

2.2 Key points: parties

2.3 Key points: types of liability

2.4 Recent cases

2.5 Analysis of questions

2.1 Introduction

This chapter briefly discusses who can sue and be sued, and the situation where there is more than one defendant.

2.2 Key points: parties

a) Minors can sue in tort, as can an unborn child both at statute law, Congenital Disabilities (Civil Liability) Act 1976, and at common law: *B* v *Islington Health Authority* [1992] NLJ 565, and spouses may sue each other. A minor cannot be sued in tort if the effect would be to enforce a legally unenforceable contract against him: *Jennings* v *Rundall* (1799) 8 Term Rep 335.

b) Note the position of the Crown and members of the armed forces. In law a company is a person, so a company may sue and be sued, and is often the defendant in a tort action as companies are vicariously liable for the torts committed by their employees in the course of their employment (see chapter 4).

c) Unincorporated associations, such as clubs, have no legal personality and so cannot sue or be sued: *Robertson* v *Ridley* (1988) The Times 28 November.

d) Trade unions have some of the attributes of legal entities and can be sued, but they cannot sue in defamation: *EETPU* v *Times Newspapers* [1980] QB 585.

2.3 Key points: types of liability

a) *Independent liability*

If the plaintiff is damaged by two separate torts he may sue each defendant separately in respect of the damage suffered: *Baker* v *Willoughby* [1970] AC 467.

b) *Several liability*

If the tortfeasors act independently and cause the same damage to the plaintiff, each tortfeasor is separately liable for the damage (although the plaintiff can only recover damages once): *The Koursk* [1924] P 140.

c) *Joint liability*

i) Here two tortfeasors damage the plaintiff following a shared intent. Joint liability can also arise in vicarious liability eg where an employer is held vicariously liable for the tort of his employee. Here both employer and employee are jointly liable. Each tortfeasor is liable for the damage, but the plaintiff can only recover once.

ii) Under the Civil Liability (Contribution) Act 1978, judgment against one tortfeasor does not bar a subsequent action against another joint tortfeasor, nor is there any rule against recovery of contribution between joint tortfeasors. See *K* v *P* [1993] 1 All ER 521 for a wide interpretation of the scope of the 1978 Act.

2.4 Recent cases

Lampitt v *Poole Borough Council* [1990] 2 All ER 887

K v *P* [1993] 1 All ER 521

2.5 Analysis of questions

Questions are rarely set on the above specific points, although a knowledge of them is frequently implicit in examination questions.

3 GENERAL DEFENCES

3.1 Introduction

Although each tort will have a number of defences that are specific to that tort (eg in negligence that no duty of care was owed) there are a number of defences that are common throughout the law of tort.

3.2 Key points

a) *Necessity*

This defence exists: *Cope* v *Sharpe* [1912] 1 KB 496; *Rigby* v *Chief Constable of Northamptonshire* [1985] 1 WLR 1242; [1985] 2 All ER 985, although it is not much favoured by the courts: *Southwark London Borough Council* v *Williams* [1971] Ch 734.

b) *Statutory authority*

Where a statute authorises an act, no action will lie either for doing that act or for any necessary consequence of the act: *Vaughan* v *Taff Vale Railway* (1860) 5 H & N 679. See *Allen* v *Gulf Oil Refining* [1981] AC 1001 on the liberal interpretation of such statutes, but note *Hampson* v *Department of Education and Science* [1990] 2 All ER 513.

c) *Consent*

This defence, usually known as the volenti defence, is based on the maxim 'volenti non fit injuria' – no wrong is done to one who consents.

Clearly few problems will occur where harm is intentionally inflicted on a consenting person. However, problems can arise where harm is accidentally inflicted: acceptance of the risk of injury must be voluntary with no constraints: *Bowater* v *Rowley Regis Corporation* [1944] KB 476; *Smith* v *Baker* [1891] AC 325, and there must be express or implied agreement between the plaintiff and defendant that the plaintiff will accept the risk of injury: *Nettleship* v *Weston* [1971] 2 QB 691; *Pitts* v *Hunt* [1990] 3 WLR 542; *Morris* v *Murray* [1990] 3 All ER 801.

Note the possible application of the Unfair Contract Terms Act 1977 to any agreement; that mere knowledge of the danger is insufficient to establish the defence (see *Smith* v *Baker* (above)); that the defence does not apply to rescue cases – *Haynes* v *Harwood* [1935] 1 KB 146; the effect of s149(3) Road Traffic Act 1988 – *Pitts* v *Hunt* [1990] 3 WLR 542, and the fact that if the 1988 Act is inapplicable, eg as between an aircraft pilot and his passenger, that the volenti defence can be successful: *Morris* v *Murray* [1990] 3 All ER 801.

d) *Illegality*

If a plaintiff suffers damage because of the defendant's tort while participating in a crime, no action will lie on the grounds of public policy – ex turpi causa non oritur actio – no right of action arises from a bad cause: *Ashton* v *Turner* [1981] QB 137; *Pitts* v *Hunt* [1990] 3 WLR 542, but note *Tinsley* v *Milligan* [1993] 3 WLR 126 in which the House of Lords rejected the 'affront to public conscience' test as a general guide to barring recovery.

3.3 Recent cases

Kirkham v *Chief Constable of Greater Manchester Police* [1990] 3 All ER 246

Pitts v *Hunt* [1990] 3 WLR 542

Morris v *Murray* [1990] 3 All ER 801

Tinsley v *Milligan* [1993] 3 WLR 126

K v *P* [1993] 1 All ER 521

3.4 Analysis of questions

Although questions are not often set on the general defences specifically, they often feature in tort questions and the possibility of the volenti defence must often be considered.

3.5 Questions

For examples of the general defences being relevant to tort questions see:

Chapter 4, Question 3; Chapter 5, Question 4; Chapter 14, Question 2.

4 VICARIOUS LIABILITY

4.1 Introduction

4.2 Key points

4.3 Recent cases

4.4 Analysis of questions

4.5 Questions

4.1 Introduction

The term vicarious liability means that one person takes the place of another as regards liability. Although the matter also arises in relation to principal and agent and partnership, the most important and commonest example of vicarious liability is that an employer is liable for the torts committed by an employee who is acting in the course of his employment.

From this statement it follows that we must be able to identify an employer and an employee and decide just what is meant by 'acting in the course of employment'.

4.2 Key points

a) *Employer* – in simple terms the person who has the right to hire and fire. In practice this gives rise to few difficulties, except

   i)   where an employee is loaned out by his original employer to a third party

   ii) Here the onus lies on the original employer to rebut the presumption that he, and not the third party, remains the employer.

   iii) This can be done by showing that the third party had, at the relevant moment, the right to control the way in which the work was done: *Mersey Docks & Harbour Board* v *Coggins & Griffith* [1947] AC 1.

   iv) A difficult presumption to rebut: original employer may run foul of the Unfair Contract Terms Act 1977: compare *Phillips Products* v *Hyland* [1987] 2 All ER 620 with *Thompson* v *T Lohan (Plant Hire) Ltd* [1987] 2 All ER 631.

b) *Employee* – original test: a person was an employee if his employer has the right to control not only what work he does but the way in which that work is done: *Yewens* v *Noakes* (1880) 6 QBD 530.

   i)   The test is right of control not whether any actual control is exercised: used by the House of Lords recently in *Smith* v *Stages* [1989] 2 WLR 529; [1989] 1 All ER 833. In *Lane* v *Shire Roofing* (1995) The Times 25 February the Court of Appeal stated that in the case of skilled employees the question should be broadened to whose business was it? Was it the workers' or the employers'?

ii) Other tests which have been suggested include:

- whether the person is employed as part of the business and his work is done as an integral part of it: *Stevenson, Jordan & Harrison* v *MacDonald & Evans* [1952] 1 TLR 101.

- whether the person is in business on her own account: *Market Investigations* v *Minister of Social Security* [1969] 2 QB 173; [1969] 2 WLR 1; *Andrews* v *King* (1991) The Times 5 July.

iii) The present approach of the courts is not to seek any single test which will apply in all cases, but to look at all the facts of the particular case. The reason for seeking to define an employee is not to recognise an employee as such, but rather to be able to distinguish between an employee and an independent contractor (see later).

c) *Course of employment*

i) The employer is liable for any torts of the employee that he authorises or ratifies.

ii) In addition he is liable for any wrongful or unauthorised modes of doing an authorised act.

iii) In other words, the employer is not only responsible for what he authorised the employee to do but for how the employee does it.

iv) The employer will only escape liability in this respect if the employee goes outside the course of his employment, ie if the employee's act is not so connected with the authorised act as to be a mode of doing it but is an independent act of the employee: compare *Century Insurance* v *Northern Ireland Road Transport Board* [1942] AC 509 with *Beard* v *London General Omnibus Co* [1900] 2 QB 530.

v) Two particular problems – frolics and detours and the effect of an express prohibition by the employer.

- Frolics and detours, eg a driver who departs from an unauthorised route – has this action taken the employee outside the course of his employment? – *Joel* v *Morrison* (1834) 6 C & P 501 and *Williams* v *A & W Hemphill Ltd* 1966 SLT 259 are examples of this test and its application and should be compared with *Whatman* v *Pearson* (1868) LR 3 CP 422.

- The related problem of whether employees travelling to and from work are in the course of their employment – see *Smith* v *Stages* (above) (note criteria applied do not apply to salaried employees).

- Express prohibitions – clear from the definition of course of employment it follows that any prohibition that the employer has placed on the conduct of the employee will not restrict the course of employment.

- However, the law does allow the employer to limit acts which lie within the course of employment, but not to restrict the mode of performing acts within the course of employment: compare *Limpus* v *London General Omnibus Co* (1862) 1 H & C 526 and *Beard* v *London General Omnibus Co* (above).

- The problem – how one defines the 'act' the employee is employed to do. In *Conway* v *Wimpey* [1951] 2 KB 266 and *Twine* v *Bean's Express* [1946] 1 All ER 202 the 'act' was defined very narrowly, but in *Rose* v *Plenty* [1976] 1 WLR 141; [1976] 1 All ER 97 a more liberal interpretation was used.
- The current attitude of the courts seems to be to adopt this wide interpretation where the employee acts carelessly, but to adopt a narrow interpretation of the act the employee was employed to do when considering a deliberate wrongful act by the employee.

vi) In considering intentional wrongful acts by the employee, the courts take a restrictive approach to the course of employment – see *Heasmans* v *Clarity Cleaning* [1987] IRLR 286; *Irving* v *The Post Office* [1987] IRLR 289; *General Engineering Services* v *Kingston & St Andrews Corp* [1989] 1 WLR 69; [1988] 3 All ER 867, *Director-General of Fair Trading* v *Smiths Concrete* [1991] 4 All ER 150.

vii) Note that where the employer is held vicariously liable he can recover an indemnity from the employee under statute: s1(1) Civil Liability (Contribution) Act 1978 and at common law: *Lister* v *Romford Ice & Cold Storage Co* [1957] AC 555.

d) *Principal and agent* – The principal is liable for the agent's acts which are carried out in the course of the agency: difficulty – determining whether or not an 'ad hoc' agency has arisen creating the relationship of principal and agent: compare *Ormrod* v *Crossville Motor Services* [1953] 1 WLR 1120 and *Morgans* v *Launchbury* [1973] AC 127.

e) *Independent contractors* – an employer is not liable for the torts of an independent contractor because he does not control the independent contractor: see *Morgan* v *Incorporated Central Council of the Girls Friendly Society* [1936] 1 All ER 404 and *D & F Estates* v *Church Commissioners* [1989] AC 177; [1988] 3 WLR 368.

f) *Partnership* – ss10 and 12 of the Partnership Act 1890.

4.3 Recent cases

General Engineering Services v *Kingston & St Andrews Corp* [1989] 1 WLR 69; [1988] 3 All ER 867

Andrews v *King* (1991) The Times 5 July

Lane v *Shire Roofing* (1995) The Times 25 February

Director-General of Fair Trading v *Pioneer Concrete* [1994] 3 WLR 1249

Racz v *Home Office* [1993] 2 WLR 23

4.4 Analysis of questions

Vicarious liability is often tested by the examiner. Although questions often turn on the course of employment and the effect of an express prohibition, the distinction between an independent contractor and an employee has also cropped up.

Where an employee commits a tort in a problem question always consider the aspect of vicarious liability as from a practical point of view it will be better for the plaintiff to sue the employer rather than the employee, who may not have the resources to satisfy judgment.

4.5 Questions

QUESTION ONE

The Moonshine Home is a private convalescent hospital. It has a permanent nursing staff, but recruits temporary nursing assistance from Mrs Nightingale's Agency when it is needed to cover for staff holidays and sickness. The agency pays the salary to its nurses and charges a fee to the hospitals which use its services. Florence was sent from the agency for two weeks as a night nurse at the Moonshine Home. On her first night George, a patient, asked Florence to give him an extra dose of his medicine as he found that it helped him to sleep. Florence told him that she was not allowed to do so without authority from a doctor. George told her untruthfully that the doctor had said that he could have an extra dose whenever he needed it and that the regular nurse had several times administered one. Florence therefore gave him an extra dose. The medicine had a stimulating effect on the heart and the extra dose caused George to suffer a non-fatal heart attack.

Advise George.

University of London LLB Examination
(for External Students) Law of Tort June 1986 Q6

Skeleton Solution

Negligence – Florence negligently gives George an extra dose of medicine causing a heart attack – Florence sent to work in hospital by a nursing agency which is vicariously liable for her conduct – facts indicate that Florence an employee of nursing agency – this raises further issue as to whether burden of liability can be shifted to hospital under the principle of lending a servant, this is unlikely on the facts – further issue arises as to whether Florence was acting within scope of her employment at relevant time – this appears to be so.

Suggested Solution

It is hardly in dispute that Florence was negligent in giving George an extra dose of his medicine merely because he requested it. As a qualified nurse she would be expected to measure up to the standard of proficiency which could be expected of an ordinary competent nurse and to conform to practices accepted as proper by a responsible section of her profession: see *Bolam* v *Friern Hospital Management Committee* [1957] 1 WLR 582. I doubt if she was conforming with proper practices in giving a patient a dose of medicine without first checking to see if it was prescribed for him in his medical records, or asking the doctor whose authority was necessary in the first place or by merely giving it to him because he asked for it.

There would appear to be little that Florence could do in defending a claim by George in negligence except, perhaps, alleging that he was contributorily negligent. Such a claim would be based on the ground that he had been less careful for his own safety than he otherwise ought to have been. Any damages he might obtain would be reduced to the extent that the court considered that he was to blame for his own misfortune: see *Nance* v *British Columbia Electric Railway* [1951] AC 601. It is doubtful if contributory negligence would have any success here because if George was ill he may have been in no fit state to consider his safety. In any event, the real cause of his injury is the administration of the extra dose rather than his asking for it. Florence could have easily refused to give it.

Having decided that there is a case in negligence against Florence the next issue is who George should sue. Obviously, he could sue Florence but it is likely that she could not pay any damages awarded against her because she probably has limited financial means. The question therefore arises whether George should sue the Moonshine Home or the Nightingale Agency on the basis that one of them is vicariously liable for Florence's negligence. An employer is vicariously liable for the tort of his employee or 'servant' where the tort is committed in the course of employment. It would appear that Florence was an employee of the Nightingale Agency since they paid her a salary and, it appears, directed her what to do. There are a number of tests to determine an employer/employee relationship; these include the 'control' test and the 'business integration' test. The former test is based on whether the alleged employee can be told not only what to do but how to do it: see *Yewens* v *Noakes* (1880) 6 QBD 530. This test is satisfactory for menial positions but is rather unsatisfactory where the alleged employee has a special skill which the employer does not have as, for example, in the case of a hospital employing doctors and nurses. See *Moren* v *Swinton and Pendlebury BC* [1965] 1 WLR 576. The courts appear to have ignored the difficulties of the control test and in cases concerning hospital doctors have held that the hospital authorities are vicariously liable for their negligence. See *Cassidy* v *Ministry of Health* [1951] 2 KB 343. On this basis the Moonshine Home would be vicariously liable for Florence if she was their employee and, if this is so, it is difficult to see why the Nightingale Agency should be in a different position if other terms of Florence's contract with them are consistent with an employer/employee relationship. The 'business integration' test was formulated by Denning LJ in *Stevenson, Jordan & Harrison Ltd* v *MacDonald & Evans* [1952] 1 TLR 101 and is used to distinguish a contract of service from a contract of services. If a person is employed as part of the business and his work is an integral part of it he is an employee under a contract of service. Considering this test in the present case it would appear that Florence is an employee of the Nightingale Agency. However, it would be appropriate to see if Florence's contract with the Nightingale Agency is consistent with this conclusion, whether she is paid gross or net of tax, if Nightingale pay employers' national insurance contributions for her, pay towards pensions schemes etc. It also seems unlikely that Florence is in business on her own account: see *Market Investigations* v *Minister of Social Security* [1969] 2 QB 173; *Andrews* v *King* (1991) The Times 5 July.

If, as appears to be the case, Florence is an employee of the Nightingale Agency this does not necessarily mean that they are liable for her negligence. It may be that in the circumstances of this case the principles concerning lending a servant apply so that the Moonshine Home is instead vicariously liable for Florence. The principles of this rule were considered by the House of Lords in *Mersey Docks and Harbour Board* v *Coggins and Griffith* [1947] AC 1 and under it, it appears that a permanent employer may be able to shift the burden of responsibility to a temporary employer. Factors which will be considered relevant to the application of the rule include whether machinery was lent with the employee, the duration of service with the temporary employer, who pays the employee, contributes towards his national insurance and pension schemes and who has the power of dismissal. In my view Nightingale Agency would not be able to invoke this rule because the period of service was too short, being two weeks only, and it seems Nightingale continued to pay Florence etc and merely collected a fee from the Moonshine Home for her services.

Thus, the proper party to sue here is the Nightingale Agency. This does not solve all difficulties because an employer is only vicariously liable for the acts of an employee if they are done in the course of the employment. Florence gave George medicine which should only have been given on the authority of a doctor so it is arguable that she acted outside the scope of her employment. I doubt if such an argument would be successful since Florence is not prohibited from giving George medicine but merely prohibited from giving it to him except on the authority of a doctor. The case is one where a prohibition exists which regulates the manner in which Florence performs her duties rather than one which defines or limits the sphere of her employment. In *Rose* v *Plenty* [1976] 1 WLR 141; [1976] 1 All ER 97 a prohibition on a milkman allowing small boys to ride on his milkfloat was treated as regulating the course of employment rather than its scope. It is difficult to see how as a matter of law, the present case could be viewed differently.

QUESTION TWO

Rodney, a twenty-year-old student, owns a motor cycle; he has had a number of convictions for driving offences. On Saturdays and some evenings he works for Scramblers Messenger Services. He uses his own motor cycle and visits the Messenger Services office once each working day to collect the messages he has to deliver. He did not tell the Messenger Services about his convictions and they did not enquire or examine his driving licence. One Saturday, while delivering a message, he rode through a halt sign without stopping. A car driven by Stewart was approaching on the main road. Stewart, who was driving at about 10 mph in excess of the speed limit, was forced to swerve, struck a tree and was killed. Stewart was aged 30 and in secure employment. He leaves a widow, Lucy, and two sons, aged four and two.

Advise Lucy.

University of London LLB Examination
(for External Students) Law of Tort June 1984 Q5

Skeleton Solution

This is a negligence and vicarious liability question which requires vicarious liability to be approached from the less usual angle of whether the tortfeasor is an independent contractor or an employee rather than whether he was in the course of employment. The question also requires discussion about damages and the heads under which the plaintiff may claim.

Suggested Solution

The issue here is whether Lucy has a cause of action against Rodney in negligence or against Scramblers Messenger Services (SMS) on the basis of vicarious liability. Lucy will be suing for damages as a dependant of Stewart on behalf of herself and the

15

children under the Fatal Accidents Act 1976, or on behalf of his estate under the Law Reform (Miscellaneous Provisions) Act 1934, both statutes having been amended by the Administration of Justice Act 1982.

In order for an action in negligence to be successful, three elements must be proved; first, the defendant, Rodney, must owe Stewart a duty of care, he must be in breach of that duty, and finally, that breach must have caused damage or injury to Stewart.

The classic statement of the duty of care is that of Lord Atkin in *Donoghue* v *Stevenson* [1932] AC 562, in which he propounded the neighbour principle, according to which the defendant, as a road user, must take reasonable care to avoid acts or omissions which he can reasonably foresee would be likely to injure fellow road users. As this is a personal injuries case then *Donoghue* is the appropriate test: *B* v *Islington Health Authority* [1991] 1 All ER 825. Taking reasonable care on the road must include compliance with road traffic signs. Rodney's conduct should be measured by the standard of the 'prudent and reasonable man' (*Blyth* v *Birmingham Waterworks Co* (1856) 11 Ex 781), who would not ride through a halt sign without stopping. A reasonable man would surely foresee the risk of damage to property or personal injury as being reasonably likely to happen on the facts of this case, especially as Rodney has ridden from a minor road on to the main road; on this analysis, Rodney is therefore in breach of his duty of care.

That breach must have caused Stewart's injuries (subject to contributory negligence) if Lucy is to recover damages. It may be argued that Stewart's act of swerving is an intervening event, but it is submitted that the chain of causation is not broken by it since his reaction was the natural and probable consequence of Rodney's breach of duty. In *Knightley* v *Johns* [1982] 1 WLR 349; [1982] 1 All ER 851, the court took the view that a consequence was reasonably foreseeable if it was a natural and probable consequence of the defendant's act; on this basis, Stewart's reaction is reasonably foreseeable, and the consequences are therefore not too remote (*The Wagon Mound (No 1)* [1961] AC 388; [1961] 2 WLR 126). Since Rodney is in breach of his duty of care and that breach has caused Stewart loss, Rodney has been negligent.

Stewart , however, is at fault to some degree as he was driving at about 10 mph in excess of the speed limit, and was therefore not taking reasonable care for his own safety, so that his contributory negligence is in issue. In the words of Lord Denning in *Jones* v *Livox Quarries* [1952] 2 QB 608; [1952] 1 TLR 1377 Stewart ought reasonably to have foreseen that if he did not act as a reasonably prudent man he might hurt himself and should have taken into account the possibility of others being careless. Under s1 Law Reform (Contributory Negligence) Act 1945 the court will therefore make 'a just and equitable reduction' in Stewart's damages for his own carelessness, since it is possible that he may not have been killed had he been driving within the legal speed limit.

Even though Lucy will have a cause of action against Rodney, there are definite financial advantages in proceeding against SMS if they are vicariously liable, but the problem here lies in proving that Rodney is an employee. The control test, used by Hilbery J in *Collins* v *Herts County Council* [1947] KB 598; [1947] LJR 789, is now considered insufficient on its own to determine this issue; it requires that for an employer/employee relationship to exist, the employer must not only control what is to be done, but *how* it is to be done. No details are given on the facts of the case of the degree of control exercised by SMS over Rodney. The inadequacy of the control test led to Lord Denning introducing the business integration test in *Stevenson, Jordan and Harrison* v *MacDonald & Evans* [1952] 1 TLR 101 which turns on whether the tortfeasor is engaged under a contract of service (in which case he will be an employee) or a contract for services (when he will be an independent contractor). This test was expanded and supplemented by MacKenna J in *Ready Mixed Concrete* v *Minister of Pensions* [1968] 2 QB 497; [1968] 2 WLR 775 so that a contract of service will exist where (i) the servant has agreed to supply his work and skill for remuneration and this has probably been agreed between Rodney and SMS; (ii) Rodney must have agreed that in performing the service, he should be subject to sufficient control to make SMS his master, but the facts as shown do not indicate such a degree of control: (iii) the other terms of the contract must be consistent with it being a contract of service eg if there is a term that the party in question must provide his own tools and equipment, that is inconsistent. Here, Rodney provides his own motorcycle; in such circumstances, according to MacKenna J, there may be a contract of service if transport is incidental to the main purpose of the contract, but here, it is the essential nature of the job.

Another factor to be taken into account is the degree of financial risk to be borne by Rodney, but that is not clear on the facts. Several circumstances and factors, however, suggest that Rodney is an independent contractor; first, if he were an employee, SMS would probably have made more stringent enquiries about his driving licence and any previous convictions: Rodney is a student, and he only works on Saturdays and some evenings (although being a part-time worker does not per se render a tortfeasor an independent contractor: see *Market Investigations* v *Minister of Social Security* [1969] 2 QB 173; [1969] 2 WLR 1.

On balance, therefore, SMS could not be vicariously liable for Rodney's negligence since he is not their employee.

Lucy may sue him on behalf of Stewart's estate under the Law Reform (Miscellaneous Provisions) Act 1934 (as amended by the AJA 1982) in which case her claim will consist of damages for funeral expenses if not claimed under the Fatal Accidents Act (which is more likely) and any special damage eg damage to the car: she cannot now claim damages for loss of expectation of life if Stewart's death occurred after 1 January 1983 (s1 AJA 1982), nor can she claim for pain and suffering if his death was, as seems probable, instantaneous. She may also claim for herself and the children as dependants under the Fatal Accidents Act 1976 for the loss of their dependancy. Lucy, as his wife, may additionally claim damages for bereavement under the new s1A of the FAA, currently fixed at £7,500. She will claim for the pecuniary loss incurred by the dependants before the trial and for future loss, by calculating a multiplicand on the basis of the annual cost of the dependancy, and a multiplier which in this case will be quite high (though not more than 16) since Stewart was relatively young. An appropriate deduction will then be made from those damages for Stewart's contributory negligence.

QUESTION THREE

Fergus is employed as a driver by the Egmont Engineering Co. It is a company rule that only their employees may be carried in their vehicles. A notice is displayed on the dashboard of Fergus's van, reading:

'Egmont employees only in this van. The company can accept no liability towards any other persons riding in this vehicle.'

One day Fergus has to drive to the premises of a supplier to collect some materials. George, an employee of a firm of electrical contractors repairing machinery at the Egmont plant, asks if he can have a lift to collect some supplies urgently needed for their repairs. Fergus agrees, but on the way he is gripped by severe chest pains, George asks him, 'Are you feeling well enough?' Fergus replies, 'Yes, just a touch of indigestion.' George allows him to continue to drive. A few minutes later Fergus loses control of the van and crashes into a lamp-post. George is thrown out of the van and is severely injured. He had not been wearing a seat belt because he felt trapped if he did so. If he had been wearing a belt, his injuries would have been slight.

It is later discovered that Fergus had had a heart attack and he can now remember nothing of the accident.

Advise George.

Written by the editor

Suggested Solution

George will base his action on Fergus' negligence, and may be in a position to sue Fergus' employers should they be vicariously liable.

He must first prove that Fergus owed him a duty of care to take reasonable steps for his safety while he is a passenger, and a duty of care has been found to exist between passenger and driver in cases such as *Froom* v *Butcher* [1976] QB 286; [1975] 3 WLR 379. Since Fergus should have George in his reasonable contemplation as he may be harmed by his carelessness, it is submitted that he is under a duty of care. A breach of that duty will be proved if a reasonable man would not have acted in the same way (*Blyth* v *Birmingham Waterworks* (1856) 11 Ex 781). On the facts, it is not per se a breach that Fergus lost control of the vehicle, but a reasonable and prudent driver may, on feeling unwell, pull into the side of the road and stop his vehicle, especially if he had a passenger, and so Fergus is in breach by continuing to drive when he feels unwell. Res ipsa loquitur has no application here since the reason for Fergus' loss of control is ascertainable (*Barkway* v *South Wales Transport* [1950] AC 185; [1950] 1 All ER 392). Fergus' breach has caused George's injuries, so that negligence has prima facie been made out.

The second issue is whether Egmont Engineering Co is vicariously liable for Fergus' negligence. Fergus must be their employee, which is apparent from the facts, but it must also be determined whether he is 'in the course of employment'. This phrase has in recent times been construed by the courts very liberally. The question to be asked is whether Fergus was performing an act which he was authorised to do or which was reasonably incidental to his employment, even though he may have been doing it in an unauthorised manner; if he was his employers will be liable.

The fact that Fergus undoubtedly knew of his employers' prohibition on the carrying of non-employees is, it is submitted, by no means decisive. In *Limpus* v *London General Omnibus Co* (1862) 1 H & C 526, contrary to his employers' express instructions, a bus driver obstructed buses from a rival company and caused an accident; it was held that the employers were still vicariously liable because the driver's act was merely a wrongful act of carrying out an authorised act, ie the driving of buses, and was not an act which he was not employed to do at all. The prohibition related to the mode of performing his job and not to the scope of his employment (cf *Beard* v *London General Omnibus Co* [1900] 2 QB 530).

A contrary view was taken as to a prohibition in *Twine* v *Bean's Express* [1946] 1 All ER 202; (1946) 62 TLR 458, a case with facts similar to those in George's case, except that in *Twine* a hitch-hiker was given a lift. It was held that an employee giving a lift to an unauthorised person is acting outside the course of his employment. Since the plaintiff was a trespasser, the employers owed him no duty of care. The latter reason now seems erroneous in the light of *British Railways Board* v *Herrington* [1972] AC 877; [1972] 2 WLR 537 and the Occupiers Liability Act 1984, where a modified duty of care was held to apply to trespassers, but the main distinction is that the court in *Twine* based vicarious liability on a duty of care owed by the employer to the plaintiff, a view which today has lost favour, so that modern courts examine instead the employer/employee relationship.

The decision in *Twine* was disapproved of by a majority of the Court of Appeal in *Rose* v *Plenty* [1976] 1 WLR 141; [1976] 1 All ER 97 where the trespassory status of the plaintiff in the milk-float was regarded as irrelevant, and in any event the presence of the boy was in effect furthering the employer's interests in helping to deliver milk.

It is submitted that *Rose* is the preferable decision to apply in this case so that the prohibition relates only to the way in which Fergus is to carry out his job as a driver and it is immaterial that George is a trespasser. It may further be argued that George's presence is indirectly furthering Egmont's interests, since he is an employee of contractors repairing machinery at the Egmont plant. As long as Fergus has not deviated from his route, he is not on a frolic of his own.

Egmont's notice should also be read in the light of s2 of the Unfair Contract Terms Act 1977, so that the employers could not rely on the notice to the extent that it purports to exclude liability for death or personal injury caused by negligence.

Fergus and Egmont would be able to claim contributory negligence against George on two possible grounds. The clearest is his failure to wear a seat-belt and he must face a reduction in his damages of 20% – 15% since his injuries would have been slight had he worn one (*Froom* v *Butcher* (above)). His aversion to seat-belts is unlikely to affect this, per Denning MR in *Froom*, unless his aversion amounted to a 'phobia': *Condon* v *Condon* [1978] RTR 483. He may also have acted without regard for his own safety by allowing Fergus to continue driving when he felt unwell; this case is different from decisions such as *Owens* v *Brimmell* [1977] QB 859; [1977] 2 WLR 943 where the plaintiff knew of the defendant's disability (drunkenness) before he accepted a lift, so that this ground is less certain to succeed.

Volenti may also be raised against George for accepting a lift in view of the notice displayed in the van. For this defence to succeed, George must have voluntarily submitted to the risk of injury, and must have had knowledge of the danger. It is therefore unlikely to succeed on these facts, since George, by ignoring the notice, has not consented to the risk of injury by Fergus' negligence (s2(3) Unfair Contract Terms Act 1977).

5 NEGLIGENCE: DUTY OF CARE

5.1 Introduction

In tort the word negligence has two meanings: it can be a mode of committing certain acts, and negligence in this sense means carelessness; or it can be an independent tort, and it is this we shall now consider.

The tort of negligence has been defined as 'the breach of a legal duty to take care which results in damage, undesired by the defendant, to the plaintiff (Winfield & Jolowicz). The tort has three elements:

1   The defendant must owe the plaintiff a duty of care.

2   The defendant must be in breach of this duty.

3   Damage must have been caused to the plaintiff by the defendant's breach and such damage must not be too remote.

The first element of the tort will be considered in this chapter and the second and third elements in subsequent chapters.

5.2 Key points

The general principle is the neighbour principle as formulated in *Donoghue* v *Stevenson* [1932] AC 562: 'You must take reasonable care to avoid acts or omissions which you can reasonably foresee would be likely to injure your neighbour. Who, then, in law is my neighbour? The answer seems to be – persons who are so closely and directly affected by my act that I ought reasonably to have them in contemplation as being so affected when I am directing my mind to the acts or omissions which are called in question.'

a) *Development*

The neighbour principle was taken further by Lord Wilberforce in *Anns* v *Merton London Borough Council* [1978] AC 728 when he proposed a two–tier test:

Firstly: as between the alleged wrongdoer and the person who has suffered damage is there a sufficient relationship of proximity or neighbourhood such that, in the reasonable contemplation of the former, carelessness on his part may be likely to cause damage to the latter, in which case a prima facie duty of care arises.

Secondly: if the first question is answered affirmatively are there any considerations which ought to negative or reduce or limit the scope of the duty

5 NEGLIGENCE: DUTY OF CARE

or the class of persons to whom it is owed or the damages to which a breach of it may give rise?

The effect of this two tier test was to expand considerably the scope of the tort of negligence, but the test has been the subject of much judicial criticism.

b) *Current formulation*

In *Peabody Donation Fund* v *Parkinson* [1985] AC 210 Lord Keith introduced the requirement that it should be just and reasonable that a duty of care should exist. Subsequent cases have emphasised this just and reasonable criterion, see especially *Davis* v *Radcliffe* [1990] 2 All ER 536.

Note the recent formulation of the test for duty of care by the House of Lords in *Caparo Industries* v *Dickman* [1990] 2 WLR 358, namely that there are three criteria for the imposition of a duty of care, viz.

foreseeability of damage

proximity of relationship

reasonableness or otherwise of imposing a duty.

In particular, in determining whether there was a relationship of proximity between the parties, the court, guided by situations in which the existence, scope and limits of a duty of care had previously been held to exist rather than a single general principle, would determine whether the particular damage suffered was the kind of damage which the defendant was under a duty to prevent and whether there were circumstances from which the court could pragmatically conclude that a duty of care existed, adopting the dictum of Brennan J in *Sutherland Shire Council* v *Heyman* (1985) 60 ALR 1.

The problem the courts have found with Lord Wilberforce's test is that it is so easy to satisfy the first requirement that too much is left to the second requirement, ie to a policy decision.

Note that *Anns* has been overruled on its facts by the House of Lords in *Murphy* v *Brentwood District Council* [1990] 2 All ER 908; in *Murphy* the House noted that reservations had been expressed regarding the two tier test and stated a preference for the incremental approach of *Sutherland Shire Council*, although in *Ravenscroft* v *Rederiaktiebolaget Transatlantic* [1991] 3 All ER 73 Ward J held at first instance that the two tier test had been overruled by *Murphy*.

The courts have also held that where the plaintiff has an alternative remedy, eg in contract or where there are statutory regulations covering the situation, that a duty of care should not be imposed which would have the effect of taking the law beyond contractual agreement or Parliamentary intention, eg *Greater Nottingham Co-operative Society* v *Cementation Piling & Foundations* [1989] QB 71; [1988] 2 All ER 971 (contractual agreement); *Reid* v *Rush & Tomkins Group* [1990] 1 WLR 212; [1989] 3 All ER 228 (contractual agreement); *Curran* v *Northern Ireland Co-ownership Housing Association* [1987] AC 718 (regulations); *Mills* v *Winchester Diocesan Board of Finance* [1989] 2 All ER 317 (regulations); *Marc Rich* v *Bishop Rock Marine* [1994] 1 WLR 1071 (Hague-Visby Rules).

In *Yuen Kun Yeu* v *AG of Hong Kong* [1988] AC 175 and *Hill* v *Chief Constable of West Yorkshire* [1989] AC 53; [1988] 2 WLR 1049 it was emphasised that mere foreseeability of harm was insufficient to impose a duty of care. Those cases decided between 1978 and 1985 in which a duty was imposed on the grounds of pure foreseeability can no longer be supported – see, for example, the criticism of *JEB Fasteners* v *Marks, Bloom* [1983] 1 All ER 583 by Lord Bridge in *Caparo* (above).

c) *Negligent misrepresentation*

The courts have been reluctant to impose a duty of care as regards the careless making of statements as opposed to liability for careless acts. But in *Hedley Byrne* v *Heller* [1964] AC 465 the House of Lords held that a duty to take care in making statements could arise. Normal *Donoghue* principles were not applied as a strict application of these principles would have led to too great a liability. Instead it was held that a duty of care would arise where there was a special relationship between the parties. For such a relationship to arise:

i)   The representor must have a special skill. Although the Privy Council in *Mutual Life* v *Evatt* [1971] AC 793 took a narrow view of this criterion, the Court of Appeal has followed the more liberal minority view: *Esso Petroleum* v *Mardon* [1976] 1 QB 801; *Howard Marine and Dredging* v *Ogden* [1978] QB 574.

ii) The representee must reasonably rely on the representation. Note that the Privy Council has taken a narrow view of this criterion also: *Royal Bank Trust* v *Pampellonne* [1987] 1 Lloyd's Rep 218. If such reliance is absent the plaintiff may, in exceptional cases, rely on ordinary *Donoghue* principles: *Ross* v *Caunters* [1980] Ch 287.

iii) The defendant must have some knowledge of the type of transaction in question: eg *Smith* v *Eric Bush* [1989] 2 WLR 790; [1989] 2 All ER 514.

Note the finding of a special relationship in *Edwards* v *Lee* [1991] NLJ 1517.

In *Caparo Industries* v *Dickman* (above) the House of Lords considered the situation where a person puts a statement into general circulation, as opposed to the situation where the defendant is aware of the transaction the plaintiff contemplated, knew the advice would be communicated to the plaintiff and knew it was likely that the plaintiff would rely on that advice (as, for example, in *Smith*, above). In the former case it was held that no duty would arise as the essential requirement of proximity was missing.

Note Lord Oliver's analysis of *Hedley Byrne* in *Caparo* and the application of *Caparo* in *Al-Nakib Investments* v *Longcroft* [1990] 3 All ER 321, *Morgan Crucible* v *Hill Samuel* [1991] 1 All ER 148 and *James McNaughton Paper Group* v *Hicks Anderson* [1991] 1 All ER 134; note especially the factors elucidated by Neill LJ in *James McNaughton* from his analysis of the cases as being relevant to the imposition or otherwise of a duty of care.

d) *Pure economic loss*

Because of the 'floodgates' argument the courts have held that no liability in negligence can arise for pure economic loss: *Cattle* v *Stockton Waterworks* (1875) LR 10 QB 453, ie economic loss which is not consequent on damage to the person or property of the plaintiff. However, in 1983 in *Junior Books* v *Veitchi* [1983]

AC 520 recovery was allowed for pure economic loss as between the owner of a building and a nominated sub-contractor. Note that this case was decided before the retreat from *Anns* (above) when foreseeability of damage played a greater part in the imposition of a duty of care – see chapter 4.1(b) above.

The courts have consistently refused to apply *Junior Books* since 1986 – see for example *Muirhead* v *Industrial Tank Specialities* [1986] QB 507; *Aswan Engineering Establishment* v *Lupdine* [1987] 1 All ER 135; *Simaan General Contracting* v *Pilkington Glass* [1988] QB 758; [1988] 2 WLR 761; *Greater Nottingham Co-operative Society* v *Cementation Piling & Foundations* [1989] QB 71.

In the House of Lords in *D & F Estates* v *Church Commissioners* [1989] AC 177; [1988] 3 WLR 368 it was said of *Junior Books* that 'the decision cannot be regarded as laying down any principle of general application in the law of tort' per Lord Bridge, and that it was 'really of no use as an authority on the general duty of care' per Lord Oliver, and perhaps the strongest criticism of all in *Simaan Contracting* where it was said that the case had been 'the subject of so much analysis and discussion with differing explanations of the basis of the case that the case cannot now be regarded as a useful pointer to any development of law... Indeed I find it difficult to see that future citation from *Junior Books* can ever serve any useful purpose' per Dillon LJ.

It thus seems unlikely that *Junior Books* will be applied in the future, and in *Nitrigin Eirann Teoranta* v *Inca Alloys* [1992] 1 All ER 854 the High Court again refused to apply *Junior Books* holding that that case was 'unique'. See also *Lancashire & Cheshire Association of Baptist Churches* v *Howard & Seddon Partnership* [1993] 3 All ER 467.

Note that in the above discussion we are considering pure economic loss resulting from a negligent *act*; pure economic loss resulting from a negligent misstatement is, of course, recoverable under *Hedley Byrne* (see 5.2(d) above). However, in three recent cases in the House of Lords it was held that *Hedley Byrne* covered negligent acts and omissions as well as negligent statements where there has been a voluntary assumption of responsibility towards the defendant: *Henderson* v *Merrett Syndicates* [1994] 3 WLR 761; *Spring* v *Guardian Assurance* [1994] 3 WLR 354 and *White* v *Jones* [1995] 2 WLR 187 – see especially the speeches of Lord Goff.

e) *Nervous shock*

By nervous shock or psychiatric damage, the law means mental injury or psychiatric illness, not merely grief or sorrow: *Brice* v *Brown* [1984] 1 All ER 997. See also the recent case of *Nicholls* v *Rushton* (1992) The Times 19 June.

Originally it was held that no duty of care arose because of the fear of fraudulent claims: *Victorian Railway Commissioners* v *Coultas* (1888) 13 App Cas 222. Gradually, however, the courts retreated from this stand and allowed recovery where the plaintiff was in fear of her own safety: *Dulieu* v *White* [1901] 2 KB 669, or in fear for the safety of her children: *Hambrook* v *Stokes Bros* [1925] 1 KB 141. However, this area of negligence was still burdened by concepts such as that the plaintiff had to witness the accident through his own senses and had to be in the vicinity of the accident. In *McLoughlin* v *O'Brian* [1983] AC 410 the House of Lords held that the appropriate test to apply was that of reasonable foreseeability. Lord Wilberforce stated that the law must limit those situations in which the plaintiff could recover for nervous shock and postulated three elements which should be present for a claim to succeed, but Lord Bridge said that Lord Wilberforce's approach was too rigid and that pure reasonable foreseeability was the test.

In *Attia* v *British Gas* [1988] QB 304 the Court of Appeal allowed recovery for nervous shock following damage to property continuing the incremental approach of allowing recovery to a range of plaintiffs, and in *Hevican* v *Ruane* [1991] 3 All ER 65 and *Ravenscroft* v *Rederiaktiebolaget Transatlantic* [1991] 3 All ER 73 the plaintiffs succeeded despite not being present at the accident or its aftermath. However, in the leading case of *Alcock* v *Chief Constable of South Yorkshire Police* [1991] 4 All ER 907 the House of Lords held a plaintiff could only recover from nervous shock if he satisfied both the test of reasonable foreseeability that he would be so affected because of the close relationship of love and affection with the primary victim, and the test of proximity to the tortfeasor in terms of physical and temporal connection between the plaintiff and the accident.

Hence a plaintiff could only recover if:

i) his relationship to the primary victim was sufficiently close that it was reasonably foreseeable that he might suffer nervous shock;

ii) his proximity to the accident or its immediate aftermath was sufficiently close both in time and space; and

iii) he suffered nervous shock through seeing or hearing the accident or its immediate aftermath.

Thus a plaintiff who suffered psychiatric illness not caused by sudden nervous shock through seeing or hearing the accident or its immediate aftermath, or who suffered nervous shock caused by being informed of the accident by a third party, did not satisfy the tests of reasonable foreseeability and proximity. Also, given the television broadcasting guidelines, persons who witnessed the Hillsborough disaster live on television had not suffered nervous shock induced by the sight or hearing of the event as they were not in the proximity to the event and would not have suffered shock in the sense of a sudden assault on the nervous system.

The House of Lords doubted that *Hevican* or *Ravenscroft* had been correctly decided, and *Ravenscroft* has been overruled by the Court of Appeal [1992] 2 All ER 470.

The House of Lords also held that the class of persons who may claim for nervous shock was not limited to particular relationships such as husband and wife or parent and child.

The House also suggested that a bystander who witnesses a particularly horrific catastrophe may recover, and that in certain circumstances a plaintiff may recover on witnessing an event on simultaneous television. However, in *McFarlane* v *Caledonia Ltd* [1994] 2 All ER 1 the Court of Appeal held that a bystander could not recover unless he was proximate in time and place and there was a close relationship of love and affection between the plaintiff and the victim. Note also

Page v *Smith* [1994] 4 All ER 522 where the Court of Appeal stressed the point that psychiatric damage had to be foreseeable to a person of ordinary fortitude before liability could arise.

f) *Third parties*

As regards a person's duty to prevent third parties from inflicting damage on the plaintiff see the House of Lords decision in *Smith* v *Littlewoods Organisation* [1987] AC 241 and especially the speech of Lord Goff.

g) *Police*

Do not have any general immunity from the law: *Rigby* v *Chief Constable of Northamptonshire* [1985] 1 WLR 1242; *Kirkham* v *Chief Constable of Greater Manchester Police* [1990] 3 All ER 246 but in many negligence situations there will be insufficient proximity to impose a duty: *Hill* v *Chief Constable of West Yorkshire* (above); *Clough* v *Bussan* [1990] 1 All ER 431; *Ancell* v *McDermott* [1994] 4 All ER 355; *Alexandrou* v *Oxford* [1994] 4 All ER 328; *Osman* v *Ferguson* [1993] 4 All ER 344. See also *Hughes* v *National Union of Mineworkers* [1991] 4 All ER 278.

h) *Judges and legal representatives*

Cannot be sued for their conduct of a case: *Rondel* v *Worsley* [1969] 1 AC 191; *Somasundaram* v *Julius Melchior* [1989] 1 All ER 129; *Gran Gelato* v *Richcliff* [1992] 1 All ER 865; but note *Walpole* v *Partridge & Wilson* [1993] 3 WLR 1093. But if a legal adviser steps outside his role liability may be imposed: *Al-Kandari* v *Brown* [1988] QB 665; [1988] 1 All ER 833.

i) *Exercise of a statutory power*

A distinction is drawn between policy and operational decisions, the latter being capable of being exercised negligently: *Sheppard* v *Glossop Corporation* [1921] 3 KB 132; *Home Office* v *Dorset Yacht* [1970] AC 1004.

In *Jones* v *Department of Employment* [1989] QB 1; [1988] 1 All ER 725 it was held that a civil servant owed no duty of care and remedy was via judicial review: see also *Mills* v *Winchester Diocesan Board of Finance* (above).

5.3   Recent cases

Caparo Industries v *Dickman Industries* [1990] 2 WLR 358

Reid v *Rush & Tomkins Group* [1990] 1 WLR 212; [1989] 3 All ER 228

Mariola Marine v *Lloyd's Register* [1990] 1 Lloyd's Rep 547

Clough v *Bussan* [1990] 1 All ER 431

Al-Nakib Investments v *Longcroft* [1990] 3 All ER 321

Davis v *Radcliffe* [1990] 2 All ER 536

Department of Environment v *Thomas Bates* [1990] 2 All ER 943

Murphy v *Brentwood District Council* [1990] 2 All ER 908

Morgan Crucible v *Hill Samuel* [1991] 1 All ER 148

James McNaughton Paper Group v *Hicks Anderson* [1991] 1 All ER 134

Alexandrou v *Oxford* [1993] 4 All ER 328

Hughes v *National Union of Mineworkers* [1991] 4 All ER 278

Edwards v *Lee* [1991] NLJ 1517

Alcock v *Chief Constable of South Yorkshire Police* [1991] 4 All ER 907

Ancell v *McDermott* [1994] 4 All ER 355

Lancashire & Cheshire Association of Baptist Churches v *Howard & Seddon Partnership* [1993] 3 All ER 467

Walpole v *Partridge & Wilson* [1993] 3 WLR 1093

Marc Rich v *Bishop Rock Marine* [1994] 1 WLR 1071

Henderson v *Merrett Syndicates* [1994] 3 WLR 761

Spring v *Guardian Assurance* [1994] 3 WLR 354

White v *Jones* [1995] 2 WLR 187

McFarlane v *Caledonia Ltd* [1994] 2 All ER 1

Page v *Smith* [1994] 4 All ER 522

Osman v *Ferguson* [1994] 4 All ER 344

5.4 Analysis of questions

The existence or otherwise of a duty of care must come up in every tort paper. Sometimes this may be a descriptive essay eg on the development of the *Anns* test or negligent misstatement, or it may occur in a problem where there are a number of possible defendants. In the latter situation the existence of a duty may be trite, eg a driver of a motor vehicle and other road users, or it may have to be argued through and a decison reached.

5.5 Questions

QUESTION ONE

Is it correct to say that since *Anns* v *Merton London Borough Council* (1978) the courts have consistently tried to restrict the scope of the duty of care and the persons to whom it is owed? If so, has this been a desirable development?

University of London LLB Examination
(for External Students) Law of Tort June 1987 Q2

Skeleton Solution

Duty of care – one of three elements of negligence – two tier test laid down in *Anns* – high water mark in the development of the duty of care – initial expansion in cases such as *Junior Books* and *McLoughlin* – then period of restriction in cases such as *Aliakmon*, *Curran* and *Yeun Kun Yeu* – misfeasance and nonfeasance – too much emphasis upon policy?

Suggested Solution

The decision of the House of Lords in *Anns v Merton London Borough Council* [1978] AC 728 is of fundamental importance to the development of the tort of negligence, and in particular to the development of the duty of care. The duty of care is a vital concept in the tort of negligence. It is one of the three essential ingredients of the tort of negligence, the other two being breach of duty and damage.

The origins of the present law relating to the duty of care lie in the judgment of Lord Atkin in *Donoghue v Stevenson* [1932] AC 562. Lord Atkin stated that there is a general principle in English law that a person must take reasonable care to avoid acts or omissions which he can reasonably foresee will be likely to injure his neighbour. For this purpose a neighbour was held to be someone who is so closely and directly affected by my act that I ought reasonably to have had him in contemplation as likely to be affected by my act. The importance of Lord Atkin's judgment lay in its willingness to recognise that this was a statement of general principle which was capable of application to new fact situations. The recognition that *Donoghue* was a statement of general principle was recognised by Lord Reid in *Home Office v Dorset Yacht* [1970] AC 1004 when he said that the time had come to apply the principle established in *Donoghue* unless there was some justification for not applying it. It was, however, in *Anns* that the clearest recognition was given to the fact that *Donoghue* was a principle of general application.

The test laid down by Lord Wilberforce in *Anns* has since been described as the 'high-water mark' in the development of the tort of negligence (see Lord Bridge in *Curran v Northern Ireland Co-ownership Housing Association* [1987] AC 718; [1987] 2 WLR 1043). The test was laid down in two parts. At the first stage the question to be asked was whether there was a relationship of proximity between the tortfeasor and the injured party which was such that, in the reasonable contemplation of the former, carelessness on his part may be likely to cause damage to the latter. If the question at the first stage was answered in the affirmative then it had to be considered whether or not there were any considerations of policy which excluded the duty or restricted its scope. This two tier test provided the judiciary with an opportunity to expand the horizons of the tort of negligence because the first tier was thought to be satisfied relatively easily and that only left the second stage, based upon consideration of policy, as a limitation upon the development of the tort of negligence.

It would not, however, be true to say that the courts have consistently tried to limit the scope of the duty of care and the persons to whom it is owed. In the period immediately post *Anns*, the courts were, in fact, prepared to extend the ambit of the duty of care. This can be seen in the following three cases. The first was the case of *Junior Books v The Veitchi Company Ltd* [1983] AC 520, where the House of Lords held that a factory owner could sue a sub-contractor in tort for failing to lay a floor properly and that they could recover damages in respect of the cost of relaying the floor and in respect of the consequent disruption to their business. The floor was not a source of danger to health or safety but it was nevertheless held that a duty of care was owed by the defendants to the plaintiffs. The effect of this judgment was to undermine, to a large extent, the doctrine of privity of contract because the factory owners were able to obtain their promised floor even though they were not privy to the contract with the sub-contractors. In many ways this was the most remarkable extension of *Anns* because it took tort into an area which had hitherto been the preserve of the law of contract.

A second case in which the courts were prepared to expand the ambit of the duty of care was *McLoughlin* v *O'Brian* [1983] AC 410 in which the House of Lords held that a mother could recover for the nervous shock which she suffered as a result of seeing her children in hospital, even though she had not actually been at the scene of the accident but had come upon its 'immediate aftermath'. The House of Lords dismissed the argument that this would open the floodgates of liability and were prepared instead to expand the range of liability. The third case is a case in which the category of persons to whom a duty of care is owed was extended. In *Emeh* v *Kensington Area Health Authority* [1985] QB 1012; [1985] 2 WLR 233 it was held that a mother could maintain an action against the defendants for the cost of upkeep of her child when it had been conceived after the defendants had negligently performed a sterilisation operation upon the plaintiff. The Court of Appeal held that there were no policy objections to holding that a duty of care was owed on the facts of the case.

However it would be true to say that since 1985 the courts have taken a more restrictive approach to the development of the duty of care and, indeed, seem to be drawing back on the advances made in *Anns*. This can be seen in the case of *The Aliakmon* [1986] AC 785; [1985] 1 QB 350 CA; [1986] 2 All ER 145 HL. There it was held that a plaintiff could not maintain an action in tort when, at the time of the damage, he had neither a possessory nor a proprietary interest in the property. Both the Court of Appeal and the House of Lords refused to re-examine the existing lines of authority in the light of *Anns*. Lord Brandon stated that Lord Wilberforce's judgment in *Anns* was given in the context of a novel factual situation and was not to be applied where there was a consistent line of authority denying the existence of a duty of care. This constitutes an attack upon the generality of the principle in *Anns*.

The retreat from *Anns* can also be seen in the treatment which has been afforded to *Junior Books*. The House of Lords has twice refused to apply it, as has the Court of Appeal. The result is that *Junior Books* has almost been distinguished out of existence and the advances which were thought to have been made by *Junior Books* have now been undone.

Perhaps the most fundamental assault upon *Anns* can be seen in the judgment of Lord Bridge in *Curran* v *Northern Ireland Co-ownership Housing Association* [1987] AC 718; [1987] 2 WLR 1043 and in the judgment of Lord Keith in *Yeun Kun Yeu* v *Attorney General of Hong Kong* [1988] AC 175; [1987] 2 All ER 705. Lord Bridge criticised the judgment of Lord Wilberforce on two grounds. The first was that it failed to take account of the distinction between misfeasance and nonfeasance. The former is concerned with cases of causing damage through a negligent act, whereas the latter is concerned with failing to prevent harm from arising. The fact situation in *Curran* neatly illustrates the distinction. The defendants were statutorily responsible for the financing of improvement grants and the work had to be executed to their satisfaction. The work on the property which the plaintiffs bought had been done negligently and so the plaintiffs sought to recover their loss from the defendants. It was held that the defendants did not owe the plaintiffs a duty of care because the statute was not enacted to protect the interests of owner occupiers but to ensure that public money was properly spent. However this was not a case in which the defendants had caused loss to the plaintiffs by a negligent act. It was a case in which it was alleged that they had failed to prevent the builders from inflicting loss on the plaintiffs. It is submitted that this restriction upon *Anns* is a perfectly desirable development because the effect of *Anns* was to obscure this fundamental distinction between misfeasance and nonfeasance. The importance of this distinction can be seen in the judgment of Lord Goff in *Smith* v *Littlewoods Organisation Ltd* [1987] AC 241; [1987] 1 All ER 710 when he held on the facts that no duty of care was owed by the defendant to prevent third parties from doing damage to the plaintiff's property. A similar analysis can be used to explain the reasoning of the Court of Appeal in *Hill* v *Chief Constable of West Yorkshire* [1989] AC 53; [1988] 2 WLR 1049.

The second reason given by Lord Bridge in *Curran* for the withdrawal from *Anns* is a judicial reluctance to place such strong emphasis upon policy as the operative factor in restricting the scope of the duty of care. This can be seen in the judgment of the Court of Appeal in *The Aliakmon* and in the judgments of the House of Lords in *Curran* and *Yuen Kun Yeu*. The fear seems to be that the first tier in the *Anns* formulation was too easy to overcome and that too much emphasis was being placed upon policy factors. This can be clearly seen in Lord Keith's re-interpretation of Lord Wilberforce's judgment in *Anns* when he said that it would only be in rare cases that the second, policy stage would be resorted to and that most cases would be resolved at the first stage.

It is submitted that, unlike the first reason given by Lord Bridge in *Curran*, this development is not a desirable one in so far as it is likely to result in the judges refusing to articulate the true reasoning behind their judgments. However, apart from this point, it is submitted that the restrictions recently placed upon the development of the *Anns* principle have been desirable in the sense that they have resulted in the restatement of the distinction between misfeasance and nonfeasance.

Finally it should be noted that *Anns* has been overruled on its facts by the House of Lords in *Murphy* v *Brentwood District Council* [1990] 2 All ER 908; in *Murphy* the House noted that reservations had been expressed regarding the two-tier test and stated a preference for the incremental approach of Brennan J in *Sutherland Shire Council* v *Heyman* (1985) 60 ALR 1, and in *Ravenscroft* v *Rederiaktiebolaget Transatlantic* [1991] 3 All ER 73 Ward J held at first instance that the *Anns* test had been overruled by *Murphy*.

QUESTION TWO

Tyrant Industries plc decided to install a light railway to transport raw materials and finished goods between its factory premises and a railway station three miles away. They reached an agreement with Farmer Fred that for part of the distance they would utilise disused tracks which ran on an embankment across Fred's land. The local authority gave planning permission on condition *inter alia* that the embankment would be suitably landscaped and that the landscaping scheme would be approved by the Foliage Consultancy Council, a body established by the government to advise on certain environmental protection policies. Tyrant Industries contracted with Sleepers plc to carry out the main construction work. The contract permitted Tyrant Industries to nominate sub-contractors to carry out parts of the work and provided that Sleepers would not be liable for the neglect or wilful default of subcontractors. Tyrant Industries nominated Greenmadness Ltd as sub-contractors for the landscaping work. Greenmadness Ltd submitted a scheme which was approved by the Foliage Consultancy Council. The work was carried out in 1988. Tyrant Industries also contracted with Cleaners Ltd that Cleaners would maintain the tracks for a period of five years for a fixed annual sum.

As a result of the dry summer of 1989 and the ensuing mild winter the trees chosen by Greenmadness grew very rapidly and proved to be unsuitable for the embankment, which has become weakened. It poses no danger in itself but is at present insufficiently strong to carry trains. Tyrant Industries have had to purchase a fleet of heavy lorries to transport goods and have to meet the much higher transport costs involved. Because the tracks are not in use, the maintenance work is much more complex and Cleaners Ltd find that their contract has become more onerous.

Advise Tyrant Industries and Cleaners whether they have any claims in tort.

University of London LLB Examination
(for External Students) Law of Tort June 1990 Q7

Suggested Solution

It is clear from the facts of the problem that the loss suffered by Tyrant Industries and Cleaners is pure economic loss. We must therefore consider the situations in which the law will allow recovery for such loss.

The traditional approach of the courts was to deny recovery of economic loss that was not consequent upon damage to the person or property of the plaintiff: *Spartan Steel & Alloys* v *Martin* [1973] 1 QB 27.

However, in 1983 in *Junior Books* v *Veitchi* [1983] AC 520 the House of Lords allowed recovery for economic loss suffered by the plaintiff when a firm of sub-contractors, with whom the plaintiff had no contractual relationship, laid a floor defectively. It was held that there was such a relationship of proximity between the plaintiff and the defendant that the defendant owed the plaintiff a duty of care to avoid economic loss. *Junior Books* was decided when the two-tier test of Lord Wilberforce in *Anns* v *Merton London Borough Council* [1978] AC 728 was still used to determine the existence of a duty of care and the House of Lords relied heavily on the fact that the plaintiff had nominated the defendant to lay the floor and had relied on the defendant to carry out this work properly, that this reliance was known to the defendants and that the damage was a direct and foreseeable result of the defendants' negligence. Interestingly, Lord Brandon dissented on the grounds that the decision effectively created contractual obligations while circumventing contractual concepts such as privity and consideration.

Recent subsequent cases have not followed *Junior Books*; in parallel with the retreat from *Anns*, which formed the basis for *Junior Books*, the latter case has been the subject of much judicial analysis and criticism. In *Muirhead* v *Industrial Tank Specialities* [1986] QB 507 *Junior Books* was not followed and in *Aswan Engineering Establishment* v *Lupdine* [1987] 1 All ER 135 it was said that where the defect renders the product less valuable the plaintiff's remedy lies in contract, and where the defect creates a danger to others the remedy lies in tort, and that *Junior Books* was the first case to cross this line.

In *Simaan General Contracting* v *Pilkington* [1988] QB 758; [1988] 2 WLR 761 there was a nominated sub-contractor situation but *Junior Books* was not applied, and in *Greater Nottingham Co-operative Society* v *Cementation Piling & Foundations* [1989] QB 71; [1988] 2 All ER 971 there was a contract between the plaintiff and the defendants who were nominated sub-contractors. The defendants carried out their work carelessly but the contract related only to the materials and not the way in which the work was to be carried out. The Court of Appeal held that no duty of care arose in tort because the contractual relationship between the parties precluded this and exhaustively defined the obligations between the plaintiff and the defendant.

In *D & F Estates* v *Church Commissioners* [1989] AC 177; [1988] 3 WLR 368 the House of Lords held that a builder was not liable in tort for the cost of remedying defects in a building constructed by him if the defects did not pose an imminent threat of physical injury to the building or occupants or damage other property of the plaintiff, and where the only purpose of the remedial works was to render the buildings fit for their intended use, which seems to be the situation in the question set. In *D & F Estates* Lord Bridge stated that the consensus of judicial opinion seemed to be that *Junior Books* cannot be regarded as laying down any principle of general application in the law of tort and Lord Oliver stated it was really of no use as an authority on the general duty of care. In *Simaan General Contracting* Dillon LJ went even further and said that the case had been the subject of so much analysis and discussion with differing explanations of the case that the case cannot now be regarded as a useful pointer to any development of law and that he found it difficult to see that future citation from *Junior Books* could ever serve any useful purpose.

Given this extensive and detailed criticism of *Junior Books* Tyrant and Cleaners must be advised that there is no chance of successfully suing Greenmadness in tort for the economic loss they have suffered. The fact that Tyrant nominated Greenmadness as nominated sub-contractors is not enough to allow Tyrant to sue: *Simaan General Contracting*, nor do Cleaners have the required proximity.

The next aspect we must consider is whether Tyrant and Cleaners can sue the Foliage Consultancy Council in negligence for the economic loss they have suffered. To see whether or not Foliage owe a duty of care to these parties one would use the test for duty of care laid down in *Caparo Industries* v *Dickman* [1990] 2 WLR 358; [1990] 1 All ER 568 by the House of Lords, viz, foreseeability of damage, proximity of relationship and the reasonableness or otherwise of imposing a duty. The problem for Tyrant and Cleaners is that in *Curran* v *Northern Ireland Co-ownership Housing Association* [1987] AC 718 the House of Lords held that although the defendants had to be satisfied under regulations that certain building work was to be carried out properly, the purpose of the regulations was to ensure that public money was spent properly and not to protect the interests of the plaintiff; see also *Mariola Marine* v *Lloyd's Register* [1990] 1 Lloyd's Rep 547. In the present problem the purpose of approval by Foliage is to protect the environment and not the interests of Tyrant or Cleaners. Hence Tyrant and Cleaners cannot sue Foliage.

There is no point in Tyrant suing Sleepers in tort because following *Greater Nottingham Co-operative* the contract between Tyrant and Sleepers would define any liability for economic loss, and it is stated in the contract that there will be no liability on Sleepers' part for the neglect or wilful default of Greenmadness.

If Cleaners were to sue Sleepers, they would be met by the earlier argument regarding the difficulties of imposing a duty of care in respect of economic loss.

Thus our advice to Tyrant and Cleaners is that they have no claims in tort.

Doris, who is six months pregnant, was on holiday with her six-year-old son Eric. Another guest at the hotel, Frank, took Eric out in his sailing dinghy on a lake about three miles away. Eric accidentally fell overboard and was swept over a weir. Frank could see him firmly grasping a rock below; as he could not see a way down and did not know the area, he sailed back to the landing stage to raise the alarm. Unknown to Frank, Doris had driven round to the lake to watch the sailing boats; when she saw Frank abandon the search, she collapsed with fright and later suffered a miscarriage as a result of the shock. In fact there was an easy descent to the spot where Eric was lying and he could easily have been saved; by the time he was eventually rescued he had suffered severely from exposure and was very ill for several weeks.

Advise Doris and Eric.

Prepared for Holborn College, September 1989

Suggested Solution

Frank's potential liability depends upon establishing a duty of care owed by him to Doris and Eric, and a breach of that duty causing to Doris' nervous shock and Eric's illness.

It is convenient to deal first with Frank's liability towards Eric. In order to establish a duty of care, Frank must reasonably foresee that any careless act or omission on his part may cause harm or injury to Eric, following *Donoghue* v *Stevenson* [1932] AC 562; see *B* v *Islington Health Authority* [1991] 1 All ER 825. There would appear to be two points in time when a duty of care could be imposed here; the first is when Frank initially takes Eric out in the boat. Even if he is not acting in loco parentis, Frank has, it is submitted, assumed a degree of responsibility for Eric so that there is a sufficient relationship of proximity and it would be reasonable to impose a duty of care. Frank is therefore under a duty to take all reasonable care in preventing Eric from injury.

We are told that Eric fell into the lake 'accidentally' and was swept over a weir. Whether these events involved a breach of the standard of the 'reasonable man' on the part of Frank is unclear and would depend upon further information not available here: had Frank ensured that Eric was wearing a life-jacket?: was Frank exercising all the supervision and control that a reasonable man would exercise to ensure Eric did not fall out?; was Frank sailing the dinghy dangerously close to the weir, thereby increasing Eric's chances of being swept over if he did fall in?; etc. On the facts we are given, there is no evidence of a breach at this stage, therefore Frank will not be liable for Eric falling out of the boat.

The second point at which he may fall within the limits of a duty of care is at the rescue stage. There is no general duty in negligence to act positively for the benefit of others in a rescue situation unless a special relationship exists between the parties, such as a parent/child relationship. It is submitted that on the facts, Frank may arguably be in loco parentis, in which case he would be under a duty to rescue Eric; otherwise, he would have to mishandle the rescue so as to create a new situation of danger in order to incur liability (see *Horsley* v *McLaren* [1971] 2 Lloyd's Rep 410). However, because of the degree of control and responsibility which Frank may be said to have assumed over Eric by taking him in the boat, he will then be in loco parentis which in turn will give rise to a special relationship. This will be such as to impose on Frank, as part of the duty of care he owes to Eric, the obligation to attempt to rescue him, as long as that attempt is, in all the circumstances reasonable (*Cutler* v *United Dairies* [1933] 2 KB 297). Considering the circumstances of the case as Frank perceived them, a rescue attempt could not be made immediately (despite the fact that an easy descent existed), and his perception of the facts must be taken into account in judging whether he was in breach of the duty of care ie whether his conduct falls below the standard of the reasonable man (*Blyth* v *Birmingham Waterworks Co* (1856) 11 Ex 781). He could see that Eric was 'safe' in some respects in that he was firmly grasping a rock and his decision to sail back to raise the alarm may arguably be reasonable in the circumstances of the case. He could only be liable to Eric if he reached the decision not to attempt a rescue in an unreasonable way, eg if the easy descent was reasonably discoverable. If Frank is in breach of his duty of care, Eric's injuries must be a reasonably foreseeable consequence of that breach, and on the facts, Frank would then be liable to Eric in negligence. Eric only has an arguable case against Frank at most.

Doris will base her action on the nervous shock cases, and primarily on the House of Lords' decision in *Alcock* v *Chief Constable of South Yorkshire Police* [1991] 4 All ER 907. She will have to prove that her relationship to Eric was sufficiently close that it was reasonably foreseeable that she might suffer nervous shock; that the proximity to the accident or its immediate aftermath was sufficiently close in time and space; and that she suffered nervous shock through seeing or hearing the accident or its immediate aftermath. Doris should have no problem with satisfying the first criterion (see *Alcock*; *Hambrook* v *Stokes Bros* [1925] 1 KB 141), though it will be open to Frank to prove (if he can) that despite the parent/child relationship the necessary relationship of love and affection does not exist in this particular case. Doris also seems to be proximate in time and space to the accident, but it is not clear from the facts whether she witnessed the accident (ie the falling overboard) or the immediate (aftermath ie Eric clinging to the rock). If she could satisfy the third criteria she should have a good case against Frank, assuming that Frank was found to be negligent towards Eric at first.

QUESTION FOUR

Green is a famous and highly paid violinist. He is travelling with his wife in a taxi to a concert in which he is to perform when the taxi is involved in a collision with a car. The collision is caused solely by the negligence of Brown, the driver of the car. Green is not injured but his Stradivarius violin, worth £50,000, is destroyed. He is also too shaken to be able to perform the concert, for which his fee was to have been £1,000. Green cannot afford to buy a new Stradivarius immediately although he knows of one for sale in London. He hires one for three months at £300 a month until he is able to buy one.

The taxi driver, White, is uninjured but the taxi is damaged so that it cannot be used for four weeks. White does not own the taxi, but hires it from Taxicab Ltd. Taxicab Ltd cannot supply another taxi, so that White cannot work for four weeks.

Violet, a pedestrian, witnesses the accident. As she is trained in first aid, she immediately rushes across the road to see if any of the occupants of the vehicles require assistance and is struck and injured by another car.

Advise Green, White and Violet.

Written by the editor

Suggested Solution

All parties concerned will base their respective claims for damages on negligence but the main issue here is whether Green and White will be able to recover their total loss in full since part of that loss is economic, as opposed to physical damage.

We are told that Brown, the defendant, has been negligent in causing the collision, but the damage caused must be a reasonably foreseeable consequence of his negligence (*The Wagon Mound No 1* [1961] AC 388; [1961] 2 WLR 126) and must be a type of loss which is recoverable.

Considering, first of all, the claim of Green, it seems that he will wish to recover for the loss of the violin, the loss of the concert fee and the cost of hiring a replacement violin. Until the decision in *Junior Books* v *Veitchi* [1983] AC 520; [1982] 3 WLR 477, a plaintiff could only recover for economic loss if it was consequential upon personal injury or damage to property; that rule was relied upon in *SCM (UK)* v *WJ Whittall* [1971] 1 QB 137; [1970] 3 WLR 694 and in *Spartan Steel* v *Martin* [1973] 1 QB 27; [1972] 3 WLR 502. Applying that principle to the facts of this case, it is quite clear that the most immediate loss flowing from the destruction of the violin is the value of the instrument itself, ie £50,000. The loss of the concert fee is not so immediately consequential. However, in considering remoteness principles, it is clear that the defendant must take his victim as he finds him, either in relation to physical weaknesses (eg *Smith* v *Leech, Brain* [1962] 2 QB 405; [1962] 2 WLR 148) or to the value of the property damaged. Since damage to Green's property is reasonably foreseeable, Green will be able to recover the value of the destroyed instrument regardless of its rarity. It is submitted that it is also reasonably foreseeable that Green will be unable to attend the concert, either through the physical effects suffered as a result of the collision or through the loss of the violin.

The £900 claim for hiring is less certain to be recovered. *The Liesbosch Dredger* v *Edison* [1933] AC 449 lays down the premise that where a plaintiff suffers a greater loss through some extraneous cause, eg his own impecuniosity, he cannot recover that loss; a plaintiff must always mitigate his own loss. Here Green has to wait for three months until he can afford another violin, although one is available.

Although a short period of hiring may be reasonably foreseeable as a temporary measure, it may be argued that, applying *The Liesbosch*, Green could not recover the whole claim for £900. However, as in *Perry* v *Sidney Phillips* [1982] 1 WLR 1297 it was said that *Liesbosch* was 'consistently being attenuated in more recent decisions', and in *Mattocks* v *Mann* (1992) The Times 19 June the Court of Appeal stated the case would only be applied in exceptional circumstances, it seems most likely that Brown would be liable for the full amount.

As far as White's claim is concerned, he has suffered economic loss alone; physical damage to the taxi is reasonably foreseeable but will be recoverable not by White but by Taxicab Ltd, the owners. White could rely on *Junior Books* v *Veitchi* on which to base his claim for loss of earnings, but unfortunately *Junior Books* has been the subject of much judicial criticism, see for example, *D & F Estates* v *Church Commissioners* [1989] AC 177; [1988] 3 WLR 368; [1988] 2 All ER 992 and *Simaan General Contracting* v *Pilkington (No 2)* [1988] QB 758; [1988] 2 WLR 761, and it would not be safe for a plaintiff to rely on *Junior Books* in the future. A similar case to White's is *The Mineral Transporter* [1986] AC 1; [1985] 3 WLR 381 in which a party who hired a ship could not claim for economic loss consequent upon physical damage to the ship.

Violet, as a rescuer, is under no duty to act positively for the benefit of others as a mere passer-by, but since she has attempted to come to the aid of the other parties, she will be owed a duty of care by Brown, whose negligence created the situation which invites rescue (*Haynes* v *Harwood* [1935] 1 KB 146; *Baker* v *Hopkins* [1959] 1 WLR 966). A defence of volenti will be unlikely to succeed against her (*Haynes* v *Harwood*) since the necessary elements of free-will and consent are missing in the urgency of a rescue. The decision in *Harrison* v *BRB* [1981] 3 All ER 679 allows the possibility of a defence of contributory negligence against a rescuer who has acted without regard for his own safety, although Boreham J stated his 'distaste' in so reducing the plaintiff's damages by 20%, although in that case the contributory negligence referred to the plaintiff's carelessness not during the act of rescue, but in bringing about the dangerous situation. This defence is unlikely to be successful in rescue cases, although Violet has immediately rushed across the road, so has in that sense acted carelessly. Brown may argue that her action constituted a novus actus interveniens and her injuries are therefore too remote. This argument is unlikely to succeed since a reasonably foreseeable result of his actions is that someone will attempt to aid the parties. Violet, in any event, would also be able to bring an action against the second driver in negligence, as well as (or instead of) against Brown, subject to a possible reduction for contributory negligence.

6 NEGLIGENCE: BREACH OF DUTY

6.1   Introduction

6.2   Key points

6.3   Recent cases

6.4   Analysis of questions

6.5   Questions

6.1 Introduction

The standard of care is that of the reasonable person: *Blyth* v *Birmingham Waterworks Co* (1856) 11 Ex 781 where breach of duty was defined as the omission to do something that a reasonable man would do, or doing something that a prudent or reasonable man would not do.

This is an objective test; the question is not did the defendant act reasonably, but would a reasonable person, placed in the position of the defendant, act as the defendant did: *Glasgow Corpn* v *Muir* [1943] AC 448. Thus, as regards drivers of motor vehicles, a learner or impaired driver is judged by the standard of the reasonably competent driver: *Nettleship* v *Weston* [1971] 2 QB 691; *Roberts* v *Ramsbottom* [1980] 1 All ER 7.

6.2 Key points

a) *Guidelines*

In considering how a reasonable person would act some guidelines or factors include:

i)   the seriousness of the injury risked eg *Paris* v *Stepney Borough Council* [1951] AC 367.

ii) the likelihood of the injury occuring, as the defendant is only required to guard against reasonable possibilities, not highly unlikely possibilities; see *Blyth* v *Birmingham Waterworks Co* (above); *Bolton* v *Stone* [1951] AC 850.

iii) the relationship of the risk to the object to be attained, eg *Daborn* v *Bath Tramways* [1946] 2 All ER 333; *Watt* v *Hertfordshire County Council* [1954] 1 WLR 835.

iv) the practicability or cost of precautions, eg *Latimer* v *AEC Ltd* [1953] AC 643; *Knight* v *Home Office* [1990] 3 All ER 237.

v)   conforming to common practice, which is evidence though not conclusive proof of lack of carelessness eg *Knight* v *Home Office* (above); *Johnson* v *Bingley* (1995) The Times 28 February.

vi) any special relationship between the plaintiff and defendant, such as spectator and participant in a sport: *Wooldridge* v *Sumner* [1963] 2 QB 43.

vii) defendant is a child. There is no English authority as to whether the standard of a reasonable person or a lesser standard is to be used. In Australia the standard of a reasonable child was used: *McHale* v *Watson* [1966] ALR 513; note that for contributory negligence the courts do apply a different standard for children (see chapter 8) which supports the Australian approach.

viii) emergencies. Where the defendant acts in an emergency, the standard of care takes into account all the circumstances of the situation: *Jones* v *Boyce* (1816) 1 Stark 493.

ix) professionals. A person who claims to possess a special skill is judged by the standard of a reasonable person having that skill: *Bolam* v *Friern Hospital Management Committee* [1957] 1 WLR 582; *Hughes* v *Waltham Forest Health Authority* (1990) The Times 9 November.

x) foreseeability. In all cases the harm to the plaintiff must have been foreseeable by a reasonable person: *Roe* v *Minister of Health* [1954] 2 QB 66.

b) *Proof of the breach*

The plaintiff must prove, on the balance of probabilities, that the defendant was in breach of his duty. Note the effect of s11(1) Civil Evidence Act 1968 and *Wauchope* v *Mordecai* [1970] 1 WLR 317.

A problem may arise where the cause of the accident is known only to the defendant. In such situations the plaintiff may seek to rely on the maxim res ipsa loquitur – the thing speaks for itself. In *Scott* v *London and St Katherine Docks* (1865) 3 H & C 596 it was said it applies where the thing is shown to be under the management of the defendant and the accident is such as in the normal course of things does not happen if those who have the management use proper care. The maxim does not apply where all the facts are known, as it depends on the absence of explanation: *Barkway* v *South Wales Transport Co* [1950] 1 All ER 392.

It has been suggested that as the maxim raises the inference that the defendant was in breach of his duty, the defendant must rebut this inference, ie that the maxim reverses the burden of proof. Despite *Henderson* v *Henry Jenkins* [1970] AC 282 and *Ward* v *Tesco Stores* [1976] 1 WLR 810, the Privy Council has held that the burden of proof does not shift to the defendant but rests on the plaintiff throughout the case: *Ng Chun Pui* v *Lee Chuen Tat* [1988] RTR 298.

6.3 Recent cases

Knight v *Home Office* [1990] 3 All ER 237

Luxmoore-May v *Messenger May Baverstock* [1990] 1 All ER 1067

Hughes v *Waltham Forest Health Authority* (1990) The Times 9 November

Worsley v *Hollins* (1991) The Times 22 March

Surtees v *Kingston Upon Thames Royal Borough Council* (1991) The Independent 27 March

Porter v *Barking and Dagenham London Borough Council* (1990) The Times 9 April

Johnson v *Bingley* (1995) The Times 25 February

6.4 Analysis of questions

Questions involving breach of duty may concern a particular type of defendant, eg a surgeon, or may concern an ordinary defendant. As with duty, a question on breach may call for a detailed examination of whether the defendant was in breach of his duty or it may be fairly obvious, eg a car driver crashes into a lamp post. In the latter type of question at the very least *Blyth* should be cited as authority for the standard of care owed by the defendant to any potential plaintiff. In the majority of questions the possibility of a breach of duty will be only one of the issues to be tackled.

6.5 Questions

QUESTION ONE

Shelley is a consultant psychiatrist. Keats is referred to him suffering from anxiety and depression. Shelley correctly diagnoses the nature of his illness and prescribes a course of injections of 'Poesy', a newly developed drug. Shelley knows that there is a risk of heart trouble developing in patients receiving 'Poesy' but does not tell Keats as he thinks it would worry him unnecessarily as Keats is in extremely good physical health. An article in a recent specialist medical journal concerned with the study of the blood has suggested that there is evidence of blood disorders developing in persons being treated with 'Poesy', but Shelley has not read this. Keats develops a blood complaint three months after starting treatment, but the cause cannot be ascertained.

Advise Keats.

University of London LLB Examination
(for External Students) Law of Tort June 1985 Q1

Skeleton Solution

The factors which must be considered are what is the nature of the duty owed to Keats, what is the standard of care, has there been a breach of duty and did this breach cause Keats's loss?

Suggested Solution

Keats will be advised to bring a case in negligence against Shelley, for which he will have to prove: (i) that Shelley owed him a duty of care; (ii) that he was in breach of that duty; and (iii) that the breach caused Keats' damage or injury, both in fact and in law.

The main difficulties which Keats will encounter here, it is submitted, are in proving (a) that Shelley is in breach of his duty, although he certainly has an arguable case on this point, and (b) that Shelley's breach caused his damage.

As far as the duty of care is concerned, a duty was recognised between a doctor and his patient even before *Donoghue* v *Stevenson* [1932] AC 562 was decided, but the problem raised by Keats's case is whether Shelley is under a duty to warn his patient of the risks involved in the proposed course of treatment. The courts, in medical negligence cases, have to consider on the one hand the patient's right of self-determination over what happens to his body, as against the doctor's desire to act in the patient's best interests, which sometimes the patient may not be in the best position to judge (for a discussion of medical negligence see Dugdale and Stanton's *Professional Negligence* (1982) Butterworth). Furthermore, the courts are also aware of the adverse consequences to the medical profession of a too highly demanding duty of care which would result in over-caution, and would hinder rather than help. An analysis of the case law reveals that there is no absolute duty on a doctor to reveal any risk inherent to treatment which he may prescribe. In *Smith* v *Auckland Hospital Board* [1964] NZLR 241 the judge at first instance took the view that a doctor was under a duty to disclose that a course of treatment would produce harmful side-effects (see also *Clarke* v *Adams* (1950) 94 SJ 599), but it is far more difficult to state with certainty how probable materialisation of the risk must be in order for a doctor to incur such a duty.

The most recent discussion of this duty has been that of the House of Lords in *Sidaway* v *Board of Governors of the Bethlem Royal Hospital* [1985] AC 871; [1985] 1 All ER 643, the ratio of which stated that a medical practitioner is under a duty to disclose to a patient 'any substantial risk involving grave adverse consequences inherent in the surgery or other treatment', which he proposes to carry out. Lord Scarman there took the view that the duty to warn was limited to 'material risks' (following *Canterbury* v *Spence* (1972) 464 F2d 772), concluding that a doctor would not be in breach of his duty if he formed the opinion that a warning would be detrimental to the patient's health. Applying this view to the facts of Keats' case, it may be argued that Shelley is not under a duty to warn Keats of the risk of heart trouble if he believes that such a warning would worry Keats unnecessarily. Evidence of the degree of the risk involved is essential here in order to determine with certainty whether that risk may be said to be material or substantial; on the facts of *Sidaway* the risk was assessed at 1 to 2 per cent, which was evidently insufficient to be 'substantial'. Yet in the Canadian case of *Reibl* v *Hughes* (1980) 114 DLR (3d) 1 a 10 per cent risk of a stroke following from the operation in question was a substantial risk, and Lord Bridge took the view that in such a case, the doctor would be under a duty to disclose in the absence of any cogent reason to withhold that information.

It is submitted in the light of the above discussion, that if the risk is not substantial, Shelley will be under no duty to disclose it to Keats. There may, however, be different considerations for disclosure of the risk of blood disorders of which Shelley is unaware, and at this point, discussion of the duty of care becomes very much linked with consideration of the standard of care and current knowledge. Lord Diplock in *Sidaway* formulated a doctor's duty of care as a duty 'to exercise his skill and judgment to improve the patient's health'. It is submitted that it is a rather different case where a doctor does not disclose risks to a patient because he is unaware of them.

At this point, the standard of care must be considered. The basic test is that enunciated in *Bolam* v *Friern Hospital Management Committee* [1957] 1 WLR 582 as 'standard of the ordinary skilled man exercising and professing to have that special skill'. Current knowledge must also be taken into account (*Roe* v *Minister of Health* [1954] 2 QB 66) in order to deal with risks which are, at the time of treatment, unforeseeable. Lord Scarman in *Sidaway* spoke out rather more strongly against the *Bolam* test than his fellow Law Lords in stating that the law imposed a duty but the medical profession imposed its own standard of care, since hitherto the courts had regard to 'responsible medical opinion' on a particular practice in determining the requisite standard (see on this point *Maynard* v *West Midlands Regional Health Authority* [1984] 1 WLR 634). The House of Lords in *Sidaway* accepted that even though non-disclosure was a proper practice, judges could still hold that disclosure is necessary if 'no reasonably prudent medical man could fail to make it'. This renders the standard of care ultimately one which is imposed by law.

Turning to the facts of Keats's case, it must be noted that the blood disorder risks have been identified in a *specialist* medical journal concerned with the study of the blood, and the question raised here is whether a consultant psychiatrist would be expected to read such a journal and thus to know of the risks. Keats must attempt to argue that part of a reasonable medical practitioner's duty is to be informed about the risk created by new drugs, and possibly *Roe* could be distinguished here on the basis that the microscopic flaws in the ampoules in Roe were a risk of which no one knew at the time, but in Keats's case, the risk of blood disorders is a foreseeable one, though perhaps only in a specialist sphere of medical practice. This raises a further question of how widespread knowledge must be within a profession before it will constitute current knowledge. Keats must also be prepared for Shelley to raise the point which was taken both in *Bolam* and *Maynard* v *West Midlands Regional Health Authority* that a doctor is not necessarily negligent merely because a body of medical opinion takes a view which is contrary to his own, although this may be countered by an argument that Shelley simply had no knowledge of the risks, and did not merely disagree with the facts.

Keats therefore has an arguable case that there has been a breach of duty by Shelley but he must further prove that that breach has caused the blood complaint. It is possible that this condition may have developed in any event but if it was triggered off by 'poesy', Keats could rely on the maxim that Shelley must take his victim as he finds him, as illustrated in *Smith* v *Leech, Brain* [1962] 2 QB 405; [1962] 2 WLR 148 on the point of remoteness. As far as factual causation is concerned, this is a case where the 'but for' test will be of little avail in the absence of medical evidence; if the condition would have happened anyway and was not triggered off by the drug, Keats's claim will fail (*Barnett* v *Chelsea and Kensington Hospital Management Committee* [1969] 1 QB 428; [1968] 1 All ER 1068). Essentially Keats must prove that the breach by Shelley caused his injury. Traditionally plaintiffs who have had a problem with pure causation have relied on *McGhee* v *National Coal Board* [1973] 1 WLR 1 as authority for the proposition that it is enough that the plaintiff shows that the defendants' breach materially increased the risk of damage or materially contributed to his injury. Unfortunately for Keats the House of Lords has recently taken a very restrictive approach to *McGhee* in *Hotson* v *East Berkshire Area Health Authority* [1987] AC 50 and *Wilsher* v *Essex Area Health Authority* [1988] AC 1074. As in *Wilsher* where Lord Bridge stated that *McGhee* 'laid down no new principle of law whatever but on the contrary affirmed the rule that the onus of proving causation lies on the plaintiff', Keats would appear to be unable to prove causation on the facts given.

In the absence of proof of causation, Keats's claim will not succeed since he has not shown to the court that Shelley's breach of duty has caused resultant loss or damage to him. A reliance on res ipsa loquitur would not avail him since that helps to prove a breach of duty rather than causation.

QUESTION TWO

Mrs White was admitted to hospital with breathing difficulties. That evening Dr Green decided to perform an emergency operation and insert a device in her windpipe. She was then transferred to intensive care under Nurse Brown. Nurse Brown was a temporary nurse hired from the Florence Agency. The agency paid her remuneration and the hospital paid a fee to the agency. Nurse Brown was instructed to summon a doctor if there was any change in Mrs White's condition. She was a very experienced nurse who had previously worked in a specialist clinic where she had tended people in Mrs White's condition. When Mrs White's windpipe became temporarily obstructed, she attempted to clear it herself but was unsuccessful. Mrs White died.

Most doctors would not have performed surgery when Dr Green did but would have waited until it was clear that she was not responding to other treatment, but some would have acted as he did. It is not clear whether Mrs White would have recovered from the emergency if Nurse Brown had summoned help or if she would have died anyway.

Advise Mrs White's executors.

University of London LLB Examination
(for External Students) Law of Tort June 1993 Q7

Skeleton Solution

Medical negligence: the duty of care; the standard of care – negligence of nurse: breach and causation – vicarious liability.

Suggested Solution

Dr Green has performed an emergency operation on Mrs White who subsequently dies. The first point to establish is the basis on which her executors can claim. Under the Law Reform (Miscellaneous Provisions) Act 1934 s1(1) all causes of action vested in a person on her death survive for the benefit of the estate and any damages recovered form part of the estate of the deceased.

Turning to Dr Green's actions, we are concerned with possible medical negligence. The duty of care of the medical practitioner has been considered in numerous cases. In *R* v *Bateman* (1925) 94 LJKB 791 it was said that 'he owes a duty to the patient to use diligence, care, knowledge, skill and caution in administering the treatment'. The standard of this care is that of the ordinary competent medical practitioner who is exercising the ordinary degree of professional skill (*Chin Keow* v *Government of Malaysia* [1967] 1 WLR 813). Further, in *Bolam* v *Friern Hospital Management Committee* [1957] 1 WLR 582, McNair J said that a practitioner was not guilty of negligence, 'if he acted in accordance with practice accepted as proper by a responsible body of medical men skilled in that particular art ... merely because there was a body of opinion who would take a contrary view'.

Applying the law to the facts, we are told that most doctors would not have performed surgery when Dr Green did, although some would have done. Presuming this minority view is also held by a body of responsible medical practitioners, the fact that Dr Green has not followed the common practice will not be sufficient to show negligence. Indeed, it was held in *Maynard* v *West Midlands Regional Health Authority* [1984] 1 WLR 634, in the House of Lords, that negligence ought not to be established by the judge having to choose between two bodies of respectable professional opinion.

The operation was an emergency, therefore it is most likely that Mrs White's consent could not be obtained. Impliedly, however, she consented to allow herself to be treated in consideration for a promise that Dr Green would exercise proper care and skill. Had her express consent been obtained, there would have been further issues as to the amount of information disclosed to her (per *Sidaway* v *Board of Governors of the Bethlem Royal Hospital* [1985] AC 871).

It would appear, then, that Dr Green has not acted in breach of his duty of care in carrying out the operation and has not been negligent. Even if that were not the case, one would still have to consider the questions of causation and remoteness, since Mrs White dies some time after the operation. Dr Green is not liable for the negligence of nurses at the hospital when they are not employed by him and it is submitted that, even if he were in breach of his duty of care, the actions of Nurse Brown may well act as an intervening cause to make Mrs White's death too remote.

If we now consider Nurse Brown's liability, we can ask the question, why did Mrs White die? There seem to be two linked answers. First, she may have died because Nurse Brown failed to summon a doctor to deal with the obstruction; second, she may have died as a result of Nurse Brown's failure to clear the obstruction herself. The omission to summon a doctor would have to be 'the omission to do something which a reasonable man ... would do', to be in breach of the duty of care (*Blyth* v *Birmingham Waterworks Co* (1856) 11 Ex 781. Certainly, there was an instruction to summon a doctor upon any change in the patient's condition and that is an important factor against Nurse Brown. But it may be that a reasonable nurse, judged by the standard of the reasonably competent nurse, would have considered this temporary obstruction too minor a change in the patient's condition to justify a doctor's attendance. Further, Nurse Brown's failure to clear the obstruction may not, in itself, be evidence of any negligence on her part. These are largely questions of fact and expert opinion.

We are also told that there is a chance that Mrs White would have died anyway. That being so, we may not be able to say that 'but for' Nurse Brown's negligence, Mrs White would not have died (*Barnett* v *Chelsea and Kensington Hospital Management Committee* [1969] 1 QB 428). It would be for the plaintiff executors to prove on the balance of probabilities that negligence was the cause of death.

Supposing that Nurse Brown is liable, she could be sued in her personal capacity. However, on the basis of suing 'the deepest pocket', the executors will want to know whether they can sue the Florence Agency and/or the hospital (ie whichever body manages the hospital). Nurse Brown is employed by the Florence Agency but works under the hospital's direction. Whether or not the agency remains vicariously liable for Nurse Brown's torts depends to an extent on the construction of the contract between the agency and the hospital. In *Mersey Docks and Harbour Board* v *Coggins & Griffith (Liverpool) Ltd* [1947] AC 1 it was held that if the servant when doing the negligent act, is merely exercising the discretion vested in him by the general employer and not obeying the specific directions given by the particular employer, he remains the servant of the general employer. It is difficult to draw the line on the facts of this case, but it is submitted that the general employer, the agency, may well remain vicariously liable.

However, while they can be sued by the executors, the hospital also owes a primary duty to its patients which it cannot delegate to employees or agencies (see *Gold* v *Essex County Council* [1942] 2 KB 293). If a nurse working in the hospital has been negligent, then the hospital is itself liable.

A final point with regard to vicarious liability concerns the nature of Nurse Brown's act. If she has been merely careless or negligent then obviously the agency cannot avoid liability. However, if they can show that her actions were wilfully wrong, that may take her actions out of the course of her employment. In other words, she is employed to do X and if she does it carelessly, the agency is still liable. But if she does Y, which she has been specifically instructed not to do, that may extinguish liability. Case law has not been so straightforward, however, and, again, the dividing line is hard to draw (see, for example, *Twine* v *Bean's Express Ltd* (1946) 62 TLR 458 and *Rose* v *Plenty* [1976] 1 WLR 141). On the facts of this case, it does not appear that her failure to obey an instruction was so much a wilful wrong as a considered judgment.

In conclusion, I would advise the executors that their action in negligence lies against the agency and the hospital, but that it is not at all clear that Nurse Brown has, in fact, acted negligently.

7 NEGLIGENCE: CAUSATION AND REMOTENESS

7.1 Introduction

Despite the defendant owing the plaintiff a duty of care and being in breach of that duty, the defendant will not be liable unless his conduct has caused the plaintiff's damage and that damage is not too remote in law.

7.2 Key points

a) *Causation*

The test generally used in determining causation is the 'but for' test in *Cork* v *Kirby Maclean* [1952] 2 All ER 402; see *Barnett* v *Chelsea & Kensington Hospital Management Committee* [1969] 1 QB 428 for a good example.

However, there are three areas in which the 'but for' test gives rise to problems:

i)   Pre-existing conditions. Where the damage is caused by a pre-existing condition rather than by the defendant's breach, the defendant will not be liable for all the damage which follows eg *Cutler* v *Vauxhall Motors* [1971] 1 QB 418; *Performance Cars* v *Abraham* [1962] 1 QB 33 (this is an example of the rule that a tortfeasor takes his victim as he finds him – see later (d)(i)).

ii) Omission. The test is difficult to apply where the breach consists of an omission, eg *McWilliams* v *Sir William Arrol & Co* [1962] 1 WLR 295.

iii) Multiple causes. Where, for example, two persons cause damage to the plaintiff, the 'but for' test would be answered in the affirmative for both defendants. In such situations the courts take a common sense view of causation.

b) *Proof of causation*

It may not always be clear that the defendant's breach was the cause of the plaintiff's damage. In such situations the plaintiff will usually rely on *McGhee* v *National Coal Board* [1973] 1 WLR 1 in which it was held sufficient that the plaintiff could show that the defendant's breach materially contributed to the injury. Note the recent restrictive developments of *McGhee* by the House of Lords in *Kay* v *Ayrshire and Arran Health Board* [1987] 2 All ER 417, *Hotson* v

East Berkshire Area Health Authority [1987] AC 50, *Wilsher* v *Essex Area Health Authority* [1988] AC 1074; [1988] 1 All ER 871, and the dictum of Lord Bridge in *Wilsher* that *McGhee* 'laid down no new principle of law whatever. On the contrary it affirmed the principle that the onus of proving causation lies on the plaintiff.'

c) *Successive causes*

Note the problems that can occur here, as exemplified by *Baker* v *Willoughby* [1970] AC 467 and *Jobling* v *Associated Dairies* [1982] AC 794.

d) *Remoteness of damage*

Once duty, breach and causation have been established, one must ascertain whether all the damage suffered by the plaintiff can be recovered or whether some or all of it is too remote.

For intentional damage the defendant is liable for all the damage which follows: *Quinn* v *Leatham* [1901] AC 495; *Doyle* v *Olby (Ironmongers) Ltd* [1969] 2 QB 158.

For unintentional damage the test for remoteness is reasonable foreseeability: *The Wagon Mound (No 1)* [1961] AC 388.

i) Damage to the person

The defendant will be liable for all the damage if he could foresee some damage to the person, even if he could not foresee the extent. This is often known as the 'egg-shell skull' rule as laid down in *Dulieu* v *White* [1901] 2 KB 669 or by the maxim that a tortfeasor takes his victim as he finds him. This is an important rule and the following examples should be noted: *Smith* v *Leech, Brain* [1962] 2 QB 405; *Bradford* v *Robinson Rentals* [1967] 1 WLR 337; *Robinson* v *Post Office* [1974] 1 WLR 1176; *Hughes* v *Lord Advocate* [1963] AC 837.

ii) Damage to property

Here the foreseeability requirement is greater, as it seems that foreseeability of damage, by itself, is insufficient but that the kind of damage needs to be foreseen: *The Wagon Mound (No 1)* (above).

e) *Damage which is too remote*

i) if it arises from a novus causa interveniens, a new intervening cause such as the plaintiff's own impecuniosity: *Liesbosch Dredger* v *Edison* [1933] AC 449. However, in *Perry* v *Sidney Phillips* [1982] 1 WLR 1297 it was said that this case was consistently being attenuated in later decisions and more recently in *Mattocks* v *Mann* (1992) The Times 19 June that *Liesbosch* would only be applied in exceptional circumstances.

ii) if it arises from a novus actus interveniens, an intervening act which breaks the chain of causation. An intervening act may arise in three ways:

– act of plaintiff

If an act of the plaintiff amounts to a novus actus interveniens the defendant will not be liable. The defendant will have to show that the plaintiff's conduct has been so careless that his damage cannot be regarded as being caused by the defendant, eg *McKew* v *Holland & Hannen & Cubbitts* [1969] 3 All ER 1621 where the plaintiff acted unreasonably. Compare *Wieland* v *Cyril Lord Carpets* [1969] 3 All ER 1006 where the plaintiff acted reasonably and the defendants were held liable. See also Slipper v BBC [1991] 1 All ER 165 for an application of novus actus in defamation.

– act of nature

If an act of nature is independent of the negligence of the defendant, the defendant will not be liable: *Carslogie Steamship* v *Royal Norwegian Government* [1952] AC 292.

– act of a third party

If an act of a third party is the true cause of the plaintiff's damage, the defendant will not be liable: *The Oropesa* [1943] P 32; *Knightley* v *Johns* [1982] 1 WLR 349, but compare *Rouse* v *Squires* [1973] QB 889, and *Wright* v *Lodge & Shepherd* [1992] NLJ 1269.

An intervening act will not break the chain of causation where:

– it is an instinctive act done in the agony of an emergency created by the defendant's tort: *Jones* v *Boyce* (1816) 1 Stark 493; *The Oropesa* (above).

– the defendant places the plaintiff in a position in which it is reasonable for him to take the risk he did (ie a non-emergency situation): *Sayers* v *Harlow UDC* [1958] 1 WLR 623.

– the act which is alleged to have broken the chain of causation is one which the defendant should have foreseen and guarded against: *Stansbie* v *Troman* [1948] 2 KB 48; *Rouse* v *Squires* (above).

7.3 Recent cases

Slipper v *BBC* [1991] 1 All ER 165

Wright v *Lodge & Shepherd* [1992] NLJ 1269

Mattocks v *Mann* (1992) The Times 19 June

7.4 Analysis of questions

Questions on causation and remoteness are common, either as essay questions or as problem questions. Again, any question on negligence will automatically bring these topics into consideration, and the egg-shell skull rule is regularly tested by the examiner as a small part of a general question on negligence.

7.5 Questions

QUESTION ONE

Sam is a trainee fireman with the Waterside Fire Brigade. While undergoing instruction in driving a fire engine, he was ordered by his instructor Tom to drive at high speed along a country road with his blue lights flashing and bell sounding. Sam could see that the driver of the car ahead, Ursula, had become agitated, but he kept going. Ursula panicked in trying to make room for the fire engine and collided with a lamp post. Ursula received serious eye injuries but was released immediately. Her passenger Violet was trapped in the car. Ursula needed urgent medical treatment and was taken to a nearby hospital. However, there had been a major railway accident a short time earlier and the hospital was unable to admit other casualties. Ursula was therefore removed to another hospital six miles away; the hospital was unable to save her sight, but this would have been possible if she had been able to receive prompt treatment. Violet was released after two hours. She was not seriously hurt but was taken by ambulance to hospital for examination. On the way the ambulance was involved in a further accident (without negligence on anyone's part) and Violet sustained two broken legs.

Advise Ursula and Violet.

University of London LLB Examination
(for External Students) Law of Tort June 1990 Q8

Suggested Solution

It is well established law that Sam as a driver owes a duty of care to all other road users and as this is a personal injuries case the nature of the duty of care is governed by *Donoghue* v *Stevenson* [1932] AC 562 – see *B* v *Islington Health Authority* [1991] 1 All ER 825 per Potts J. In carrying out this duty of care Sam must act as a reasonable man: *Blyth* v *Birmingham Waterworks* (1856) 11 Ex 781; this is an objective test which means that the standard of care required of a trainee driver is the same standard as required of an experienced and competent driver: *Nettleship* v *Weston* [1971] 2 QB 691, and it is by this standard that Sam must be judged. When Sam drives at high speed along a country road he is prima facie in breach of his duty as a reasonable man would not act in this way. If Sam were en route to an emergency then his actions would be those of a reasonable man: *Watt* v *Hertfordshire County Council* [1954] 1 WLR 835, but this is not the situation here. Ursula's collision is caused by Sam's breach of duty so prima facie Sam is liable for any injuries caused. Sam may seek to argue that Ursula did not make room for the fire engine to pass, but acted instead in a careless manner and that she caused her own injuries, ie that her panic and collision was a novus actus interveniens. As Ursula has been placed in an emergency or difficult situation by Sam's negligence however, the court is unlikely to make this finding if Ursula acted reasonably in the agony of the moment, even if with hindsight she could have avoided the accident: *Jones* v *Boyce* (1816) 1 Stark 493. But it is open to the court to find contributory negligence on Ursula's part and to reduce any damages awarded by s1 Law Reform (Miscellaneous Provisions) Act 1945 having regard to Ursula's fault in causing the accident. All that Sam will have to show is that Ursula failed to look after herself properly: *Davies* v *Swan Motor Co* [1949] 2 KB 291.

Hence Sam is liable for the eye injury initially suffered by Ursula (subject to any reduction in damages); the question arises, however, is Sam liable for Ursula's subsequent loss of sight or is the earlier railway accident a novus actus interveniens? The new act (ie the railway accident) is an act of a third party and we must decide whether this act is the true cause of Ursula's loss of sight. From the facts of the problem it seems that the loss of Ursula's sight was caused only by the delay, and so Sam would not be liable for this additional damage: *Knightley* v *Johns* [1982] 1 WLR

47

349. It is not a situation where the delay was a natural and probable consequence of the first accident and was foreseeable as in *Rouse* v *Squires* [1973] QB 889; instead there has been a break in the chain of causation. [Note that the question that must be decided here is one of causation and not foreseeability as Sam is liable for any personal injury that ensues in the accident as he need only foresee the kind of damage and not the extent: *Smith* v *Leech, Brain* [1962] 2 QB 405].

Similarly Sam will be liable for Violet's slight injuries suffered in the collision but not for her two broken legs, as the cause of the broken legs was a novus actus interveniens which was not a natural and probable consequence of the first collision (see above).

As we are told that Sam was undergoing instruction and is a trainee fireman, it is clear that Sam is an employee, the Waterside Fire Brigade (or the appropriate local authority) is his employer, and Sam was acting in the course of his employment. The fact that Sam was doing so in a negligent manner is irrelevant: *Century Insurance* v *Northern Ireland Road Transport Board* [1942] AC 509.

Thus the Waterside Fire Brigade (or the appropriate local authority) will be responsible for Sam's actions and Ursula and Violet are advised to sue the Fire Brigade in respect of the injuries first suffered in the collision; as regards the later more serious injuries they are without a remedy. Ursula and Violet should also be advised that if they failed to wear seat belts and the wearing of a seat belt would have reduced their injuries, a reduction will be made for contributory negligence on their part: *Froom* v *Butcher* [1976] QB 286; [1975] 3 WLR 379.

QUESTION TWO

'The "but for" test is no more than an aid, for the choice of cause rests ultimately on common-sense evaluation. Dictates of common-sense lead sometimes to the disregard of the "but for" test.' (Dias and Markesinis).

Discuss.

University of London LLB Examination
(for External Students) Law of Tort June 1988 Q8

Skeleton Solution

But for test – *Barnett* – competing causes – role of common sense evaluation – policy – *Wilsher* – contrast between CA and HL – successive causes – contrast between *Baker* and *Jobling* – departures from 'but for' – multiple causes – omissions? – competing causes.

Suggested Solution

Causation is a particularly difficult issue in the law of tort. As the question implies the basis of the doctrine of causation is the 'but for' test but this test is not applied as a philosopher would apply it but, according to the judges, it is applied as a matter of common sense.

The application of the 'but for' test can be seen in the case of *Barnett* v *Chelsea and Kensington Hospital Management Committee* [1969] 1 QB 428. The plaintiff's husband went to a casualty department of a hospital complaining that he had been vomiting.

The doctor refused to examine him and he was told to go home and consult his own doctor in the morning. The plaintiff's husband was, in fact, suffering from arsenical poisoning and he died some five hours later. The plaintiff sued the hospital alleging that they had been negligent in the treatment of her husband and that as a result of their negligence her husband had died. It was held that the defendants were not liable as their negligence had not caused the death of the plaintiff's husband. Even if the doctor had examined the husband and treated him the husband would still have died and so the defendant's negligence was not a cause of the husband's death.

In this case we can see an example of a pure application of the 'but for' test. So the general rule is that if the damage would not have occurred but for the fault of the defendant then the fault is a cause of the damage, but if it would have happened anyway the fault of the defendant is not the cause of the damage.

But it is true that the choice of cause 'rests ultimately on common-sense evaluation' provided that common sense is understood as including the judge's view of the policy issues at stake. A good illustration of these competing views of policy arises where one of a number of competing possible causes could have been the actual cause of the damage which the plaintiff has suffered. In *Wilsher* v *Essex Area Health Authority* [1988] AC 1074; [1988] 1 All ER 871 the plaintiff was born prematurely and suffered from, amongst other things, oxygen deficiency. The negligence of one of the defendant's doctors resulted in the plaintiff later being given an excess of oxygen. The plaintiff alleged that this excess of oxygen had caused incurable damage to his retina which had left him virtually blind. The problem for the plaintiff was that there were a number of other possible causes of the damage to his retina and none of these other possible causes were attributable to the fault of the defendants. The Court of Appeal held, applying the decision of the House of Lords in *McGhee* v *National Coal Board* [1973] 1 WLR 1, that the plaintiff was entitled to succeed because the defendants had materially increased the risk of damage to the plaintiff. Mustill LJ recognised that there was an element of policy in his judgment because he held that the effect of the decision mitigated the rigour of the rule that the plaintiff must prove that the breach of duty caused the loss. This policy consideration was also clearly expressed by Lord Wilberforce in *McGhee* when he said that it was the defendants, who admittedly had been at fault, who were the ones who had to shoulder the evidential difficulty of showing the cause of the loss to the plaintiff.

But this 'pro-plaintiff' approach was abandoned by the House of Lords in reversing the decision of the Court of Appeal in *Wilsher*. The House of Lords affirmed that in all cases the plaintiff must establish the requisite causal connection on a balance of probabilities. They rejected the approach of Lord Wilberforce in *McGhee* and said that the law required proof of fault causing damage as the basis of liability and that if the law was to be changed it was for Parliament to do it and not the courts acting out of some misplaced sense of 'justice'. In this type of case human knowledge simply does not know what was the cause of the loss and while scientific evidence can help to establish the cause of the damage it cannot prove what was actually the true cause. So inevitably the courts are left to apply a test based on their perception of common sense and their perception of the competing policy issues.

Evidence of common sense evaluation can also be seen in the judgments of the House of Lords in *Baker* v *Willoughby* [1970] AC 467 and *Jobling* v *Associated Dairies* [1982] AC 794. In the former case the court was concerned to ensure that the plaintiff was not undercompensated by the application of the 'take your victim as you find him' rule. In the latter case the court knew that the crippling back disease would have overcome the plaintiff anyway and held that the defendants were therefore not liable for the loss of earnings after the onset of the back disease. It is true that the policies appear to conflict, in that the court in *Baker* was concerned to avoid plaintiff undercompensation whereas the concern in *Jobling* was to prevent plaintiff overcompensation, but the point to note is that in each case the court was seeking to come to a conclusion which it felt was a fair one on the facts of the case and which satisfied their view of common sense. The recent Court of Appeal decision in *Mattocks* v *Mann* (1992) The Times 19 June is another example of the courts' common sense approach to the question of causation.

It is also true that on occasions these considerations of common sense or policy lead a court to disregard the 'but for' test. An example of a disregard of the 'but for' test is provided by Professor Atiyah. Two fires started independently by A and B unite and spread to C's house which is destroyed. The 'but for' test would appear to acquit both parties because if the question is asked, 'would the damage have occurred but for the negligence of A?', the answer would be 'yes' and the same answer would be given if the question is asked, 'would the damage have occurred but for the negligence of B?' This absurd result would not, however, be reached by the courts. In *Cook* v *Lewis* [1952] 1 DLR 1 the plaintiff was injured by a gun shot and it was unclear which of the two defendants had caused the injury as both parties had fired shots simultaneously. It was held that both parties were liable because the burden of proof lay on the defendants to show that they had not been negligent and they had failed to discharge that burden. In this case, as Professor Fleming has noted, the law prefers a 50 per cent chance of doing injustice to the certainty of doing injustice.

But is is submitted that it is only in rare cases that the courts actually disregard the 'but for' test. In many cases they are trying to apply the 'but for' test but that test does not yield a conclusive answer on the facts of a particular case and so the courts have to apply it with a dose of common sense. A good example of this is provided where the negligence of the defendant takes the form of an omission. In *McWilliams* v *Sir William Arrol* [1962] 1 WLR 295 the plaintiff fell to his death at work because he was not wearing a safety belt. The defendants were in breach of their statutory duty in failing to supply safety belts but there was evidence that, even if they had supplied a safety belt, the plaintiff would not have worn it. Here the but for test yields no conclusive answer because we do not know what would have happened if the defendants had actually supplied the safety belts. So the court has to do the next best thing and attempt to ascertain from the parties' past practices whether the plaintiff would have worn a safety belt had one been supplied. The court concluded that he would not have worn one so that the defendants were not liable. However it would be a mistake to see these cases as a court disregarding the 'but for' test. Rather, as was the case in our consideration of competing causes, the court is seeking to apply the 'but for' test with due regard to considerations of common sense and the policy issues at stake.

QUESTION THREE

Where human action forms one of the links between the original wrongdoing of the defendant and the loss suffered by the plaintiff, that action must at least have been something very likely to happen if it is not to be regarded as novus actus interveniens breaking the chain of causation.' (*Home Office* v *Dorset Yacht Co Ltd* (1970), per Lord Reid).

Discuss this proposition and explain how since 1970 the courts have dealt with the problem of intervening *deliberate* human conduct.

University of London LLB Examination
(for External Students) Law of Tort June 1993 Q6

Skeleton Solution

Explanation of the proposition – case law since 1970: *Lamb* v *Camden*; *Ward* v *Cannock Chase*; *Rouse* v *Squires*; *Knightley* v *Johns*; *Smith* v *Littlewoods* – conclusion.

Suggested Solution

'I feel bound to say with respect that what Lord Reid said in the *Dorset Yacht* case [*Home Office* v *Dorset Yacht Co Ltd* [1970] AC 1004] does nothing to simplify the task of deciding for or against remoteness, especially where the fresh damage complained of has been caused by the intervening act of a third party': Watkins LJ in *Lamb* v *Camden London Borough Council* [1981] QB 625.

Lord Reid's dictum in the *Dorset Yacht* case concerns the principle that the consequence is too remote if it follows a break in the chain of causation. This break in the chain of causation, or novus actus interveniens, could be as a result of a natural event (as in *Carslogie Steamship Co Ltd* v *Royal Norwegian Government* [1952] AC 292, the act or omission of the plaintiff (as in *McKew* v *Holland & Hannen & Cubitts (Scotland) Ltd* [1969] 3 All ER 1621, or the act or omission of a third party. It is with this last that we are concerned.

In the leading case of *The Oropesa* [1943] P 32 – which pre-dates Lord Reid's dictum – it is said: 'to break the chain of causation it must be shown that there is something which I will call ultroneous, something unwarrantable, a new cause which disturbs the sequence of events, something which can be described as either unreasonable or extraneous or extrinsic' (per lord Wright). In other words, the defendant's breach of duty has been followed by the truly independent, but not necessarily tortious, act of a third party which causes the plaintiff's damage.

Lord Reid has restated the principle in this way: unless the act of the third party was something very likely to happen, it will break the chain of causation. Therefore something that was merely foreseeable would be seen as a novus actus interveniens. As Lord Reid went on to say later in the same judgment, 'I do not think that a mere foreseeable possibility is or should be sufficient'.

There have been a number of cases on this point since 1970, but briefly one should place the *Dorset Yacht* case in context. It was an attempt to broaden the scope of the 'neighbour principle' of *Donoghue* v *Stevenson* [1932] AC 562 and Lord Reid suggested that the time had come to regard that principle as applicable in all cases where there was no justification or valid explanation for its exclusion. His obiter statement regarding third party interference was not reflected in the other speeches in that case.

However, if one turns to case law since 1970, one reaches the conclusion that it is very difficult to say where exactly the dividing line is drawn between those third party acts which terminate the defendant's liability and those which do not, but the test is essentially whether the intervening act is reasonably foreseeable.

In *Lamb* v *Camden London Borough Council* (above), the plaintiff's house was damaged through the defendant's negligence. The house became unoccupied and squatters moved in on two occasions, causing further damage. The Official Referee held that the squatting was a 'foreseeable' risk but not a likely one and, applying Lord Reid's speech in the *Dorset Yacht* case, he held that the damage they caused was too remote. However, whilst upholding this decision, the Court of Appeal was critical of Lord Reid's proposition, as has been noted above.

In contrast, in *Ward* v *Cannock Chase District Council* [1986] Ch 546, on similar facts, the defendants were held liable. The difference between the two may lie in the degree of wilful wrongdoing by the third party. A third party's negligence will be more foreseeable than its wilful conduct. But ultimately what the court is looking at is whether the reasonable man would foresee the intervening acts in question. While squatting may be foreseeable, the actual conduct of the squatters – particularly if it is wilfully wrong – is not a reasonably foreseeable consequence which can be attributed to the defendant's negligence.

To contrast two further cases which are factually similar: in *Rouse* v *Squires* [1973] QB 889, a lorry jack-knifed across a motorway owing to the first defendant's negligent driving. A second lorry, also being driven negligently, crashed some minutes later into the pile-up, killing someone who was assisting at the scene. The first defendant's negligence was held to have caused his death, Cairns LJ saying that, having negligently created the danger to other road users, the first defendant was responsible for the further accident, despite the second lorry driver's negligence. Only if this latter had deliberately or recklessly driven into the obstruction would the chain of causation be broken.

In *Knightley* v *Johns* [1982] 1 WLR 349, on the other hand, a subsequent collision was held too remote where the first defendant's negligent driving caused the blocking of a busy tunnel. A police inspector, who took charge, at first negligently failed to close the tunnel, but then sent a police motorcyclist (the plaintiff) the wrong way along the tunnel to close it. He collided with another motorist. This accident was too remote, because there had been so many errors between the initial negligence and the subsequent collision.

These cases suggest, therefore, that it is a question of fact where the line is precisely drawn, the need to draw a line and its general position being a question of policy, although policy based on common sense. As Oliver LJ said in *Lamb*: 'I confess that I find it inconceivable that the reasonable man, wielding his pick in the road in 1973, could be said reasonably to foresee that his puncturing of a water main would fill the plaintiff's house with uninvited guests in 1974.'

This passage from his judgment was endorsed by Lord Mackay in *Smith* v *Littlewoods Organisation Ltd* [1987] AC 241 in the House of Lords. Referring also to the speech of Lord Reid, his Lordship concluded that the only way it would be possible to persuade a judge that an outcome was not only possible but reasonably foreseeable was to show that it was also highly likely. In other words something more than mere foreseeability would be required. Despite the criticism of Lord Reid, this does not seem far from what Lord Reid was saying. It is perhaps the perennial difficulty in tort, and particularly in negligence, of trying to reach a definition using indefinable terms.

Perhaps the last word should go to Lord Denning, who said in *Lamb*: 'The law has to draw a line somewhere. Sometimes it is done by limiting the range of persons to whom duty is owed ... At other times it is done by saying that the consequence is too remote to be a head of damage ... But ultimately it is a question of policy for the judges to decide.'

8 CONTRIBUTORY NEGLIGENCE

8.1 Introduction

8.2 Key points

8.3 Recent cases

8.4 Analysis of questions

8.5 Questions

8.1 Introduction

Section 1 Law Reform (Contributory Negligence) Act 1945 provides that where the plaintiff is partly responsible for the damage suffered the damages recoverable shall be reduced to such an extent as the court thinks just and equitable having regard to the plaintiff's share in the responsibility for the damage.

8.2 Key points

a) *Fault by the plaintiff*

The plaintiff must be at fault or he can recover in full, see for example *Tremayne* v *Hill* [1987] RTR 131, but he need not owe a duty of care to the defendant: *Nance* v *British Columbia Electric Railway* [1951] AC 601.

b) *Standard of care*

The defendant must prove that the plaintiff failed to take reasonable precautions for his own safety: *Davies* v *Swan Motor Co* [1949] 2 KB 291; *Jones* v *Livox Quarries* [1952] 2 QB 608.

i) Children

In *Gough* v *Thorne* [1966] 1 WLR 1387 Lord Denning stated that a very young child could not be guilty of contributory negligence; see also *Yachuk* v *Oliver Blais* [1949] AC 386. However, in *Morales* v *Eccleston* [1991] RTR 151 an eleven-year-old boy was held to be guilty of contributory negligence.

ii) Workmen

The courts are reluctant to find an employee guilty of contributory negligence when he sues his employer for breach of statutory duty, eg *Caswell* v *Powell Duffryn Associated Collieries* [1940] AC 152, but are more willing to do so where the employee is suing in negligence only eg *Bux* v *Slough Metals* [1974] 1 All ER 262; *Jayes* v *IMI* [1985] ICR 155.

iii) Rescuers

The courts are also reluctant to find contributory negligence on the part of a rescuer, although they will do so in appropriate cases, eg *Harrison* v *British Railways Board* [1981] 3 All ER 679.

iv) Emergencies

Again the courts are reluctant to make a finding of contributory negligence against a plaintiff who makes a wrong decision in the agony of the moment: *Jones* v *Boyce* (1816) 1 Stark 493.

c) *Causation*

The plaintiff's carelessness need not contribute to the accident; it is enough if it contributes to the damage the plaintiff suffers.

Thus in *Froom* v *Butcher* [1976] QB 286; [1975] 3 WLR 379 the non-wearing of a seat belt was held to amount to contributory negligence, as was the failure of a motor cyclist to wear a helmet: *O'Connell* v *Jackson* [1972] 1 QB 270, or to wear a helmet but not to fasten the strap: *Capps* v *Miller* [1989] 2 All ER 333. If a person accepts a lift from a driver who he knows has consumed large quantities of alcohol, that too can amount to contributory negligence: *Owens* v *Brimmell* [1977] QB 859.

d) *Apportionment*

The damages are to be reduced to such an extent as the court thinks just and equitable. For seat belts *Froom* v *Butcher* (above) suggested that if the wearing of a seat belt would have completely prevented the injuries the reduction should be 25%; if the seat belt would have reduced the severity of the injuries 15% is appropriate.

In *O'Connell* a reduction of 15% was made and in *Capps* a reduction of 10% was made.

In *Pitts* v *Hunt* [1990] 3 WLR 542 it was held that for s1 of the 1945 Act to operate there must be fault on the part of both parties. This presupposes that the person suffering damage will recover some damages, and thus the claimant cannot be held 100 per cent responsible for the damage.

Where there is more than one defendant it was held by the House of Lords in *Fitzgerald* v *Lane* [1989] AC 328; [1988] 2 All ER 961 that first the apportionment between the plaintiff and the defendants should be decided, then the apportionment between the defendants inter se, and that at the first stage the plaintiff's conduct was to be compared with the totality of the defendant's conduct rather than to each defendant separately.

8.3 Recent cases

Pitts v *Hunt* [1990] 3 WLR 542

Morales v *Eccleston* [1991] RTR 151

8.4 Analysis of questions

Questions on just contributory negligence are rare, but contributory negligence often appears in negligence questions and often has to be considered in the examination, although figures for a reduction will not be required other than mentioning the guidelines above for road accident cases.

8.5 Questions

For examples of the way in which contributory negligence appears as part of negligence questions see:

Chapter 4, question 3; chapter 7, question 1; chapter 9, question 3.

9 BREACH OF STATUTORY DUTY AND EMPLOYERS' LIABILITY

9.1 Introduction

9.2 Key points

9.3 Recent cases

9.4 Analysis of questions

9.5 Questions

9.1 Introduction

A breach of statutory duty may give a cause of action in tort. The problem is, what statutes give rise to such an action? The statute may expressly exclude a civil right, eg the Guard Dogs Act 1975, or the statute may give a cause of action where none previously existed. Usually, however, the statute is silent as to whether or not it gives rise to an action in tort.

9.2 Key points

a) *Breach of statutory duty*

   i) Does the breach give rise to a tort?

      • to answer this question the courts must find the intention of Parliament. See the recent spate of child care cases where the courts attempted to ascertain the intent of Parliament: *M* v *Newham Borough Council* [1994] 2 WLR 554; *E* v *Dorset County Council* [1994] 3 WLR 853; *T* v *Surrey County Council* [1994] 4 All ER 577.

      • in *Lonrho* v *Shell Petroleum Co (No 2)* [1982] AC 173 Lord Diplock stated that the initial presumption was that if the statute contained an obligation together with a means of enforcing that obligation (eg a criminal penalty) then the obligation could not be enforced in any other way.

      • but there are two exceptions to this presumption, namely where the statute was enacted for the benefit of a particular class of persons, and where the statute created a public right and the plaintiff had suffered damage over and above the damage suffered by the public at large.

   ii) *Remedy within statute*

      • if the Act imposes a duty but provides no remedy for breach, the presumption is that breach gives rise to an action in tort, eg *Thornton* v *Kirklees Metropolitan Borough Council* [1979] QB 626.

      • if the Act provides a remedy it is harder to show that breach gives the right to sue: *Atkinson* v *Newcastle Waterworks* (1877) 2 ExD 441, although a civil action was allowed in *Groves* v *Lord Wimborne* [1898] 2 QB 402.

iii) Note also the effect of an existing common law remedy on the readiness or otherwise of the courts to hold that a civil remedy lies for a breach of statute; compare *Phillips* v *Britannia Hygienic Laundry* [1923] 2 KB 832 with *Monk* v *Warbey* [1935] 1 KB 175.

iv) Statutes for the benefit of a class

* the plaintiff has an action in tort if he is a member of that class; the problem is what constitutes a class of persons.

* it is clear that employees are a class of persons as regards industrial safety legislation: *Groves* v *Lord Wimborne* (above). But see *Richardson* v *Pitt-Stanley* [1995] 2 WLR 26.

* this apart, however, it seems difficult to ascertain what is meant by a class; see *Phillips* v *Britannia Hygienic Laundry* (above) and *McCall* v *Abelesz* [1976] QB 585, and note *Cutler* v *Wandsworth Stadium* [1949] AC 398.

v) Additional damage

The second exception in *Lonrho* v *Shell Petroleum* (above) is where the statute creates a public right and a particular person suffers particular, direct and substantial damage other and different from that suffered by the rest of the public. Note the restricted interpretation of this exception in *Lonrho* v *Shell Petroleum* (above).

vi) Scope of statute

The plaintiff must prove three things:

* the act which caused the damage is regulated by statute
* he is one of the persons the act is intended to protect
* the damage suffered is of the kind the Act was intended to prevent.

See the leading case of *Gorris* v *Scott* (1874) LR9 Exch 125.

b) *Employers' liability*

Employers owe various duties to their employees at common law and under a number of statutes. The common law duties are often described as four separate duties, although some authors prefer to say that an employer owes his employee the common duty of care in all the circumstances of the case. In any event, we shall describe the four common law duties if only as examples of the overall duty of care.

i) Competent staff

The employer owes a duty to his employees to select competent fellow employees: see *Hudson* v *Ridge Manufacturing Co* [1957] 2 QB 348 and compare *Smith* v *Crossley Bros* (1951) 95 Sol Jo 655.

ii) Proper plant and equipment

The employer must provide properly maintained plant and equipment: *Smith* v *Baker* [1891] AC 325. Note the effect of the Employers' Liability (Defective Equipment) Act 1969 and the ruling of the House of Lords in *Coltman* v *Bibby Tankers* [1988] AC 276 that the term 'equipment' in the 1969 Act is not restricted to parts of a larger entity.

iii) Safe place of work

The employer must provide a safe place of work, but this is not an absolute duty and merely requires the employer to take reasonable steps to provide a safe place of work: *Latimer* v *AEC Ltd* [1953] AC 643; *Gitsham* v *Pearce* [1992] PIQR 57.

iv) Safe system of work

The employer is also under a duty to provide a safe system of work: *General Cleaning Contractors* v *Christmas* [1953] AC 180. In the recent case of *Walker* v *Northumberland County Council* [1994] NLJ 1659 this was held to cover a duty not to cause an employee psychiatric damage by the volume and character of the employee's workload, where such psyciatric damage was foreseeable.

Note that the duty the employer owes to his employee is an individual duty to each and every individual employee, and must take into account the attributes of that particular employee: *Paris* v *Stepney Borough Council* [1951] AC 367.

Note also that this duty is a personal non-delegable duty, and the employer cannot discharge his duty merely by entrusting it to another person: *McDermid* v *Nash Dredging and Reclamation* [1987] AC 906; *Morris* v *Breaveglen* (1992) The Times 29 December.

The duty is only to safeguard the employee's physical safety; it does not extend to protecting the employee's economic welfare: *Reid* v *Rush & Tomkins* [1990] 1 WLR 212.

Finally, note the different attitudes of the courts to contributory negligence on the part of an employee as regards employers' breach of statutory duty and breach of common law duties (see chapter 8.2(b)(ii) and the fact that an employer many owe a duty of care to members of an empoluee's family: *Hewett* v *Alf Brown's Transport* (1992) The Times 4 February.

9.3 Recent cases

Gitsham v *Pearce* [1992] PIQR 57

West Wilts DC v *Garland* [1995] 2 WLR 439

Hewett v *Alf Brown's Transport* (1992) The Times 4 February

Pape v *Cumbria County Council* [1992] 3 All ER 211

Morris v *Breaveglen Ltd* (1992) The Times 29 December

M v *Newham County Council* [1994] 2 WLR 554

E v *Dorset County Council* [1994] 3 WLR 853

T v *Surrey County Council* [1994] 4 All ER 577

Richardson v *Pitt-Stanley* [1995] 2 WLR 26

Walker v *Northumberland County Council* [1994] NLJ 1659

9.4 Analysis of questions

The liability of employers frequently arises as part of a question, and breach of statutory duty has arisen often in recent years.

9.5 Questions

QUESTION ONE

Alan, Bill and Cyril are employed by the lighting department of Gleaming District Council. When working on street lights they travel in a vehicle which has a cage which can be raised so that the workers can reach the lights. Statutory regulations make it an offence for the vehicle to be moved while the cage is in the raised position or for workers to travel in the cage when the vehicle is in motion. In one street where a number of lights close together required repair, Alan drove from one lamp to the next without lowering the cage and with Bill and Cyril riding in the cage. They came to a low bridge. Alan did not lower the cage as he knew there was sufficient clearance. Bill also knew this, but Cyril panicked and clambered out of the cage, falling to the ground. A passer-by shouted a warning and Alan suddenly stopped, throwing Bill from the cage. Bill landed on a pram containing Donald, aged three months. Donald was killed and Bill and Cyril were injured.

Advise Bill, Cyril and Donald's mother.

University of London LLB Examination
(for External Students) Law of Tort June 1989 Q9

Skeleton Solution

B and C should have claims for breach of statutory duty against GDC but B might fail if the duty was delegated to him. B and C also have claims at common law. D would have had a claim and his parents have claim for bereavement. Reductions for contributory negligence on parts of B and C. GDC vicariously liable for negligence of employees.

Suggested Solution

Bill, Cyril and Donald's mother must respectively show the breach of a legal duty by one or other actor here, causing their losses.

Presumably the statutory regulations are primarily intended for the protection of employees, and therefore, analogously with the Factories Acts, create a civil liability to injured employees, but not to outsiders. The breach of duty will impose a liability on Gleaming D C. Since the employer, particularly if a corporation, will of necessity delegate the task of seeing that the statute is carried out to an employee, the employee so designated may be unable to recover if he is injured too (see *ICI* v *Shatwell* [1965] AC 656; [1964] 2 WLR 329). Whether lighting operatives have the same autonomy and discretion as shot-firers in a mine might be doubted, and so it is possible that even if Bill were in charge here he would not be precluded from recovering.

Cyril's unwarranted, if understandable, decision to dismount, though unusual, is well within the range of foolish acts which the purpose of the regulations is to prevent. Accordingly he can recover for the breach of them.

Bill's injuries likewise are exactly such as the regulations were intended to prevent, since a sudden stop, for any cause, is far from unusual in traffic, and must be the most likely reason for injury to anyone travelling in the cage. Donald, on the other hand, is not the beneficiary of the regulations, and cannot claim in respect of their breach. He must rely solely on the common law. Additionally Bill and Cyril can rely on it, which they will wish to do in the alternative, since statutory duties, though strict and precise, may leave some circumstances not covered. Hence the common law duty of care may fill in the gaps, and will be invoked for many injuries at work.

The propinquity necessary to a duty of care is almost invariably found as between any road users who are involved together in any accident, the pavement being included for this purpose. Clearly Alan's sudden stop, in the normal way, must have been negligent towards his passengers sitting precariously above him. However what is negligent depends on all the circumstances, and a driver who when driving is suddenly apprised of a sudden and perhaps unspecified danger to unseen pesons outside his line of vision perhaps does not act negligently in stopping suddenly to investigate further. If so then neither Bill nor Donald (and his mother) can claim. However, the cause of the mishap is not the vehicle's sudden stop in itself, but the starting of the journey with the men travelling in the cage in the first place, with Alan's knowledge and consent. Even if not necessarily dangerous, this clearly carried some risk of mishap, including the risk of vertigo or fright. Since the arrangement was a joint decision it seems that Alan and Cyril are liable to Bill, Alan and Bill and Cyril to Donald, and probably Alan and Bill to Cyril too.

Under the Fatal Accidents Acts Donald's parent or parents will be entitled to claim the fixed sum of £3,500 (or £7,500 if the death occurred after 1 April 1991) for bereavement. Both Bill and Cyril will because of their participation in the dangerous plan and in Cyril's case of his loss of nerve, will suffer a reduction in any damages awarded either for breach of the duty imposed by the regulations or at common law because of contributory negligence.

The Gleaming D C, although liable directly only for the breach of the regulations, is liable vicariously for the torts of its employees committed within the course of their employment. This includes both illegal and forbidden acts which were nonetheless intended to forward the employer's concerns and (as here) were evidently likely to do so. It would seem clear that there is a case of vicarious liability here, since an observer, asked what was going on, would not say 'They are doing something dangerous with their employer's equipment', but 'They are doing their job in a dangerous way'. The conclusion follows that the employer is liable (subject to deductions where appropriate for contributory negligence) to both of its injured employees and to Donald's parent(s), along with its respective employees.

QUESTION TWO

Regulations made under statutory authority provide: 'Employers shall ensure that all workers engaged in the manufacture of chemicals wear the protective clothing prescribed in these regulations at all times when they are exposed to danger and shall ensure that such clothing is maintained in a sound state of repair.' These regulations apply to the premises of Burns plc. Scald, an employee of Burns, who is noted for bad time-keeping, turning up late for work. In his haste to put on his protective overalls, he ripped them down one side. He discarded them and put on a spare pair which were hanging on a peg. Later that day one of the workers in the laboratory collapsed with a suspected heart attack. Flame, a medical orderly employed by Burns, went into the laboratory to assist; he put on the overalls abandoned by Scald, but did not notice that they were torn. In the laboratory, a quantity of acid was spilled on him and penetrated through the tear in the overalls. Flame was severely injured.

Advise Flame.

University of London LLB Examination
(for External Students) Law of Tort June 1987 Q6

Skeleton Solution

Breach of regulations – no remedy provided in the regulations – does it give rise to civil liability in negligence? – breach of duty by employers in failing to provide safe system of work – provision of competent staff – vicarious liability for negligence of Scald – action against Scald? – contributory negligence.

Suggested Solution

Flame was injured at work when acid, which had been spilt, penetrated through the overalls which he was wearing because the overalls were ripped. There are three potential causes of action which Flame has against Burns plc. The first is for breach of statutory duty, the second is for breach of their common law obligations towards him and the third is that Burns are vicariously liable for Scald's negligence. We shall consider each in turn.

Burns plc are clearly in breach of the statutory regulation which requires that overalls such as the one which Flame was wearing must be maintained in a 'sound state of repair'. The wording of the regulations is crucial in deciding the standard of care demanded of Burns plc. It appears that the regulations impose upon Burns an absolute obligation to ensure that their clothing is maintained in a sound state of repair. The regulations state that the employers 'shall ensure that such clothing is maintained in a sound state of repair'. There is no suggestion that the employers' obligation is limited to that which is reasonably practicable. The imperative nature of this provision suggests that Burns have no defence in terms of the wording of the regulations. It seems that his injury was of a type that the regulation was intended to prevent (*Gorris* v *Scott* (1874) LR 9 Ex 125).

The difficult question which then arises is whether or not breach of the regulations gives rise to a cause of action in tort. The test to be applied is whether the regulations, on their true construction, confer upon Flame a cause of action in respect of the personal injury which he has suffered as a result of the breach of the regulations (*Cutler* v *Wandsworth Stadium Ltd* [1949] AC 398). In *Lonrho* v *Shell Petroleum Co (No 2)* [1982] AC 173 the House of Lords held that the initial presumption was that where the regulations provided their own means of enforcing the obligations enshrined in the regulations, for example, by imposing a criminal penalty, then the obligations cannot be enforced in any other way. We are not told that there is any such provision in the regulations. However the existence of such a provision would make it much harder for Flame to establish that the breach of the regulations gives him a remedy for breach (see *Atkinson* v *Newcastle Waterworks Co* (1877) 2 Ex D 441) but it is not necessarily impossible (see *Groves* v *Lord Wimborne* [1898] 2 QB 402).

In *Lonrho* v *Shell Petroleum* Lord Diplock held that there were two exceptions to the initial presumption that no cause of action arose in tort where the statute created its own means of enforcement. The first of these two exceptions is relevant here. That exception arises where the statute is enacted for the benefit of a particular class of individuals and the plaintiff is a member of that class. Here it is at least highly arguable that these regulations were enacted for the safety of employees at work and that therefore employees injured at work as a result of the breach of the regulations may maintain an action in tort for injury suffered as a result of breach. Such was the conclusion reached in the case of *Groves* v *Lord Wimborne* (above) where it was held that an employee could bring an action in tort in respect of a breach of the industrial safety legislation.

Flame may also have a cause of action against Burns plc in negligence. Employers owe a threefold duty towards their employees. The first is to provide a competent staff, the second is to provide proper plant and equipment and the third is to provide a safe system of work. The vital feature to note about these duties is that they are non-delegable so that an employer cannot simply discharge his responsibility by delegating the work to his employees or to independent contractors (see *McDermid* v *Nash Dredging and Reclamation Co Ltd* [1987] AC 906; [1987] 2 All ER 878). Burns plc may have breached their duty towards Flame in two respects.

The first is that they may have failed in their obligation to provide a competent staff of fellow employees. In *Hudson* v *Ridge Manufacturing Co Ltd* [1957] 2 QB 348) an employer was held to be in breach of this duty when one employee was injured as the result of a foolish prank carried out by a fellow employee. The employee who carried out the prank was known by the employer to have a propensity to carry out such pranks and the employer was held to be in breach of his duty in failing to take proper steps to halt these pranks. Here Scald was known to be a bad time keeper and the rip to the overall arose out of his haste after turning up late for work. So it is at least arguable that Burns are in breach of this duty to Flame and that that breach has been the cause of damage to Flame.

Alternatively Flame could argue that Burns have failed to maintain and operate a safe system of work. In *General Cleaning Contractors Ltd* v *Christmas* [1953] AC 180 it was held that the duty imposed on the employers was an onerous one. Here it is arguable that Burns plc have failed to provide a safe system of work because they have failed to provide adequate facilities for the disposal of torn garments and to provide sufficient numbers of new garments. Even if Burns could prove that the system was in fact safe, Flame could still argue that Burns were in breach of their duty in failing to operate it safely. In *McDermid* v *Nash Dredging and Reclamation Co Ltd* (above) the plaintiff's injury arose out of a failure to operate a system which was safe if operated properly. It was held that the employers were liable because they had failed to discharge their duty to their employees.

Alternatively Flame could argue that Burns are vicariously liable for the negligence of Scald. To establish liability here it must be shown that Scald was an employee of Burns, that he committed a tort and that he committed the tort in the course of his employment. It is clearly the case that Scald is an employee of Burns. The second question is whether Scald has committed a tort. It is submitted that Scald has committed the tort of negligence. He owed a duty of care to his fellow employee, the doctrine of common employment no longer being part of English law. He was in breach of that duty in leaving his ripped overall lying around without properly disposing of it. The fact that he was working in a laboratory where acids were in use means that he should take care of his overalls because of the serious risk which is posed by the use of materials such as acid. The fact that Scald was in a rush because he was late for work is irrelevant in fixing the standard of care. Thirdly it must be shown that the breach of duty caused damage to the plaintiff. There are two points which arise here. The first is that it could be argued that the breach did not cause the damage to Flame because it was his own decision to put on the ripped overall. Thus his action constituted a novus actus interveniens (*McKew* v *Holland, Hannen and Cubitts* [1969] 3 All ER 1621). However it is submitted that such an argument would fail because Flame was acting in an emergency to deal with someone who had had a heart attack, so it could not be said that his actions were so unreasonable as to break the chain of causation. Alternatively it could be argued that Scald was not responsible for the spilling of the acid which was the real cause of the damage. But applying the 'but for' test, if Flame had been wearing the proper protective clothing the accident would not have occurred and so, but for Scald's negligence the accident would not have arisen. Lastly, it could be argued that the loss was too remote because it was not reasonably foreseeable that Flame would suffer damage in such a way. But it is submitted that it was reasonably foreseeable that, if an employee did not wear the proper protective clothing, he would suffer burns and so the damage was not too remote.

On the third point it is clear that Scald committed the tort within the course of his employment. At the time of the negligent act he was in the course of his employment in preparing to go into the laboratory. The fact that he was doing his job negligently is not sufficient to take Scald out of the course of his employment because at the time of the incident he was doing his job in an unauthorised manner; he was not doing an unauthorised act. Lastly it may be argued that Flame's damages should be reduced on the ground that he was guilty of contributory negligence in going into the laboratory without checking that his overalls were not ripped. However at the time of the alleged contributory negligence Flame was acting in an emergency situation because an employee had collapsed with a suspected heart attack. In *Jones* v *Boyce* (1816) 1 Stark 493 it was held that a person who acted in the heat of the moment was not guilty of contributory negligence if he acted as a reasonable and prudent man would have done in the circumstances. It is submitted that Flame acted as a reasonable man would have done in the circumstances and that therefore he is not guilty of contributory negligence.

QUESTION FOUR

'Neither the liability of an employer to an employee on the basis of breach of statutory duty nor vicarious responsibility for fellow employees adds much to the liability resulting from the employer's personal duty of care.'

Discuss.

University of London LLB Examination
(for External Students) Law of Tort June 1991 Q1

Skeleton Solution

Employers' liability at common law; non-delegable nature – breaches of statutory duties; non-delegable nature and extent of such duties; pure economic loss – vicarious liability; effect of Law Reform (Personal Injuries) Act 1948, liability for dishonest employees.

Suggested Solution

At common law an employer's personal duty of care to an employee comprises a 'threefold obligation' namely the provision: of competent staff; of adequate equipment; and of a safe system of work (per Lord Wright in *Wilsons & Clyde Coal Co* v *English* [1938] AC 57 HL.

This definition is not exhaustive and has been extended to cover a duty to warn a prospective employee of inherent risks involved in the work before the employee accepts the job: *White* v *Holbrook Precision Castings* [1985] IRLR 215.

The burden is on the employee to prove that the employer either deliberately or negligently breached the personal duty of care and that as a result the employee sustained damage recoverable at law. The personal duty is a non-delegable (or primary) duty.

The injured employee may also be able to rely on two other forms of employers' liability which overlap but do not precisely coincide with the employer's personal duty. These forms are breach of statutory duty and vicarious liability for the torts of an employee acting in the course of his employment.

In regard to statutory duties, it will be a matter of construction whether the particular duty was intended by Parliament to be strict, such as in the case of the duty to fence dangerous machinery. If the duty is strict the employee is relieved of the burden of proving fault (though he must still prove a breach of the statutory duty and consequent damage): *Groves* v *Wimborne* [1898] 2 QB 402 CA and per Lord Wright in *LPTB* v *Upson* [1949] AC 155 HL, who emphasised the importance of the conceptual distinction between employers' personal and statutory duties. A statutory duty of the strict kind is, however, similar to the personal duty in being non-delegable in character.

The statutory duty may be interpreted to include a duty to protect the employee from suffering pure economic loss if that kind of loss is within the ambit of the relevant statute; for example an Act to protect the performing rights of film actors could protect correlative financial interests. By contrast the employer's personal duty does not extend to protect his employee from such loss because common law regards their relationship as being insufficiently proximate, with no assumption of special responsibility by the employer. This is consistent with recent common law hostility to the imposition of tortious duties to prevent pure economic loss, especially where a contract exists between the parties which may either expressly or impliedly deal with such loss in a more satisfactory manner than the law of tort: see *Reid* v *Rush and Tompkins* [1989] 3 All ER 228 CA where the Court of Appeal held no duty to insure an employee or to warn him of the wisdom of self-insurance in a case where the employee was being sent to work overseas.

In regard to vicarious liability there was a considerable expansion in the scope of such liability following the passage of the Law Reform (Personal Injuries) Act 1948.

Before that Act the employer had a defence called common employment which prevented an employee suing him for the torts of a fellow employee. The Act abolished this defence so that where the employee can prove fault by a fellow employee a claim under the principles of vicarious liability will succeed. Nevertheless the continued existence of the employer's personal duty to provide a competent staff may still be of relevance, as where the injured employee cannot prove fault but can establish that the other employee was not suitably qualified or experienced to perform the job in question.

Further there may be one area where the personal duty is wider in scope than vicarious liability. That area covers dishonest conduct by an employee. As a general rule an employer is not vicariously liable for such conduct even though he may have placed the dishonest employee in a position where he had the opportunity to steal from fellow employees (or others), unless it was a special position of trust akin to an agency: *Armagas* v *Mundogas (The Ocean Frost)* [1986] AC 717 HL. However an employer may be held liable for breach of his personal duty if he had knowingly employed a dishonest servant. Finally, the personal duty is non-delegable and therefore constitutes an important exception to the principles of vicarious liability under which there is no liability for the acts of an independent contractor: see *McDermid* v *Nash Dredging* [1987] 2 All ER 878 where the D employer had put the P employee under the control of a tugmaster who operated an unsafe system of work on the tug. It was held that D was liable for not providing a safe system of work. The House of Lords made it clear that the threefold obligation of the employer's personal duty was non-delegable in all of its three parts.

Hence issue is taken with the statement in question. There are sound practical reasons for the distinctions between an employer's personal duty, his statutory duties and his vicarious liability. Further, as Brazier points out in her 8th edition of Street on Torts, the conceptual distinctions between the three torts remain the basis of judicial thinking on the subject, and the developments and implications of the cases cannot be understood if this is not grasped.

QUESTION FIVE

Hamlet was employed as a gardener and groundsman at the Elsinore District Council playing fields. The council employed Guildenstern plc to service all the gardening equipment every six months. Last autumn Hamlet was using a heavy mechanical digger to remove the grass from a football pitch preparatory to returfing. Laertes and Ophelia, aged 7 and 9, had been allowed to play on the grass behind the goal posts. They lived in a house opposite the playing fields and their father Polonius was watching from an upstairs window.

As Hamlet reached the end of a row, he found that the steering had jammed and the digger ran off the pitch behind the goal towards the children. They managed to scramble out of the way at the last moment and were not injured. Polonius, who could not see exactly what had happened, collapsed. Since the incident he has suffered from sudden fits and all his hair has fallen out. Hamlet was very shaken by what happened and has not been able to return to work.

Inspection has shown that part of the steering mechanism which was not immediately visible had become badly corroded and had seized up.

Advise Hamlet and Polonius.

University of London LLB Examination
(for External Students) Law of Tort June 1993 Q1

Skeleton Solution

Employer's liability: safe plant and equipment; Defective Equipment Act - proving negligence: res ipsa loquitur - vicarious liability: employees; independent contractors - nervous shock - contributory negligence.

Suggested Solution

Hamlet is injured whilst at work. The first question to ask is whether his employers, Elsinore, are liable for his injuries. An employer owes a duty of care to his employees and the extent of this duty has been defined in many cases, most notably in *Wilsons & Clyde Coal Co* v *English* [1938] AC 57. One aspect of this duty is to provide adequate plant and equipment. Hamlet is using a heavy mechanical digger and the steering mechanism jams. Therefore his injury is caused by defective equipment.

The employers, Elsinore, are under a duty to inspect and maintain the digger (*Murphy* v *Phillips* (1876) 35 LT 477). However, they will argue that Guildenstern were employed to service the equipment. If the seizure of the steering mechanism is Guildenstern's fault, then, under the Employers' Liability (Defective Equipment) Act 1969, the injury is held to be attributable to the employer also. This means that Hamlet need only sue Elsinore who would presumably join Guildenstern as a third party.

This is presuming that there has been negligence, because we are told that the fault was not immediately visible on inspection. It is for Hamlet to show, on the balance of responsibilities, that there has been negligence, that is to say, whether it is reasonable to expect an inspection to be thorough enough to spot the defects.

Hamlet may well raise the maxim res ipsa loquitur. The requirements are that the digger is shown to be under the control of Guildenstern and that the seizure must be such as could not in the ordinary course of things have happened without negligence (*Scott* v *London and St Katherine Docks Co* (1865) 3 H & C 596). The effect of raising the maxim is not to shift the formal burden of proof (*Ng Chun Pui* v *Lee Chuen Tat* [1988] RTR 298) but to raise an inference of negligence which the defendants should rebut. *Henderson* v *Henry E Jenkins & Sons* [1970] AC 282 - which involved mechanical defects in a lorry which were not immediately apparent - indicates that the defendants may have to go some way to rebut the inference and it is submitted that Guildenstern's inspection may be held to be too cursory for such a machine.

On the other hand, it is also said that there must be an absence of explanation. In *Barkway* v *South Wales Transport Co Ltd* [1950] 1 All ER 392 it was held that where the cause of the accident is known, the maxim does not apply. If the cause of this incident is known, then the facts do not speak for themselves. Nevertheless the facts suggest negligence.

Hamlet will be suing for damages to compensate him for his injury and inability to return to work. There is no indication that he has been contributorily negligent although Elsinore might argue that a reasonable groundsman would have carried out his own checks on the vehicle. In the circumstances, it is submitted that his action is likely to succeed.

Polonius has suffered from fits and all his hair has fallen out since the incident. First, who could he sue? Hamlet owes a duty of care to the children but he is not in breach unless, as above, it can be shown that he might reasonably have inspected the vehicle and detected the fault.

In any event, Hamlet does not have the deepest pocket and Polonius would wish to know whether he can recover from Elsinore and/or Guildenstern. The accident occurred through the negligence of Elsinore and/or Guildenstern. Since Elsinore employs Hamlet, it is vicariously responsible for him. However, if Hamlet has not been negligent, although the accident occurred during the course of his employment, he has not committed a tort.

Is Elsinore vicariously liable for Guildenstern? Guildenstern owe a duty of care to those likely to be injured by mechanical failures to vehicles they service and they are in breach of that duty. However, although we are told they are 'employed' by Elsinore, we do not know the nature of the contract between them and it is much more likely, given the fact that Guildenstern are a limited company, that Elsinore has engaged the services of independent contractors. The test as to whether the contract is one of service or for services is contained in *Ready Mixed Concrete (South East) Ltd* v *Minister of Pensions* [1968] 2 QB 497.

Presuming it is the latter then, in principle, the employer is not vicariously responsible for the torts of the independent contractor (*D & F Estates Ltd* v *The Church Commissioners* [1989] AC 177). (Note, therefore, that the duty owed by Elsinore to Hamlet would be primary rather than vicarious.) If Elsinore has selected a reputable firm and taken reasonable steps to ensure that Guildenstern are carrying out the duties delegated to them in a responsible way, then they would not be held responsible. If, on the other hand, Polonius can show that Elsinore have not acted reasonably - for example, that a six-monthly check is inadequate - then they might be held responsible, but it would because of a breach in their primary liability.

I would advise Polonius, at this stage, that he is most likely to succeed against Guildenstern plc. His claim will be for damages to compensate him for nervous shock. This must constitute 'a positive psychiatric illness' to justify a claim (per Lord Bridge in *McLoughlin* v *O'Brian* [1982] 2 All ER 298). Clearly Polonius satisfies that requirement. The other requirements have recently been stated in the House of Lords' decision, *Alcock* v *Chief Constable of South Yorkshire Police* [1991] 4 All ER 907. It must be reasonably foreseeable that a person would suffer nervous shock in those circumstances. As father of Laertes and Ophelia, Polonius is presumed to have the necessary ties of love and affection. He is also very close to the incident and might reasonably have believed that his children had been hit by the vehicle. The fact they were not is irrelevant to his claim. What he saw with his unaided senses suggested to him that they had been killed or injured.

Was he contributorily negligent in that a reasonable father would not have let his children play anywhere near a mechanical digger? We are not given enough facts to answer this but it may be a consideration. There is an analogy with occupier's liability, where, at common law, an occupier may assume a degree of care for a child's safety will be exercised by the parent (*Phipps* v *Rochester Corporation* [1955] 1 QB 450). Guildenstern might argue that Polonius would never have suffered nervous shock if he had behaved responsibly.

10 PRODUCT LIABILITY

10.1   Introduction

10.2   Key points

10.3   Recent cases and statute

10.4   Analysis of questions

10.5   Questions

10.1 Introduction

Liability in law for defective products has undergone two major changes: the first was in 1932 when *Donoghue* v *Stevenson* exploded the 'contract fallacy' and the second was the passing of the Consumer Protection Act 1987.

10.2 Key points

a) *Common law position*

The Consumer Protection Act 1987 has not repealed the common law rules on defective products which must still be considered.

i) Note the explosion of the 'contract fallacy' in *Donoghue* v *Stevenson* [1932] AC 562 and Lord Atkin's statement: 'A manufacturer of products, which he sells in such a form as to show that he intends them to reach the ultimate consumer in the form in which they left him with no reasonable possibility of intermediate examination, and with the knowledge that the absence of reasonable care in the preparation, or putting up of the products will result in an injury to the consumer's life or property, owes a duty to the consumer to take reasonable care.'

ii) The statement has been extended from manufacturers to any supplier who is under a duty to inspect the goods.

iii) Note the wide meaning attributed to 'products' and 'consumers' and the meaning of 'reasonable probability of intermediate examination': *Grant* v *Australian Knitting Mills* [1936] AC 85.

iv) An express warning of the danger will discharge the manufacturer's duty: *Kubach* v *Hollands* [1937] 3 All ER 907.

v) Since *Aswan Engineering Establishment* v *Lupdine* [1987] 1 All ER 135 it is clear that the damage covered is that to other property of the consumer; if the defect only renders the goods less valuable then any claim is in contract (see Chapter 5.2(d)).

vi) The manufacturer's duty is to take reasonable care, and the plaintiff usually proves lack of care by showing that the defect arose in manufacture because nothing that happened to the product after it left the manufacturer could have caused the defect: *Mason* v *Williams & Williams* [1955] 1 WLR 549. However, if the product has been handled and used for some time this may be difficult: *Evans* v *Triplex Safety Glass* [1936] 1 All ER 283.

b) *Statutory position*

   i) The general principle of the Consumer Protection Act 1987 is found in s2: 'Where any damage is caused wholly or partly by a defect in a product, every person to whom subsection (2) applies shall be liable for the damage.'

       Subsection (2) applies to the producer, the importer into the European Community and sometimes the supplier of the goods.

       Note the extended definition of producer, and those situations in which the supplier may be held liable.

  ii) By s3(1) a defective product is one in which the safety of the product is not such as persons generally are entitled to expect. Obviously any product is capable of being misused in an unsafe manner (eg a kitchen knife), so note the guidelines in s3(2) as to what matters shall be taken into account.

 iii) The Act allows various defences in s4. The most important are that the defect did not exist in the product at the relevant time and the 'state of the art defence' ie 'that the state of scientific and technical knowledge at the relevant time was not such that a producer of products of the same description as the product in question might be expected to have discovered the defect if it had existed in his products while they were under his control'.

       This defence is likely to be very important with, for example, drug manufacturers and side effects. The defendant must prove this defence, ie he must prove that the defect was not one a producer might be expected to discover. Thus the manufacturer will only be liable if he knew or reasonably ought to have known of the defect which is just what the plaintiffs would have to prove in negligence. The only practical difference is that under s4 the burden of proof lies on the defendant while in negligence it would lie on the plaintiff. (Note the state of the art defence in s4(2)(e) is much wider than that allowed in the original EC directive 85/374/EEC Article 7(a), and there is still debate between the UK government and the European Commission as to whether or not the UK has validly enacted the directive, which could give rise to problems as to which state of the art defence a defendant could actually rely on.)

  iv) The plaintiff must still prove causation, although there is no requirement of foreseeability.

   v) By s5 the damage covered is death or personal injury to the plaintiff or damage to his private property other than the product itself.

  vi) The Act does not apply to damage below £275, and liability under s2(1) cannot be excluded or restricted.

10.3 Recent cases and statute

Hobbs v *Baxendale Chemical Co* [1992] 1 Lloyd's Rep 54

Consumer Protection Act 1987

EC Directive 85/374/EEC

10.4 Analysis of questions

The passing of the 1987 Act seems to have jolted the examiner's memory on this topic, as can be seen from the 1988 and 1989 examination papers.

10.5 Questions

QUESTION ONE

'The provisions of Part I of the Consumer Protection Act 1987 are to be welcomed, but there is scope for the role of fault in the law of tort to be further diminished.'

Discuss.

University of London LLB Examination
(for External Students) Law of Tort June 1988 Q5

Skeleton Solution

CPA – strict liability – who is liable – defective – defences – damage – is Act welcome? – other examples of strict liability – *Rylands*, animals, fire, vicarious liability, nuisance? res ipsa loquitur? – other extensions? – causation and *Wilsher* – replacement of present system by comprehensive no-fault accident compensation scheme.

Suggested Solution

The provisions of Part I of the Consumer Protection Act (CPA) 1987 were introduced to implement the provisions of an EEC Directive relating to product liability. The CPA 1987 purports to introduce a regime of strict liability in the sphere of product liability. Before considering whether or not the Act is to be welcomed it is necessary to outline the principal provisions of the Act.

The main provision of the Act is contained in s2(1) which states that where any damage is caused wholly or partly by a defect in a product then certain persons shall be liable for the damage which is occasioned. The persons who may be liable are the producer of the goods, any person who holds himself out as being a producer of the goods, the importer of the goods into the EEC and, in certain circumstances, the supplier of the product. The liability of the supplier is, however, a secondary liability; that is to say that the supplier may discharge liability by identifying the producer of the goods and it is only where he fails to so this that he will be liable. A product is defined in s1(2) as any 'goods or electricity' and goods is further defined in s45.

The consumer is left with a problem, however, in establishing that the product was defective. A product is defective where the 'safety of the product is not such as persons generally are entitled to expect' (s3(2)). Thus the product must in some way be unsafe; it will not generally suffice to say that the goods simply did not live up to expectations. A court is to have regard to all the circumstances of the case in considering whether a product is defective but relevant factors include the marketing of the product, any warnings contained on the product and the use to which the product might reasonably be put.

The Act contains a number of defences, the most important of which is the 'state of the art' defence contained in s4(1)(e) which states that it is a defence to show that the state of scientific knowledge at the relevant time was not such that a producer of products of the same description might be expected to have discovered the defect. The presence of this defence makes it difficult to say that the role of fault has been completely eliminated under the CPA because the factors to which a court will have regard in considering whether the state of the art defence has been established are similar to the factors which a court will have regard to in a negligence action.

Finally it should be noted that only certain types of losses are recoverable under the Act. Damages are recoverable for personal injury and death and in relation to damage to private property (provided that it exceeds £275) but damages are not recoverable for the defect in the product itself (s5).

The provisions of the Act are generally to be welcomed in that they improve the position of the consumer who suffers injury as a result of a defective product. But difficulties will remain due to the presence of the state of the art defence which may be invoked by many manufacturers, particularly in relation to the manufacture of drugs. Difficulties will also remain in showing that the product was defective and where the goods themselves are defective and do not cause any other injury no remedy will lie under the Act and the remedy (if any) will be in contract.

These provisions of the CPA are not, however, the only example of liability without fault in English law. Other examples of strict liability in English law are the rule in *Rylands* v *Fletcher* (1868) LR 3 HL 330, vicarious liability (as the employer does not commit a tort), liability under the Animals Act 1971 and liability for the escape of fire. More debatable examples of strict liability are nuisance (although the role of fault within this tort is unclear: see Lord Reid in *The Wagon Mound (No 2)* [1967] 1 AC 617) and res ipsa loquitur. Another source of strict liability is contractual liability, particularly in relation to the merchantable quality provisions of the Sale of Goods Act 1979. Liability depends on proof that the goods are unmerchantable and not on proof that the vendor was in some way at fault.

Despite the fact that there are a number of areas in which English law recognises liability without fault there is no general principle in English law of liability without fault and there is still room for the extension of no fault liability as can be seen from the recent case of *Wilsher* v *Essex Area Health Authority* [1988] AC 1074; [1988] 1 All ER 871. The House of Lords held that the plaintiff must in all cases prove on a balance of probabilities that the negligence of the defendant was the cause of the loss to the plaintiff. This is likely to cause problems for plaintiffs in medical negligence cases such as *Wilsher* where it is uncertain which of a number of competing causes was the cause of the damage to the plaintiff. If the plaintiff can surmount the problems of proof he can recover for all his losses; if he cannot surmount this hurdle he will recover nothing. It seems rather arbitrary that enormous sums of money should hinge on such difficult evidential questions.

Wilsher also demonstrates other deficiencies of a fault based system. The plaintiff's parents have now been fighting for a number of years to recover damages for their son but as a result of the decision of the House of Lords they are now no nearer to recovery than they were when the case first started. Large amounts of time and money have so far been spent on seeking to show that the defendant's fault was the cause of the damage to the plaintiff. The Pearson Committee discovered that the cost of operating the tort system accounted for some 85 per cent of the sums paid to accident victims.

Similarly it is questionable whether the presence of fault should make such a difference to the plaintiff in *Wilsher*. His needs are the same whether the negligence of the defendants was the cause of his loss or not. It is difficult to justify a system in which he recovers extremely large sums of money if he can prove the necessary causal link but nothing if he fails. It may be said that the presence of fault is the differentiating factor but in cases such as *Nettleship* v *Weston* [1971] 2 QB 691 the role of personal fault in a negligence action appears to have almost entirely disappeared.

Dissatisfaction with the tort system in New Zealand was such that the tort action has been abolished in relation to personal injury cases and replaced by a comprehensive no-fault accident compensation scheme which covers all accidental injury, except diseases (other than occupational diseases) and is financed by a levy on motor vehicles, employers and employees and out of general taxation.

Such a scheme is likely to ensure a greater extent of equality as between different victims of misfortune in society. It is true that such a system would be expensive to operate but at least more of the money would get to the claimants and not be tied up in administration as in the present fault based system. It is therefore suggested that there is scope for the extension of no-fault liability in English law and that serious consideration should now be given to implementing a comprehensive no-fault accident compensation scheme.

QUESTION TWO

Critically examine the provisions of Part I of the Consumer Protection Act 1987 relating to product liability. To what extent do these provisions constitute an improvement upon the common law rules?

Written by the editor

Skeleton Solution

CPA – strict liability – product – who is liable? – defect – defences – common law – fault – state of the art defence – causation – liability of supplier – losses recoverable.

Suggested Solution

The provisions of Part I of the Consumer Protection Act (CPA) 1987 were introduced to implement the provisions of an EEC Directive relating to product liability. The CPA 1987 purports to introduce a regime of strict liability in the sphere of product liability. The main provision of the Act is contained in s2(1) which states that where any damage is caused wholly or partly by a defect in a product then certain persons shall be liable for the damage which is occasioned. The persons who may be liable are the producer of the goods, any person who holds himself out as being a producer of the goods, the importer of the goods into the EEC and, in certain circumstances, the supplier of the product. The liability of the supplier is, however, a secondary liability; that is to say that the supplier may discharge liability by identifying the producer of the goods and it is only where he fails to do this that he will be liable.

A product is defined in s1(2) as any 'goods or electricity' and goods is further defined in s45. The consumer is left with a problem, however, in establishing that the product was defective. A product is defective where the 'safety of the product is not such as persons generally are entitled to expect' (s3(2)). Thus the product must in some way be unsafe; it will not generally suffice to say that the goods simply did not live up to expectations. The Act contains a number of defences, the most important of which is the 'state of the art' defence contained in s4(1)(e) which states that it is a defence to show that the state of scientific and technical knowledge at the relevant time was not such that a producer of products of the same description might be expected to have discovered the defect.

In subjecting these provisions to critical analysis it is necessary to give a brief consideration to the defects in the common law which prompted the enactment of the 1987 Act. The common law was based upon *Donoghue* v *Stevenson* [1932] AC 562, according to which a manufacturer could be liable to a consumer where he had failed to take reasonable care in the preparation of the goods with the result that injury was caused to the consumer's life or property. It is only by understanding the deficiencies in the common law that we can begin to engage in a critical appraisal of the Act. There were a number of defects in the common law which led to the enactment of the 1987 Act. We shall consider each deficiency and the response of the Act to the particular problem.

The first problem at common law was the difficulty which was experienced in showing that the manufacturer was at fault in relation to the defect in the product. The manufacturer was only required to take reasonable care and could argue, for example, that the state of human knowledge did not enable him to discover the defect. This defect has been dealt with to some extent because the Act purports to introduce a regime of strict liability. But it is likely to remain a problem due to the width of the state of the art defence. Indeed the inclusion of the state of the art defence and the width of that defence is the most controversial aspect of the Act.

Secondly, at common law, it could be difficult for a consumer to show that the defect arose during the manufacturing process. In *Evans* v *Triplex Safety Glass Ltd* [1936] 1 All ER 283 the plaintiff was unable to show that the defect in the windscreen of the car which he purchased was present when the car left the manufacturing process and that it did not materialise during the intervening year when he was using the car. This difficulty has not been dealt with by the Act because there is no provision in the Act which deals with causation, apart from s2(1) which states that the damage must be caused '*wholly or partly*' by a defect in the product. Thus causation is likely to remain a problem in such cases as actions against drug manufacturers.

Thirdly, at common law, it was difficult for a consumer to succeed against a supplier in tort. It is true that in many cases the consumer had an action in contract against the supplier but this was of no use to the person who was injured when he received the product as a gift because then there was obviously no contractual relationship between the supplier and the injured party. This difficulty has been resolved by the Act because, although the liability of a supplier is only secondary, if the supplier can identify his supplier the plaintiff will take an action against that person and if the original supplier cannot identify his supplier then the original supplier himself will be liable. Thus either way the plaintiff will have a remedy.

Finally at common law there was a difficulty where the goods were simply less valuable, in the sense that they were not as good as the purchaser thought they were. Again the existence of a contract would protect most persons but problems arose when there was no contractual relationship because, unless the case fell within the narrow confines of *Junior Books* v *Veitchi* [1983] AC 520, there was no remedy available in tort. The Act does not resolve this problem because damages are recoverable under the Act only in respect of 'death or personal injury or any loss of or damage to property' (s5(1)). But crucially s5(2) provides that a defendant shall not be liable in respect of the 'loss of or damage to the product itself or for the loss of or any damage to the whole or any part of the product which has been supplied with the product in question comprised in it'. Also the Act does not protect disappointed expectations, unless it can be shown that the *safety* of the product was not such as persons generally are entitled to expect.

The CPA does constitute an improvement upon the common law but it cannot claim to be a wholly satisfactory piece of legislative reform. It remains to be seen how the courts will interpret this legislation, but the width of the state of the art defence means that the Act cannot be said to remedy the deficiencies of the common law completely.

QUESTION THREE

Fanny and Gordon were married last year. They received a very expensive record player and stereo system manufactured by Botchit Ltd as a wedding present from Henry, a business associate of Fanny's father. For the first few weeks the equipment caused much trouble. There were unexplained surges of power and the equipment would cut out. The service engineer reported (correctly) that the motor was faulty and could not be repaired. They had to buy a new motor unit at considerable expense.

Two months later smoke started to pour from the turntable. It seems that the original surges of power had damaged the turntable drive, which had now started to overheat when in use. Fanny and Gordon had to buy a new turntable and had to buy new curtains and redecorate the room as the smoke had destroyed the original curtains and decorations.

Fanny and Gordon do not know where Harry bought the equipment and do not want to tell him that his present has caused such trouble. Advise them whether they have a remedy against Botchit Ltd.

University of London LLB Examination
(for External Students) Law of Tort June 1993 Q2

Skeleton Solution

Consumer Protection Act: who is a producer?; what is a product?; what is a defect?; what damage is covered?; are there any defences? – position at common law.

Suggested Solution

This problem concerns a defective product manufactured by Botchit Ltd, the potential defendants. The plaintiffs are put to expense in mending the product and then replacing it, as well as in repairing the damage it causes to their property.

One should first look to the Consumer Protection Act 1987 to see if Fanny and Gordon are afforded statutory protection. The stereo system is a product covered by the Act, since s1 defines product as meaning any goods. Under s2(2) of the Act, the producer of the product is liable for the damage caused by a defect in the product. Botchit Ltd, we are told, manufactured the system and are therefore producers covered by this section. F and G do not know the name of the supplier and do not want to ask H where he bought it. While the supplier can also be held liable under s2(3) of the Act, this would be where the supplier fails, upon request being made within a reasonable period after the damage occurs, to identify the producer. Therefore F and G are unaffected by their lack of knowledge of the supplier.

The next question that F and G need to consider is whether there has been a defect within the meaning of the Act. A defect exists, under s3, 'if the safety of the product is not such as persons generally are entitled to expect'. 'Safety' is construed widely and includes safety in the context of risks of damage to property. The problems that occurred in this case arose from the faulty motor, both before and after it was replaced, and meant that the system was not of the safety that one would reasonably expect in a new product. Therefore, the defect falls within the definition of the Act.

Next, the plaintiffs must consider the damage. Unfortunately for them, the Act restricts recovery for property damage in that there is no liability in respect of loss of or damage to the product itself (s5(2)). Therefore they cannot recover under the Act for the defective motor unit and turntable. They can only recover for the damage the product causes to their property. Presumably this damage is quite extensive and, in any case, is above the £275 threshold demanded by the Act.

It does not appear that any of the defences provided by s4 of the Act will apply, unless this is a 'state-of-the-art' stereo and Botchit can claim that 'the state of scientific and technical knowledge at the time was not such that a producer of products of the same description as the product in question might be expected to have discovered the defect if it had existed in his products while they were under his control' (s4(1)(e)). This is the so-called 'development risks' defence.

Therefore Fanny and Gordon can recover under the Act for the damage to their property but not for their outlay on repairing and then replacing the stereo. The next question, then, is whether that expense can be recovered. Obviously there is no contract between plaintiffs and defendants and Fanny and Gordon do not want to involve Henry, who was a party to the contract. So any remedy must lie in tort.

Liability at common law for defective products was most famously stated in *Donoghue* v *Stevenson* [1932] AC 562. However, it applies where the product causes damage to other property than the product itself. There is no general liability at common law for loss to the product. This is despite the House of Lords' decision in *Junior Books* v *Veitchi Co Ltd* [1983] 1 AC 520 which purported to allow such liability but which has since been disapproved. This is properly the sphere of contract law and I would advise the plaintiffs that they will not recover for damage to the property itself in tort.

11 OCCUPIERS' LIABILITY

11.1 Introduction

11.2 Key points

11.3 Recent cases

11.4 Analysis of questions

11.5 Questions

11.1 Introduction

Occupiers' liability is a specialised aspect of the tort of negligence, but rather than being covered by common law it is subject to statute, namely the Occupiers' Liability Act 1957 and the Occupiers' Liability Act 1984. Thus in this area close attention must be paid to the exact words of the relevant statute while still being aware of the common law concepts such as breach of duty, etc.

11.2 Key points

a) *The Occupiers' Liability Act 1957*

Under this Act the occupier of premises owes a duty of care to his visitors.

i) Occupier was defined in *Wheat* v *Lacon* [1966] AC 552: 'Wherever a person has a sufficient degree of control over premises that he ought to realise that any failure on his part to take care may result in injury to a person coming lawfully there, then he is an "occupier" and the person coming lawfully there is his "visitor"'.

Note Lord Denning's four categories of occupier in *Wheat* and the fact that these categories are not exhaustive: *Harris* v *Birkenhead Corporation* [1976] 1 WLR 279.

ii) Visitors include invitees and licensees. As regards implied licences see *Robson* v *Hallett* [1967] 2 QB 393 concerning callers, and the restrictive approach to implied licences involving children in *Edwards* v *Railway Executive* [1952] AC 737. The occupier may limit the permission he gives to a visitor to enter the premises as regards space: *The Calgarth* [1927] P 93; *Gould* v *McAuliffe* [1941] 2 All ER 527; purpose of visit: *R* v *Smith & Jones* [1976] 1 WLR 672 and time: *Stone* v *Taffe* [1974] 1 WLR 1575.

iii) Premises are widely defined by s1(3)(a).

iv) Duty

The duty owed by the occupier is the common duty of care, s2(1), which he may extend, restrict, modify or exclude in so far as he is free to.

The occupier must 'take such care as in all the circumstances of the case is reasonable to see that the visitor will be reasonably safe in using the premises for the purposes for which he is invited or permitted by the occupier to be there.' It is the visitor, not the premises, which must be reasonably safe, and the duty is clearly similar to that in negligence. Note *Hogg* v *Historic Buildings Commission* (1989) Current Law March para 285; *Cunningham* v *Reading Football Club* (1991) The Independent 20 March; *Gitsham* v *Pearce* [1992] PIQR 57 and compare *Murphy* v *Bradford Metropolitan Council* [1992] PIQR 68. Additionally, the 1957 Act provides for four specific situations:

- Children

  Section 2(3)(a) provides that 'an occupier must be prepared for children to be less careful than adults': see *Latham* v *Johnson & Nephew* [1913] 1 KB 398; *Glasgow Corporation* v *Taylor* [1922] 1 AC 44 and compare with *Liddle* v *Yorks (North Riding) CC* [1934] 2 KB 101. As regards very young children anything can be a danger, but occupiers and guardians are each entitled to assume that the other will act reasonably: *Phipps* v *Rochester Corporation* [1955] 1 QB 450.

- Common calling

  Section 2(3)(b) of the 1957 Act provides that an occupier may expect that a person, in the exercise of his calling, will appreciate and guard against special risks ordinarily incident to it. The fact that a visitor possesses a special skill does not, of itself, discharge the duty owed: *Salmon* v *Seafarer Restaurants* [1983] 3 All ER 729; *Ogwo* v *Taylor* [1987] 2 WLR 988, and note the interpretation of 'ordinarily incident' in *Bird* v *King Line* [1970] 1 Lloyd's Rep 349.

- Warning of danger

  Section 2(4)(a) provides that a warning *may* discharge the duty of care *providing* that in all the circumstances of the case it is enough to enable the visitor to be reasonably safe: see *Roles* v *Nathan* [1963] 1 WLR 1117; *Rae* v *Mars UK* (1989) The Times 15 February.

- Independent contractors

  Section 2(4)(b) provides that the occupier is not liable for the fault of an independent contractor if he acted reasonably in entrusting the work to an independent contractor and took reasonable steps to see that the contractor was competent and the work properly done. As to what steps (if any) the occupier need take to check the work compare *Haseldine* v *Daw* [1941] 2 KB 343 with *Woodward* v *Mayor of Hastings* [1945] KB 174.

v) Defences

Both volenti, s2(5), and contributory negligence, s2(3) can apply: see *Simms* v *Leigh Rugby FC* [1969] 2 All ER 923; *Stone* v *Taffe* (above).

b) *Non-visitors*

i) Governed by the Occupiers' Liability Act 1984. For the definition of a trespasser see *Robert Addie* v *Dumbreck* [1929] AC 358 and note the House of Lords decision in *British Railways Board* v *Herrington* [1972] AC 877 which was the common law precursor of the 1984 Act.

ii) It is vital to note the conditions that have to be satisfied under s1(3) 1984 Act for the duty to arise, namely:

- the occupier is aware of the danger or has reasonable grounds to believe that it exists;

- the occupier knows or has reasonable grounds to believe that the non-visitor is in the vicinity of the danger or may come into the vicinity of the danger; see *White* v *St Albans City & District Council* (1990) The Times 12 March; and

- the risk is one against which in all the circumstances the occupier may reasonably be expected to offer the non-visitor some protection.

iii) The duty, when it arises, is defined by s1(4) 1984 Act as a duty 'to take such care as is reasonable in all the circumstances to see that the non-visitor does not suffer injury on the premises by reason of the danger concerned.

This duty may be discharged by a warning or by discouraging persons from incurring the risk: s1(5).

c) *Exclusion of occupiers' duty*

i) Occupiers' Liability Act 1957

Section 2(1) 1957 Act allows the occupier to extend, restrict, modify or exclude his duty in so far as he is free to do so. The major restriction on the occupier's freedom to exclude his duty lies in the Unfair Contract Terms Act 1977, as the duty of care under the 1957 Act is expressly covered by the Unfair Contract Terms Act 1977. However, the 1977 Act, by s1(3) only applies to business liability, so an occupier is free to exclude his non-business liability. For business liability the effect of s2 1977 Act is to render void an attempt to exclude or restrict liability for death or personal injury, and for other loss or damage to make the restriction subject to the requirements of reasonableness.

ii) Occupiers' Liability Act 1984

Although the point is undecided, note the arguments which claim that the duty owed under the 1984 Act cannot be excluded.

11.3 Recent cases

Cunningham v *Reading Football Club* (1991) The Independent 20 March

Gitsham v *Pearce* [1992] PIQR 57

cf *Murphy* v *Bradford Metropolitan Council* [1992] PIQR 68

White v *St Albans City & District Council* (1990) The Times 12 March

McGeown v *Northern Ireland Housing Executive* [1994] 3 All ER 53

11.4 Analysis of questions

Occupiers' liability is a popular area with examiners and seems to come up each year. Sometimes the question involves pure occupiers' liability and sometimes other actions are present. Occupiers' liability must sometimes be considered in questions involving animals or nuisance or *Rylands* v *Fletcher*.

11.5 Questions

QUESTION ONE

Lord Steeple opened his mansion house and gardens to the public one day. All proceeds were to be donated to the local church restoration fund. A notice at the entrance read: 'All visitors enter these premises at their own risk.' Lord Steeple's private quarters were not open to the public and notices were clearly placed on doors, saying, 'Private. Closed to Visitors.' In the grounds are the ruins of an earlier house. A notice at the outside read: 'This building is dangerous. Visitors are asked to keep their children under control.'

Vestry visited the house, accompanied by his small son Pew. While visiting the ruins, Pew struggled free of Vestry's grasp and squeezed under a railing. He fell six feet to a lower level and suffered severe cuts and bruises and a broken arm. When Vestry saw that he was injured, he ran into the main house and through a door marked 'Private. Closed to Visitors.' He was set upon by an alsatian dog which Lord Steeple's butler, Aisle, had, without Lord Steeple's knowledge, been training as a guard dog. The dog caused Vestry severe injuries.

Advise Vestry and Pew.

University of London LLB Examination
(for External Students) Law of Tort June 1990 Q4

Suggested Solution

Lord Steeple is the occupier of the mansion house and its grounds under the Occupiers' Liability Act 1957, *Wheat* v *Lacon* [1966] AC 552, and Vestry and Pew are his visitors and as such are owed the common duty of care by the occupier, Lord Steeple; s2(1) 1957 Act.

As regards Pew, by s2(3) 1957 Act an occupier must be prepared for children to be less careful than adults. In the case of very young children both the guardian of the child and the occupier must act reasonably and each is entitled to assume that the other will act reasonably: *Phipps* v *Rochester Corporation* [1955] 1 QB 450. In view of the warning notice by the ruins, and the fact that we are told Pew 'squeezed' under a railing, it could be argued that Lord Steeple is not in breach of the common duty of care that he owes to Pew. This would be especially true if the danger was obvious, even to a child: *Liddle* v *Yorks (North Riding) CC* [1934] 2 KB 101.

Turning to the warning by the ruins, s2(4)(a) 1957 Act provides that a warning is not by itself sufficient to discharge the occupier from liability unless in all the circumstances it was enough to enable the visitor to be reasonably safe. In Lord Steeple's case there is not only a warning but also a railing which would seem to discharge the duty under the 1957 Act. It was held in *Hogg* v *Historic Buildings Commission* (1989) Current Law March para 285 that the antiquity of a building is a factor to be taken into account in determining whether or not the occupier has taken reasonable care, and in *Rae* v *Mars UK* (1989) The Times 15 February it was held that where an unusual danger exists, the visitor should not only be warned but a barrier or notice should be placed to show the immediacy of the danger. Taking these factors and those in the previous paragraph into account Lord Steeple appears to have complied with the duty imposed as regards Pew.

Lord Steeple may also seek to rely on the defence that by the notice at the entrance he has excluded any duty he owes under the 1957 Act. By s2(1) of the 1957 Act the occupier can exclude his duty by agreement or otherwise (ie via a non-contractual notice) in so far as he is free to. Such an exclusion clause will be subject to the provisions of the Unfair Contract Terms Act 1977 by s1(1)(c) of that Act. However the Unfair Contract Terms Act 1977 only applies to business liability (s1(3) 1977 Act) and as Lord Steeple only opens his house on one day per year and donates all proceeds to the church restoration fund it would seem that Lord Steeple is not granting access for his business purposes and thus the Unfair Contract Terms Act 1977 will not apply to the notice and it will be a valid exclusion of duty to Pew.

Considering now Vestry, when Vestry ran through the door marked 'Private. Closed to Visitors', Vestry was no longer Lord Steeple's visitor. An occupier may give a visitor permission to enter some parts of his premises but not others: *The Calgarth* [1927] P 93. An occupier who wishes to do this must take steps to bring the limitation to his visitor's attention: *Gould* v *McAuliffe* [1941] 2 All ER 527 and Lord Steeple has done this by means of the notice on the door. Hence as regards this part of the premises Vestry is a trespasser and any duty owed to Vestry is governed by the Occupiers' Liability Act 1984. By s1(3) of the 1984 Act the occupier of premises owes a duty of care to a non-visitor if:

a) he is aware of the danger or has reasonable grounds to believe it exists,

b) he knows or has reasonable grounds to believe that the visitor is in the vicinity of the danger concerned or may come into the vicinity of the danger, and

c) the risk is one against which, in all the circumstances, he may reasonably be expected to offer the non-visitor some protection.

In Vestry's case, Lord Steeple does not satisfy conditions (a) or (b) as he is unaware that the dog is being trained as a guard dog and is unaware of Vestry's presence in the private quarters. Thus a duty under the 1984 Act will not arise.

We must now consider whether any liability to Vestry arises under the Animals Act 1971 or the Guard Dogs Act 1975.

Lord Steeple is the keeper of the dog (assuming that Lord Steeple owns the dog) by s6(3) of the Animals Act 1971, and the dog is a non-dangerous species as defined by s6(2) of the 1971 Act. By s2(2) 1971 Act the keeper will be liable if:

a) the damage is of a kind which the animal, unless restrained, was likely to cause or which, if caused by the animal, was likely to be severe; and

b) the likelihood of the damage or of its being severe was due to characteristics of the animal which are not normally found except at particular times or in particular circumstances; and

c) those characteristics were known to that keeper or were at any time known to a person who had charge of the animal or that keeper's servant.

Requirements (a) and (b) are met in this case, the damage from a bite by an alsatian dog being likely to be severe and alsatians are not normally vicious except in the particular circumstances of their being kept as guard dogs: *Cummings* v *Grainger* [1977] QB 397. In addition, the servant of the keeper must have charge of the animal to make his knowledge relevant, which seems to be the case here. Thus Lord Steeples is prima facie liable to Vestry under s2(2) 1971 Act and note that s2(2) does not require negligence on the part of the keeper: *Curtis* v *Betts* [1990] 1 All ER 769.

However, Lord Steeple has several defences available to him under s5 of the 1971 Act. By s5(1) he will not be liable if the damage is wholly due to Vestry's fault, and while this is unlikely to succeed, by s10 Lord Steeple may rely on contributory negligence on Vestry's part to reduce any damages payable. If Vestry voluntarily accepted the risk there will be no liability, but again this seems unlikely in the given circumstances. Section 5(3) of the 1971 Act provides a defence against a trespasser if the animal was not kept for the protection of persons or property, but we are told it was being trained as a guard dog, or if it was kept for this purpose that it was reasonable to do so. In *Cummings* v *Grainger* it was held reasonable to have a guard dog in a scrap metal yard 'in the East End of London where persons of the roughest type come and go' (per Lord Denning). Whether it would be reasonable to have a guard dog in a stately home would be a matter for the court to decide, but in view of the burglaries that occur in such premises a court might well find that the keeping of a guard dog was not unreasonable. Although criminal liability may arise under s1 Guard Dogs Act 1975, s5(1) of that Act expressly provides that it confers no civil right of action.

Hence the advice to Pew is that he cannot sue Lord Steeple, and the advice to Vestry is that if he sues Lord Steeple he at best only has a slight chance of success.

QUESTION TWO

The Sporting Manufacturing Co Ltd are the owners and occupiers of a football ground provided for the benefit of their employees to which the public are admitted as spectators on payment for a ticket.

Consider the liability of the company in the following cases:

a) Ben, a member of a visiting team, falls during a match against the company's team and severely damages his knee as a broken beer bottle has been left on the pitch after a match on the previous day.

b) Edward, who has purchased a ticket, is injured by the collapse of a stand when he and other spectators move forward to leave the ground at the end of the match.

c) Percy, who has contrived to enter the ground without buying a ticket, trips over the damaged edge of one of the stairways, falls and breaks his leg.

Prepared for Holborn College, September 1993

Skeleton Solution

Occupiers' liability – occupiers and visitors – volenti – effect of UCTA 1977 – trespassers – OLA 1984.

Suggested Solution

a) By s2(2) Occupiers' Liability Act 1957 an occupier of premises owes a duty to his visitors to take such care in all the circumstances of the case as is reasonable to see that the visitor will be reasonably safe in visiting the premises for which he is permitted or invited to be there.

On the authority of *Wheat* v *Lacon* [1966] AC 552; [1966] 2 WLR 581 a person is an occupier for the purposes of the 1957 Act if he has a sufficient degree of control over the premises. On the basis of this definition the Sporting Manufacturing Co Ltd are occupiers of the sporting stadium. Ben, as a visiting member of another team, is clearly a lawful visitor and is therefore owed the common duty of care under s2(2) of the 1957 Act. There seems little doubt that leaving a broken bottle on the pitch from the previous day falls short of the required standard of care.

The defence of volenti non fit injuria is permitted under s2(5) of the 1957 Act. The Court of Appeal in *Wooldridge* v *Sumner* [1963] 2 QB 43; [1962] 3 WLR 616 held that spectators at games and sporting events assume the risk of any harm caused by the players unless it results from intentional or reckless conduct. It can be assumed, therefore, that Ben consents to ordinary risks that may occur whilst playing football according to the rules. However, this does not extend to the presence of broken bottles on the pitch.

The Sporting Manufacturing Co will therefore be liable to Ben.

b) Edward, having purchased a ticket, enters under a contract and under s5 the Occupiers' Liability Act 1957 applies. The common duty of care is incorporated into the contract, and the terms of the contract will determine liability. The duty owed, however, will be the common duty of care under s2(2) of the 1957 Act. This is because, although the Act states that the duty may be modified by an occupier, it is qualified by the words 'insofar as he is free to do so'. The freedom to exclude or restrict liability is subject to the Unfair Contract Terms Act 1977, which applies to the occupation of premises for business purposes. Section 2(1) of the 1977 Act provides that it is not possible to exclude liability for personal injury caused by negligence, which is defined as including breach of the common duty of care under s2(2) of the 1957 Act.

It could be argued that spectators are volenti to certain risks associated with the game – such as a football being kicked into the crowd, and s2(5) of the 1957 Act permits the use of the doctrine of volenti when considering liability under the Act. The injuries suffered here, however, are not of a type to which the spectator would consent (see *White* v *Blackmore* [1972] 2 QB 651; [1972] 3 WLR 296).

The Sporting Manufacturing Co Ltd will, therefore, be liable to Edward.

c) The 1957 Act applies only to lawful visitors, eg people who enter in pursuance of an invitation or who have express or implied permission to enter. When Percy enters onto the land, he does so as a trespasser, and his position is governed by the Occupiers' Liability Act 1984, which was an attempt to clarify the position of trespassers.

In *Addie* v *Dumbreck* [1929] AC 358 a trespasser was defined as one 'who goes on the land without invitation of any sort and whose presence is either unknown to the proprietor or, if known, practically objected to'. This case held that a trespasser enters the land of another at his own risk, and is owed no duty other than that of not inflicting damage intentionally or recklessly if the trespasser is know to be present.

In 1972 the House of Lords overruled this decision, exercising their power to depart from their previous decisions, in *British Railways Board* v *Herrington* [1972] AC 877; [1972] 2 WLR 537. Although their Lordships rejected the idea that no duty whatsoever was owed, they unanimously agreed that, because the trespasser has no right to be on the premises and thus cannot force a neighbour relationship on the occupier, liability will arise only in exceptional circumstances and the duty owed is one of common humanity. The trespasser must take the occupier, rather than the land, as he finds him. This implies a subjective test rather than an objective test, and due weight will be given to such factors as the occupier's wealth and resources.

Other relevant factors are the gravity of the danger and the degree of likelihood of the trespasser's presence. It is unlikely that Percy will be able to recover compensation here, for it does not appear that the defendants are in breach of the duty of common humanity.

Percy's position is now governed by the Occupiers' Liability Act 1984. Section 1(3) provides that an occupier owes a duty of care to a trespasser if:

i) he is aware of the danger or has reasonable grounds to believe that it exists;

ii) he knows or has reasonable grounds to believe that the other is in the vicinity of the danger concerned or that he may come into the vicinity of the danger; and

iii) the risk is one against which in all the circumstances of the case he may reasonably be expected to offer the other some protection.

This clearly goes further than *Herrington* in that an occupier will be liable if he knows or ought to know of the presence of the trespasser and the danger to him.

In the instant case the company should be aware of the danger if the stairway has been damaged for some time, and they should foresee the likelihood of the trespasser being in the area. The danger is one they should guard against, either by repairing the step or placing a warning notice. Therefore, they owe a duty of care to Percy, and that duty is to take such care as is reasonable in all the circumstances of the case to see that the entrant does not suffer injury. It is submitted that the duty is breached, and therefore the company should be liable. However, if they had placed a warning notice, this would have been sufficient to absolve them from liability if Percy was an adult. Thus it can be seen that the position of an adult trespasser has been improved in the new legislation.

QUESTION THREE

Gordon is the owner of a country mansion set in several acres of ground. He is a supporter of the Essex Nationalist Party and allows the party to hold its grand summer fete at the mansion. One field was used as a car park but this year many more visitors than expected arrived and cars were parked along the edge of the country road leading to the mansion. Volunteer party members erected a large marquee with a wooden stage on which teas were served. In the middle of the afternoon the stage collapsed because its wooden supports were not sufficiently strong. The stage collapsed on Herbert, aged six, who had been allowed to play on his own by his mother and had managed to crawl under the stage. Herbert's leg was broken. A huge urn of tea was overturned when the stage collapsed and scalded Isabel, a visitor standing in the tea queue. An ambulance was called but did not arrive for over an hour because it was impeded by the cars parked on the approach road. Herbert has now recovered, but Isabel is still in hospital, as the delay in receiving treatment made her burns much more difficult to heal and she faces several painful operations.

Advise Herbert and Isabel.

University of London LLB Examination
(for External Students) Law of Tort June 1988 Q9

Skeleton Solution

Gordon – occupier – Herbert – visitor – child – s2(3)(a) – role of parent – s2(4)(b) – competence of volunteers – check on work – liability of ENP – occupiers? – contributory negligence.

Isabel – who is liable? – reasonable foresight – burns – delay – cars parked – novus actus – act of a third party – public nuisance – knowledge of Gordon and ENP.

Suggested Solution

Gordon is the occupier of the mansion and of the grounds. He has given permission to the Essex Nationalist Party (ENP) to hold its annual fete at the mansion, thus establishing those attending the fete as visitors and entitled to the protection of the Occupiers' Liability Act 1957. Herbert is the first person who is injured when the stage collapsed. Herbert is a visitor and thus must be treated in accordance with the common duty of care (s2(1)). The collapse of the stage suggests that reasonable care has not been taken to see that Herbert is reasonably safe in using the premises for the purpose for which he is invited to be there.

In addition s2(3)(a) of the 1957 Act states that an occupier must be prepared for children to be less careful than adults and this will apply to Herbert when he crawled under the stage. However in the case of very young children regard must also be had to the responsibility of the parents (*Phipps* v *Rochester Corporation* [1955] 1 QB 450). *Phipps* establishes that the guardian of the child and the occupier must both act reasonably and that each is entitled to expect that the other will act reasonably. Here it could be argued that Herbert's mother has acted unreasonably in leaving Herbert to play on his own and thus Gordon may not be responsible for the injuries suffered by Herbert.

Secondly Gordon may argue that he is not responsible for the erection of the wooden stage and for the inadequacy of its wooden supports. Here Gordon may seek to rely on s2(4)(b) of the 1957 Act but the first difficulty which he will encounter is in establishing that the persons who erected the stage were independent contractors. They are all volunteer members of ENP and, although Gordon is a supporter of ENP, it is submitted that these volunteers are independent of Gordon. For s2(4)(b) to apply the volunteers must be involved in work of construction, maintenance or repair. This is satisfied here because they are involved in a work of construction. Secondly it must have been reasonable for Gordon to entrust the work to independent contractors. It is submitted that this requirement is satisfied here. Thirdly Gordon must have taken reasonable care to ensure that the contractors were competent to do the job. Here Gordon may experience a problem because they are only volunteer helpers and so may not be competent. It will be necessary to examine in some detail the steps which Gordon took, if any, to ensure that the volunteers were competent. Finally Gordon must take reasonable care to check, where possible, that the work has been properly carried out. Much here will depend on whether the inadequacy of the wooden supports was visible to a layman. In *Haseldine* v *Daw* [1941] 2 KB 343 it was held that the occupier could not reasonably be expected to check the maintenance of a lift but in *Woodward* v *Mayor of Hastings* [1945] KB 174 it was held that the defendants should have noticed the ice on a step at the school.

If Gordon can successfully invoke s2(4)(b) as a defence then Herbert will wish to take an action against the ENP. If they are an unincorporated association the members will be jointly and severally liable for torts of their own. Alternatively Herbert could take an action against the individual volunteers responsible for the construction of the stage. If an action is raised against ENP Herbert may wish to consider whether ENP are occupiers so that he can bring his action under the 1957 Act. A person is an occupier if he has sufficient control over the premises (*Wheat* v *E Lacon & Co Ltd* [1966] AC 522). Here it is ENP who are actually holding the summer fete and so they may have sufficient control to establish themselves as occupiers. If so it is likely that they will have breached the common duty of care which they owed to Herbert (the considerations will be similar to those discussed in relation to Gordon, except s2(4)(b) is not relevant). If they are not occupiers then Herbert can allege that they have breached their duty of care to him at common law (ie *Donoghue* v *Stevenson* [1932] AC 562) and the issues will be similar to those considered under the 1957 Act.

Either ENP or Gordon may wish to argue that Herbert was guilty of contributory negligence in crawling under the stage but it is submitted that such a defence is unlikely to succeed. In *Gough* v *Thorne* [1966] 1 WLR 1387 Lord Denning stated that a young child cannot be guilty of contributory negligence. It is questionable whether or not this statement represents the law but, even if it does not, the standard which is required of a young child is so low that it would be virtually impossible for ENP or Gordon to establish that Herbert was guilty of contributory negligence.

This overturning of the tea urn scalds Isabel. Isabel is a visitor and thus is covered by the 1957 Act. Although the 1957 Act only applies to the occupancy duty and not the activity duty, the injury which she has suffered has arisen out of the state of the premises because it was caused initially by the collapse of the stage. If it is held that Gordon is unsuccessful in invoking s2(4)(b) as a defence then it is submitted that he will be liable for the injury to Isabel because it is reasonably foreseeable that if the stage was built on inadequate supports that the tea urn would overturn and burn someone within close proximity (the teas were served on the stage). On the other hand if Gordon is successful in invoking the defence then it will be ENP who are liable for the injuries to Isabel for the reasons given above.

The delay in getting the ambulance to the scene has made it much more difficult for Isabel's burns to heal and she now faces several painful operations. The question is whether the parking of the cars constitutes a novus actus interveniens and thus breaks the chain of causation. The cars parked in the country road may constitute a public nuisance. In *Dymond* v *Pearce* [1972] 1 QB 497 it was held that the defendant had committed a public nuisance in leaving his lorry parked on the highway. Thus there is no requirement that the highway be completely blocked before the tort is committed.

Thus Gordon and ENP may argue that they are not responsible for the blockage of the road and the consequent injury which that has caused to Isabel. It is true that the independent and wrongful act of a third party can have the effect of breaking the chain of causation (*Knightley* v *Johns* [1982] 1 WLR 349). The difficulty for Gordon and ENP is that they must have known that the road was blocked. They have made some effort to accommodate the cars because we are told that they have provided one car park for the visitors to the fete but that this has proved to be insufficient because of the large numbers attending the fete. However in *The Oropesa* [1943] P 32 it was held that the act of the third party must be truly independent of the wrong of the defendant before it can be held to break the chain of causation. In that case it was held that the decision of the captain to take to sea in the lifeboat did not break the chain of causation because his decision was a reasonable one in the circumstances. Lord Wright said that there must be something which is unwarrantable or unreasonable before there can be a break in the chain of causation. Here it could be argued that the parking on the road was not wholly unreasonable if Gordon and ENP had failed to provide sufficient car parking space and that therefore there has been no break in the chain of causation. On the other hand if there were other places to park in the immediate vicinity it may be that the decision to park in the roadway was an unreasonable one which will break the chain of causation. If there has been a break in the chain of causation Isabel may wish to contemplate an action against the car drivers in public nuisance for the damage which she has suffered through the worsening of her condition but such an action would be beset with difficulties because she would be unable to show that any one particular car driver was responsible for her further injuries.

QUESTION FOUR

Swiftbuild plc are building a block of flats on land which they own. The site is unattended at weekends but is protected by a high perimeter fence. James, aged 11, and his brother Kevin, aged 9, discovered that, if one of them forced up the corner of the fence at one part of the site, the other could wriggle underneath. While they were coming out after playing on the site, Kevin let the corner of the fence down too soon and James's leg was very badly gashed. Lena, a district nurse on her rounds, washed and bandaged James's wound. She then took James and Kevin home in her car and left them outside their house. She did not tell them to go to the hospital or give them any advice about treatment. James told his mother that a nurse had helped him. The fence which injured James had been very rusty and his wound became severely infected. By the time this was discovered, it was too late to give effective treatment. James was very ill for several weeks and his leg had to be amputated.

Advise James's father.

University of London LLB Examination
(for External Students) Law of Tort June 1987 Q3

Skeleton Solution

Swiftbuild's statutory liability – occupiers – status of James – trespasser or visitor? – OLA 1984 – s1(3) and s1(4) – duty and standard of care – contributory negligence – Swiftbuild's common law liability – building owners – *Dutton* and *Anns* – Lena's intervention – novus actus interveniens – standard of care required of Lena – liability of parents.

Suggested Solution

James's father will wish to bring an action to recover damages in respect of the damage which James has suffered. James's father may wish firstly to pursue an action against Swiftbuild either under the Occupiers' Liability Act or at common law in negligence.

In relation to the Occupiers' Liability Act it appears to be clear that Swiftbuild are occupiers of the premises. As owners of the premises, Swiftbuild have the requisite degree of control to constitute themselves the occupiers of the premises (see *Wheat* v *E Lacon & Co Ltd* [1966] AC 552). The next issue is whether James was a visitor or a trespasser. It seems clear that James did not have the express permission of Swiftbuild to be on their land and so the only way in which he could be a visitor is to show that he had the implied permission of Swiftbuild to be on their land. However since the decision of the House of Lords in *Edwards* v *Railway Executive* [1952] AC 737 it has been much harder to show that a child has been given implied permission to enter upon the land because repeated trespass was held to be insufficient of itself to create a licence and that there has to be evidence of conduct on the part of the landowner which was such that he could not be heard to say that he did not give any permission. As no facts are given which suggest that Swiftbuild have given their implied permission to the presence of James, we must assume that he is a trespasser and is thus governed by the Occupiers' Liability Act 1984 (OLA).

Section 1(3) of the Act lays down three conditions which must be satisfied before it can be held that an occupier owes a duty of care to a trespasser. The first is that Swiftbuild must have been aware of the danger or had reasonable grounds to believe that it existed. They were aware of the existence of the fence and it would be a question of fact whether they were aware or had reasonable grounds to believe that it could have been lifted up by little boys. There is no suggestion that the fence was particularly loose because the boys had to 'force' it up. On the other hand it could be argued that the fact that the fence was forced up by little boys shows that the fence could never have been particularly secure. Secondly Swiftbuild must have known or have had reasonable grounds for believing that a child would be in the vicinity of the fence or their land. Again it would depend on the facts whether or not children played with sufficient regularity to enable Swiftbuild to know of their likely presence or whether the land would constitute an allurement to children. Thirdly it must be shown that the risk is one against which Swiftbuild could on the facts of the case reasonably be expected to have offered James some protection. This would depend upon such factors as the practicality of taking precautions against such an entry on to their land and the risk of injury as a result of entering the premises in this way.

Once s1(3) is overcome it must be shown under s1(4) that Swiftbuild failed to take such care as was reasonable to see that James did not suffer injury on the premises because of the danger. This is the familiar objective standard in the tort of negligence. What constitutes reasonable care will depend on the facts of the case and here the court will have regard to the age of James, the nature of the premises and the cost of taking precautions.

Swiftbuild may be able to argue that they have discharged their duty to James under s1(5) of the Act by taking reasonable steps to discourage James from incurring the risk by putting up the fence to keep him and other children out. The difficulty for Swiftbuild is that the method which they have adopted for keeping James out is defective because the children can lift the fence up and so Swiftbuild may not be able to show that they have taken reasonable steps to discourage James from incurring the risk. Alternatively Swiftbuild may seek to reduce their liability to James on the ground that he was guilty of contributory negligence. However the standard which is expected of James and of Kevin is the standard of the reasonable child of their age and it may be the case that a reasonable 11- or 9-year-old would not understand the risks involved in forcing up the fence and then crawling underneath it. In *Gough* v *Thorne* [1966] 1 WLR 1387 Lord Denning did not expect a high standard of behaviour from a 13 1/2-year-old plaintiff and it is submitted that a similar approach here would result in the conclusion that James was not guilty of contributory negligence, although in *Morales* v *Eccleston* [1991] RTR 151 an 11-year-old boy was held to be contributorily negligent to an extent of 75 per cent.

Alternatively James's father may wish to frame his cause of action at common law. Swiftbuild owe James a duty of care at common law and that they may also have breached that duty, for the reasons given above when discussing James's action under the OLA 1984.

Swiftbuild may also be liable for the subsequent injuries suffered by James and the eventual amputation of his leg. This depends on whether or not there has been a novus actus interveniens. Lena has washed and bandaged James's wound but has failed to advise him about securing any further treatment. The act of a third party can have the effect of breaking the chain of causation. If Lena was not negligent it is unlikely that the chain of causation was broken because, as was demonstrated in *The Oropesa* [1943] P 32, a reasonable decision which is taken by the third party will not break the chain of causation. However if Lena has been negligent then it is much easier to show that the chain of causation was broken (*Knightley* v *Johns* [1982] 1 WLR 349). It is not necessarily the case, however, that a negligent act by a third party breaks the chain of causation, as can be seen from *Rouse* v *Squires* [1973] QB 889 where it was held that the second road accident was a natural and probable consequence of the pile up created by the first accident and that therefore there was no break in the chain of causation. It is submitted that the present case is distinguishable from *Rouse* on the ground that the negligence of Lena was not a probable consequence of the negligence of Swiftbuild and that, if Lena was indeed negligent, then there was a break in the chain of causation.

The crucial question then becomes whether or not Lena was negligent. It might be argued that Lena owed no duty of care to James because she was under no obligation to go to his rescue but having attempted to alleviate his position, she cannot now turn round and say that she did not owe James a duty of care. The standard required of her is the standard of the reasonably competent district nurse (*Bolam* v *Friern Hospital Management Committee* [1957] 1 WLR 582 and *Wilsher* v *Essex Area Health Authority* [1988] AC 1074; [1987] 2 WLR 425). It seems clear that she has discharged that duty in bandaging the wound, but the difficulty arises as to whether she has been negligent in failing to advise James or his parents to seek additional medical help. In *Sidaway* v *Board of Governors of the Bethlem Royal Hospital* [1985] AC 871 as considered by the Court of Appeal in *Gold* v *Haringey Area Health Authority* [1988] QB 481; [1987] 2 All ER 888, it was held that the *Bolam* test was to be applied to advice as well as diagnosis and treatment and so the question to be asked is whether or not Lena acted in accordance with a view held by a responsible body of district nurses. If she did not then she was negligent and the chain of causation as regards the negligence of Swiftbuild has been broken.

Assuming that Lena was indeed negligent Swiftbuild would be liable for the gash to the leg and Lena would be liable for the damage done to the already damaged leg, on the ground that a tortfeasor takes his victim as he finds him. There may, however, be an argument as to whether Lena's employers are liable for her negligence because she may not have been acting within the course of her employment in treating James. James was not one of her patients and so it could be argued that in attempting to help James and in driving him to his home she had gone outside her course of employment. However it is submitted that, relying upon cases such as *Rose* v *Plenty* [1976] 1 WLR 141, a court would not take such a restrictive approach to identifying the course of employment and would hold that Lena's acts were sufficiently incidental to her employment as to render her employers liable.

Lena or her employers may argue that the failure of James's parents to take James to hospital at an earlier stage was a break in the chain of causation so that they were not necessarily liable for the amputation.

Once again this raises the question of whether or not the parents were negligent in failing to take James to hospital at an earlier date and whether taking him to hospital at such an earlier date would have saved the need to amputate his leg. We are not given sufficient facts to be able to tell whether or not the parents were negligent, but it seems likely that they should have made some inquiry about the state of their son's leg. If they have been negligent then once again the chain of causation may have been broken and James would have to look to his parents for the remainder of his damages.

QUESTION FIVE

Peggy works part-time at the old people's home run by the Satanic District Council. She is on duty for four hours each day preparing and serving lunch for residents. One Monday she obtains permission from Lucy, the matron, to bring her six-year-old son, Tom, who is very deaf, to work with her on Tuesday as his teachers are to be on strike, and she cannot find anyone with whom he can stay at short notice. Lucy agrees, provided that Tom stays in her office, where she lays out toys and books for him. Tom eventually becomes bored and wanders outside into an area where workmen employed by Jerrybuilders plc are constructing an extension to the home for the Council. The area is not fenced off, but a workman tells Tom not to come near as it is dangerous. Tom does not hear him and falls through some loose planks, breaking his leg. Peggy hears his shouts and in her agitation overturns an urn of tea, scalding herself severely.

Has Peggy or Tom a cause of action in tort?

University of London LLB Examination
(for External Students) Law of Tort June 1986 Q2

Skeleton Solution

Peggy – has no cause of action in tort on the facts as she was not a foreseeable plaintiff in incident leading to Tom's injury. See *Bourhill* v *Young* (below). Tom – possible cause of action against Council and Lucy, for whom Council probably vicariously liable, under OLA 1957 as they have not discharged duty under s2(2) and especially 2(3)(a) in ensuring he was reasonably safe as a visitor. Also possible cause of action against Council if he was a non-visitor of Council under OLA 1984, to the building site but unlikely to be a cause of action against Jerrybuilders as the conditions for application of duty under s1(4) of 1984 Act as laid down in s1(3) are probably not satisfied.

Suggested Solution

It is doubtful if Peggy has any causes of action in tort which are worth pursuing because of the events related in the question. As for Tom there is a possibility that he might recover damages for his injuries under the Occupiers' Liability Act 1957 or the Occupiers' Liability Act 1984 or in negligence.

Considering Peggy's position first, she spilled some hot tea on herself which resulted in severe scalding when she heard Tom's shouts. Peggy has no prospect of a cause of action against either Jerrybuilders or Satanic District Council who run the home on the ground that her injury arose because of the incident involving Tom, see for example *Flynn* v *Vange Scaffolding* (1987) The Times 26 March. If either Jerrybuilders or the Council were negligent in causing injury to Tom because of the state of the building works, this in itself would not enable Peggy to recover. A defendant is only liable in negligence to those who are foreseeable plaintiffs; ie those who are within the area of foreseeable danger. In *Bourhill* v *Young* [1943] AC 92 the plaintiff failed to recover for nervous shock she suffered after going to see the aftermath of a road accident. At the time of the accident she had been a passenger in a tram and not within the area of danger. Her claim failed as the negligent driver who caused the accident only owed a duty of care to those who might be injured by his negligence, ie other road users, and in the circumstances of the case, this did not include the plaintiff. Peggy is in a similar position, she was outside the area of foreseeable danger. It may however be the case that Peggy could sue the Council in negligence if the tea urn or the circumstances in which she was employed to use it were such as to be unsafe. There are no indications that this was so. Any claim on this basis would be based on negligence generally or on a breach of the non-delegable duties of an employer under *Wilsons & Clyde Coal Co* v *English* [1938] AC 57 in that the Council failed to provide adequate plant or equipment, ie a suitable tea urn, or a safe system of work. Even if Peggy were to find evidence to establish a cause of action in this way she could find that any award of damages would be substantially reduced because of contributory negligence. The facts given certainly give rise to a strong inference of contributory negligence.

Tom's prospects in bringing an action for his injuries are rather better than those of Peggy. He might consider an action under both the Occupiers' Liability Acts of 1957 and 1984 and in negligence. The claims under the Occupiers' Liability Acts of 1957 and 1984 would arise because his injury arose because of a defect in the state of the premises or a danger in them, ie his falling through loose planks. The 1957 Act sets out the duty of care owed by 'occupiers' to 'visitors' to their premises whilst the 1984 Act sets out the duty of care owed by 'occupiers' to 'non-visitors' to their premises. In dealing with the claims under the Occupiers' Liability Acts it is necessary to determine who is the 'occupier' or 'occupiers' for present purposes, whether Tom was a 'visitor' or a 'non-visitor', and in one or the other or either case whether the appropriate duty of care owed to him by the occupier was breached.

The Council is undoubtedly the occupier of the old people's home since it runs it. In *Wheat* v *Lacon* [1966] AC 552 the House of Lords considered that an 'occupier' was one who exercised 'control' over the premises such as the right to admit or exclude persons therefrom or indicate the terms and conditions upon which they entered. There can be two or more occupiers of premises as *Wheat* v *Lacon* indicates so that Lucy may also be treated as an 'occupier' since it was she who could decide who entered the premises. However, as she is probably a Council employee, it would be better to sue the Council either as occupier or as vicariously liable for her actions. See *Rose* v *Plenty* [1976] 1 WLR 141. It may also be that Jerrybuilders are 'occupiers' of the area where the building work was going on because they had a sufficient degree of control over that area. Decisions such as *AMF International Ltd* v *Magnet Bowling Ltd* [1968] 1 WLR 1028 and *Fisher* v *CHT Ltd (No 2)* [1966] 2 QB 475 clearly indicate that a builder may be an 'occupier' of a building site. There may also be joint occupation of the building site involving Jerrybuilders and the Council. Whether Tom should claim under the 1957 or 1984 Act is irrelevant insofar as the meaning of the term 'occupier' is concerned. See s1 OLA 1984.

A difficult issue arises in determining whether Tom was a 'visitor' or a 'non-visitor' to the premises. He was clearly a visitor to Lucy's office but his injury happened at the building site where it appears he did not have permission to go. If Tom were an adult the answer here would be easy, he would clearly be a non-visitor when injured and outside the terms of the 1957 Act. This is because a person who is given permission to enter a particular part of a building does not have permission to go to any other part. As Scrutton LJ said in *The Calgarth* [1927] P 93 'when you invite a person into your house to use the stairs, you do not invite him to slide down the banisters'. However, it may be that the dicta in *The Calgarth* need modification when applied to a child, particularly one of Tom's age, since it is unreasonable to expect them to observe the boundaries of permission. It may be possible to treat Tom as a 'visitor' on the basis that he was lawfully on the premises although confined to Lucy's office and that as a visitor to this part of the premises the occupier, whether the Council or Lucy, failed to satisfy the common duty of care under s2(2) in failing to take account of the fact that children will be less careful than adults, as s2(3)(a) requires. If Tom was merely left in the room with the door closed then it would be foreseeable that at six years of age he could open it and wander out, especially if left there for some time on his own. It will therefore be necessary to determine if the door was properly secured or if a responsible person was asked to keep an eye on Tom because of the danger of the building works. From the point of view of Jerrybuilders, it is probable that Tom would be treated as a non-visitor when he entered the building site and suffered injury. They had not invited him to be there and I doubt if the Court would be prepared to infer that he was 'their' visitor on the basis of an implied licence because they were carrying on a dangerous activity which was attractive to children. Such implied licences were inferred in old cases such as, for example, *Glasgow Corporation* v *Taylor* [1922] 1 AC 44, to avoid children been treated as mere trespassers at a time when the law gave very little protection to trespassers. This is no longer the case; since the decision of the House of Lords in *British Railways Board* v *Herrington* [1972] AC 877 the duty owed to trespassers is more substantial. See now the Occupiers' Liability Act 1984. The more recent cases on child trespassers show that the courts will also take into account the measures prudent parents would take for the safety of their children and an occupier is entitled to assume that they would take such prudent measures: see *Phipps* v *Rochester Corporation* [1955] 1 QB 450. I therefore conclude that Tom was a 'visitor' from the point of view of the Council and Lucy and a 'non-visitor' from the point of view of Jerrybuilders.

The next issue is to determine whether the duty of care owed by the Council and Lucy, and Jerrybuilders, has been breached or not. As a 'visitor' Tom was owed the common duty of care under s2(2) of the 1957 Act, ie to take such care as in all the circumstances of the case is reasonable to see that the visitor will be reasonably safe in using the premises for the purposes for which he is there. This duty was not discharged by the Council or Lucy, if, as stated above, they failed to take account of s2(3)(a) of the 1957 Act having regard to the fact that there were building works going on and also a likely to be a number of things in the home which could be injurious to a wandering six year old boy. As a 'non-visitor' to the building site, Jerrybuilders – and possibly the Council also, owed Tom the duty of care in s1(4) of the 1984 Act, ie to take such care as is reasonable in all the circumstances of the case to see that the non-visitor does not suffer injury on the premises by reason of the danger. However, the duty laid down in s1(4) only arises if the test in s1(3) of the Act is satisfied. Under s1(3)(a) it must be shown that the occupier was aware of the danger or had reasonable grounds to believe it existed. This requirement would clearly be satisfied. Under s1(3)(b) the occupier must know or have reasonable grounds to believe that the non-visitor is in the vicinity of the danger or that he might come within the vicinity thereof. I doubt if this condition is satisfied in the case of Jerrybuilders, who do not appear to have been warned of Tom's presence, and a child of his age is the last thing they might expect to find at an old people's home. But, if the Council and Lucy were sued this condition would be satisfied as Lucy knew that Tom might come into the vicinity of the danger. Finally, under s1(3)(c) the risk must be one against which, in all the circumstances, the occupier could reasonably be expected to offer the non-visitor some protection. This is a question of fact. All the requirements in s1(3) must be fulfilled before the duty of care under s(1)(4) arises. This is not so in the case of Jerrybuilders but may be so in the case of the Council in that Lucy may not have taken sufficient steps to offer Tom protection against the building work. Thus, Tom may have a cause of action against the Council and Lucy under either of the Occupiers' Liability Acts and also for negligence on similar grounds.

12 PRIVATE AND PUBLIC NUISANCE

12.1 Introduction

Nuisance, especially private nuisance, can be a complex and confusing topic. This confusion arises because there are few hard and fast rules as to what is a nuisance; rather there are a number of guidelines or factors which the courts may or may not decide are relevant in determining whether an activity amounts to a nuisance. (When we refer to nuisance we mean private nuisance – public nuisance will always be referred to by its full name.)

12.2 Key points

a) *Private nuisance*

  i) Definition

    Nuisance is an unreasonable interference with a person's use or enjoyment of land, or of some right over, or in connection with it.

  ii) Plaintiffs

    As nuisance is concerned with a person's use or enjoyment of land, only persons with an interest in land can sue: *Malone* v *Laskey* [1907] 2 KB 141. Thus an owner or tenant can sue, but not members of the owner's family or guests, although the necessity for this interest was recently doubted by the Court of Appeal in *Khorasandjian* v *Bush* [1993] 3 WLR 476.

  iii) Type of harm covered

    It is not possible to classify each and every possible activity that may be actionable in nuisance, but three main groups may be identified:

    • Encroachment, ie physical objects actually interfere with the plaintiff's land: eg tree roots, *Davey* v *Harrow Corporation* [1958] 1 QB 60

    landslides onto land, *Leakey* v *National Trust* [1980] QB 485

    • Physical damage to land: eg overflow of water, *Sedleigh-Denfield* v *O'Callaghan* [1940] AC 880

    vibrations, *Hoare* v *McAlpine* [1923] 1 Ch 167

- Interference with enjoyment of property: eg noise, *Tetley* v *Chitty* [1986] 1 All ER 663

  smell, *Adams* v *Ursell* [1913] 1 Ch 269

  sex shop in residential area, *Laws* v *Florinplace* [1981] 1 All ER 659

iv) Unreasonable interference: factors

Not all interferences give rise to liability; there must be give and take between neighbours and the interference must be substantial and not fanciful: *Walter* v *Selfe* (1851) 20 LJ Ch 433. Some factors that the courts taken into account include:

- Duration of the interference

  The shorter the duration of the interference the less likely it is to be found unreasonable: *Harrison* v *Southwark & Vauxhall Water Co* [1891] 2 Ch 409.

  In *Bolton* v *Stone* [1951] AC 850 it was said that an isolated happening could not constitute a nuisance – what is required is a wrongful state of affairs, even if only temporary: see *Midwood* v *Mayor of Manchester* [1905] 2 KB 597.

- Sensitivity of the plaintiff

  No account is taken of abnormal sensitivity of persons or property: *Robinson* v *Kilvert* (1884) 41 Ch D 88; *Heath* v *Mayor of Brighton* (1908) 98 LT 718. So if the only reason for the damage is such an abnormal sensitivity the plaintiff will be without a remedy.

- Character of the neighbourhood

  This is a relevant factor where interference is with health and comfort: *Bamford* v *Turnley* (1860) 3 B & S 62, but not where physical damage to property has been caused: *St Helens Smelting Co* v *Tipping* (1865) 11 HL 642. Note the dictum in *Sturges* v *Bridgman* (1879) 11 Ch D 852 'What would be a nuisance in Belgrave Square would not necessarily be so in Bermondsey.' Note also that if planning consent has been given for a development, the character of the neighbourhood must be decided by reference to that development and not as it was previously: *Gillingham Borough Council* v *Medway (Chatham) Dock Co* [1992] 3 WLR 449. However, see also *Wheeler* v *Saunders* (1995) The Times 3 January.

- Utility of the defendant's conduct

  This may be particularly relevant as regards certain activities, eg construction works. However, it is only a factor and may be overriden by other factors in the case: *Bellew* v *Cement Co* [1948] Ir R 61; *Adams* v *Ursell* [1913] 1 Ch 269.

- Malice

  Malice is not a necessary ingredient of nuisance, but its presence may make an otherwise non-actionable act actionable: *Hollywood Silver Fox Farm* v *Emmett* [1936] 2 KB 468.

- Fault by the defendant

  Negligence is not an essential ingredient of nuisance, although it may be present, and it is no defence to nuisance to show that the defendant took all reasonable, or even all possible, care.

  Note that the defendant's carelessness in allowing an annoyance to become excessive may make him liable in nuisance: *Andreae* v *Selfridge* [1938] Ch 1.

v) Defendants

- creator of nuisance

  The creator of the nuisance by misfeasance rather than non-feasance may be sued even if he no longer occupies the land from which the nuisance emanates: *Southport Corporation* v *Esso Petroleum* [1956] AC 218; [1954] QB 182; [1953] 3 WLR 773.

- occupier of the land

  The occupier is liable if he creates the nuisance: he is also liable if an independent contractor creates the nuisance following the occupier's instructions and such nuisance was foreseeable.

  In *Sedleigh-Denfield* v *O'Callaghan* (above) it was held that an occupier would be liable for a nuisance created by a trespasser where he continued or adopted the nuisance. The occupier is also liable for a nuisance arising out of the natural condition of his land if he knows of the risk and fails to take appropriate action: *Goldman* v *Hargrave* [1967] 1 AC 645; *Leakey* v *National Trust* (above).

vi) Landlords

Generally a landlord who has leased premises is not liable for any nuisance subsequently arising therefrom, unless:

- the nuisance existed prior to the granting of the lease and the landlord knew this
- the landlord granted the lease for a purpose which constitutes a nuisance: *Tetley* v *Chitty* (above)
- the landlord has reserved the right to enter and repair. Here the landlord is liable whether or not he knows of the defect that gives rise to the nuisance: *Wringe* v *Cohen* [1940] 1 KB 229.

vii) Defences

- prescription

  Continuing a nuisance for 20 years will legalise it by prescription. Time does not begin to run until the plaintiff is aware that the nuisance exists: *Sturges* v *Bridgman* (above).

- statutory authority

  If statute permits, either expressly or by implication, interference with the plaintiff's rights, no action will lie. See *Allen* v *Gulf Oil Refining* [1981] AC

1001 as regards implied authorisation. This defence will only operate where the interference is an inevitable result of the authorised act: *Corporation of Manchester* v *Farnworth* [1930] AC 171.

- other defences

  Volenti, contributory negligence, act of God or a stranger and ignorance, where the nuisance is caused 'by a secret and unobservable operation of nature': *Noble* v *Harrison* [1926] 2 KB 332.

viii) Invalid defences

There are a number of defences to nuisance that are not valid:

- that the plaintiff came to the nuisance

  The ineffectiveness of this defence is shown by *Sturges* v *Bridgman* (above). Note the anomalous dicta in the Court of Appeal in *Miller* v *Jackson* [1977] QB 966 which have not been followed in later cases.

- usefulness of the defendant's activity

  eg *Adams* v *Ursell* (above); *Bellew* v *Cement Co* (above).

- defendant one of many

  It is no defence that the nuisance was caused by a number of persons acting together and the defendant's actions, by themselves, would not have amounted to a nuisance: *Lambton* v *Mellish* [1894] 3 Ch 163.

ix) Remedies

- injunction
  - Discretionary remedy that will only be granted where damages are not an adequate remedy
  - Note private interests prevailed over public interests in *Pride of Derby* v *British Celanese* [1953] Ch 149 and in *Kennaway* v *Thompson* [1981] QB 88, and that *Miller* v *Jackson* (above) is anomalous in giving priority to public interests.

- abatement

  Allowed subject to three conditions:

  - notice to defendant

  - no unnecessary damage

  - least cost to defendant

  see *Burton* v *Winters* [1993] 1 WLR 1077

- damages
  - usually sought for past nuisance or where property damage has occurred
  - whether damages can be recovered for personal injuries is an undecided point: *Malone* v *Laskey* (above) suggests yes; *Cunard* v *Antifyre* [1933] 1 KB 551 suggests no. However, the tenor of the recent House of Lords' decision in *Cambridge Water Co* v *Eastern Counties Leather plc* [1994] 2 WLR 53 strongly suggests, albeit obiter, that no recovery is possible.

- it is also uncertain whether pure economic loss is recoverable, although *British Celanese* v *Hunt* [1969] 1 WLR 959 suggests that it is.

- the test for remoteness of damage is reasonable foreseeability: *The Wagon Mound (No 2)* [1967] AC 617.

- the court may award damages in lieu of an injunction: s50 Supreme Court Act 1981. This power is sparingly used according to the principles in *Shelfer* v *City of London Electric Lighting Co* [1895] 1 Ch 287, ie only if:

  the injury is small;

  capable of being estimated in money;

  damage can be compensated by a small money payment; and

  it would be oppressive to the defendant to grant the injunction.

b) *Public nuisance*

Public nuisance is a crime as well as a tort. Similar to private nuisance except in public nuisance it is well established that there is no need to have an interest in the land affected and prescription is not a defence. However, the plaintiff must prove:

i)   the persons affected by the nuisance are the public or a section of the public: *Attorney-General* v *PYA Quarries* [1957] 2 QB 169

ii) he has suffered damage in excess of annoyance suffered by public at large: *Rose* v *Miles* (1815) 4 M & S 101

iii) special rules cover public nuisance and the highway:

- unreasonable obstruction of the highway constitutes a public nuisance: *Dymond* v *Pearce* [1972] 1 QB 497, even if the obstruction is temporary: *Barber* v *Penley* [1893] 2 Ch 447

- a danger on the highway, eg a pile of rubble, is a public nuisance: *Clark* v *Chambers* (1878) 3 QBD 327

- a danger close to the highway is a public nuisance, so an occupier of premises close to the highway must keep his premises in repair: *Tarry* v *Ashton* (1876) 1 QBD 314 whether or not he is aware of the danger: *Wringe* v *Cohen* (above). There is an exception where the damage arose from a secret and unobservable operation of nature – see *British Road Services* v *Slater* [1964] 1 WLR 498

- condition of the highway. Section 41 Highways Act 1980 places a duty on highway authorities to maintain highways and s58 provides the defence that reasonable care was taken.

12.3 Recent cases

Gillingham Borough Council v *Medway (Chatham) Dock Co* [1992] 3 WLR 449

Khorasandjian v *Bush* [1993] 3 WLR 476

Burton v *Winters* [1993] 1 WLR 1077

Wentworth v *Wiltshire County Council* [1993] 2 WLR 175

Wheeler v *Saunders* (1995) The Times 3 January

Hunter v *Canary Wharf* (1994) The Independent 20 December

Cambridge Water Co v *Eastern Counties Leather plc* [1994] 2 WLR 53

12.4 Analysis of questions

Nuisance is a regular topic in the examination – it may be the sole topic of a question or combined with elements of *Rylands* v *Fletcher* or negligence or animals, etc.

12.5 Questions

QUESTION ONE

Anna, Betty, Clara and Daphne occupied adjoining houses in a terrace. Clara had a temporary posting overseas for two years starting in October 1989. She let her house for two years to Edward, whose hobby is carpentry. Edward has spent a great deal of time building furniture and other large wooden objects in the garden at the back of the house. This has annoyed Daphne, a nurse, who is frequently on duty at nights and is unable to sleep during the day when Edward is working. Edward has refused to desist from noisy work when Daphne is trying to sleep. Sawdust has blown over the fence into Betty's garden. Some of this was eaten by a dog belonging to Betty's sister, Emily, who came to stay permanently with Betty in January. The dog was severely ill as a result and eventually died. The sawdust was extremely difficult to pick up and after a heavy rainstorm in April sawdust was carried into the drain in Betty's garden. The drain was blocked and, in the ensuing flood, water flowed into Betty's and Anna's houses. During the storm a piece of coping blew off the roof and damaged Anna's car which was parked in the road. Neighbours had told Edward earlier that they could see that the coping had worked loose.

Advise Daphne, Emily, Betty and Anna.

University of London LLB Examination
(for External Students) Law of Tort June 1990 Q5

Suggested Solution

Edward's activities may constitute a private nuisance. Nuisance may be defined as an unreasonable interference with a person's use or enjoyment of his land. It thus follows that only a person who has an interest in land may bring an action for private nuisance: *Malone* v *Laskey* [1907] 2 KB 141, although the need for this requirement was recently doubted by the Court of Appeal in *Khorasandjian* v *Bush* [1993] 3 WLR 476, and that the interference must be unreasonable.

As regards Daphne, it is well established that noise can constitute a nuisance: *Halsey* v *Esso Petroleum* [1961] 1 WLR 683; *Tetley* v *Chitty* [1986] 1 All ER 663, and while there must be give and take between neighbours, so not all interferences give rise to liability: *Walter* v *Selfe* (1851) 20 LJ Ch 433, an amount of noise which prevents sleep is unreasonable. We are told that Edward spends a great deal of time on his hobby, which is relevant, as a short or temporary disturbance is not likely to be a nuisance: *Harrison* v *Southwark & Vauxhall Water Co* [1891] 2 Ch 409. The character of the neighbourhood will also be a relevant factor in determining whether an interference with health and comfort amounts to a nuisance: *Bamford* v *Turnley* (1860) 3 B & S 62, but even if the terrace lies in a town centre the interference would seem to be unreasonable. Daphne has one problem, however, which is that Edward could claim that she is an abnormally sensitive plaintiff as she is trying to sleep in the day. In *Robinson* v *Kilvert* (1884) 41 Ch D 88 and *Heath* v *Mayor of Brighton* (1908) 98 LT 718 it was held that a person cannot increase his neighbour's liability by putting his land to a special use, and Daphne by sleeping in the day may not be able to bring an action in nuisance.

Turning to Betty, the sawdust blowing into her garden may constitute a nuisance: *Leakey* v *National Trust* [1980] QB 485. The fact that the sawdust was difficult to pick up affords Edward no defence as it is no defence in nuisance to show that the defendant took all reasonable, or even all possible, care. Provided the defendant caused the nuisance he is liable. Thus Edward is liable for the intrusion of the sawdust into Betty's garden. As regards the blocked drain the question arises as to whether or not this damage is too remote to impose liability on Edward. It was held in *The Wagon Mound (No 2)* [1967] AC 617 that in nuisance the test for remoteness of damage was reasonable foreseeability. It would seem reasonably foreseeable that if large quantities of sawdust are left to blow into a neighbour's garden that a drain may become blocked and flooding ensue, and if so Edward would be liable for the flooding of Betty's and Anna's houses.

The traditional legal view regarding Emily is that she can only sue in nuisance if she has some interest in land, eg as a tenant: *Malone* v *Laskey* (above). However, the need for an interest in land has recently been doubted by the Court of Appeal in *Khorasandjian* v *Bush* (above) so that Emily may be able to sue in nuisance for any damage that has actually occured, eg vet's bills and the cost of a replacement dog.

Anna can sue Edward for the flooding to her house as discussed above. Edward may claim that Betty's failure to sweep up the sawdust broke the chain of causation, but as we are told that the sawdust was extremely difficult to pick up this seems unlikely to succeed as Betty's failure to sweep up the sawdust was foreseeable and is just the sort of event Edward should have foreseen and guarded against: *Stansbie* v *Troman* [1948] 2 KB 48. Turning to the damage to Anna's car, Edward as occupier of premises close to the highway is under a duty to keep his premises in repair: *Tarry* v *Ashton* (1876) 1 QBD 314, and in *Wringe* v *Cohen* [1940] 1 KB 229 it was said that this duty arose whether the occupier knew of the danger or not. As Edward was aware of the coping being loose he cannot claim the benefit of the exception to the rule in *Wringe* v *Cohen*, namely that the damage arose from a 'secret and unobservable operation of nature' and hence Edward is liable for the damage to Anna's car.

Clearly all the plaintiffs should be advised to sue Edward as he is the creator of the nuisance. Clara would only be liable if she let the premises for purposes which constitute a nuisance: *Tetley* v *Chitty*, which she has not done.

Edward may also be liable for the escape of the sawdust under the rule in *Rylands* v *Fletcher* (1868) LR 3 HL 330, as all the criteria for the operation of the rule appear to be satisfied. Betty and Anna may wish to plead this as an alternative cause of action in respect of the flooding. It would not apply to the escape of the coping as the coping was not brought onto the land by Edward nor was its presence a non-natural use of the land.

Edward may also be liable in negligence. Edward is under a duty to ensure that his activities do not cause harm to others – see *Caparo Industries* v *Dickman* [1990] 2 WLR 358; [1990] 1 All ER 568 for the most recent formulation of the criteria for imposing a duty of care. He is in breach of this duty by failure to sweep up the sawdust and this breach caused the damage which followed and this damage was reasonably foreseeable as regards the flooding and a similar liability in negligence will arise in respect of the damage to Anna's car. Whether it is reasonably foreseeable that Emily's dog would eat the sawdust and die is debateable.

As regards Daphne, as Edward's actions are deliberate rather than careless any alternative action would lie in trespass to the person rather than negligence, and as there has been no direct interference with her person Daphne has only the questionable action in nuisance against Edward.

Thus the advice to Daphne would be that she has only a slim chance of success in nuisance; Betty has a good case in both nuisance and negligence, and also *Rylands* v *Fletcher*. Emily has some chance of success in nuisance, but a limited chance of success in negligence; Anna can claim for the flooding and the damage to her car in both nuisance and negligence and claim under *Rylands* v *Fletcher* for the flooding.

QUESTION TWO

W owns a farm which he leases to X for fruit-growing. X finds that, in order to prevent birds eating fruit off the trees, he is forced to instal and keep in operation a 'scare-gun' which goes off every hour during daylight hours with a bang as loud as a shotgun. On two or three occasions he has forgotten to switch it off overnight. On his farm down the road, Y breeds mink which are so disconcerted by the bangs that their rate of breeding drops considerably. From Y's farm noxious smuts rain down on X's fruit trees from the chimney of a very large oil-fired central heating system recently installed by Y to keep the mink dens at a constant high temperature. The smuts prevent some of the blossom forming fruit, and cause a scab disease to much of X's fruit. Y, who is a highly-strung man, is made moody and irritable by the scare-gun bangs, and his elderly mother, who lives with him on the farm, is unable to take her normal afternoon sleep with the result that her health suffers. One windy day, a tile from W's farmhouse leased to Y, loosened many years previously by quarry blasting which used to go on in the vicinity, blows off the roof and injures Z who happens to be passing at the time in the adjacent lane.

Advise X, Y and Z on their rights in tort, if any.

University of London LLB Examination
Mid-sessional, 1989

Suggested Solution

The remedies (if any) for the injuries suffered by X and Y depend on the law relating to private nuisance. Private nuisance may be defined as an unreasonable interference with a person's use or enjoyment of land. It has thus been held that only a person who has an interest in land may bring an action in private nuisance: *Malone* v *Laskey* [1907] 2 KB 141, although the need for this interest was recently doubted by the Court of Appeal in *Khorasandjian* v *Bush* [1993] 3 WLR 476. Clearly the interference of which the plaintiff complains must be unreasonable.

a) X's fruit trees are prevented from blossoming and develop a scab disease because of the noxious smuts coming from Y's chimney. This amounts to an unreasonable interference with the enjoyment of land, in which he also has a proprietary interest, being a lessee. He can sue Y in private nuisance.

There is a distinction made between nuisance which produces material injury to property and nuisance causing sensible personal discomfort. In assessing whether the latter constitutes an actionable nuisance one must take into account the nature of the locality. On the other hand, in the case of the injury to the value of the property, these considerations do not apply and neither the locality nor the particular activity being carried on by the defendant can absolve him from liability (see *St Helen's Smelting* v *Tipping* (1865) 11 HL Cas 642).

It is therefore easier to establish a nuisance causing material damage to property than one causing personal discomfort. The damage is tangible, more easily observed and measured. X will want damages and an injunction to prevent further damage.

Y may also be able to bring an action under the rule in *Rylands* v *Fletcher* (1868) LR 3 HL 330 if Y has made a non-natural use of his land by accumulating something likely to do mischief, which escapes and causes damage. However, in view of the narrow interpretation taken by the courts in recent decisions as to what constitutes a 'non-natural user' of the land, it is unlikely that X will succeed here.

In *Read* v *Lyons* [1947] AC 156; [1946] 2 All ER 471 the court held that in an industrial society to use land for a factory making explosives did not amount to a non-natural user in modern times.

b) Y suffers because of the continual bangs from the scare-gun. Y can establish an interest in the land, as it appears that he owns the farm. His mother, however, who is also disturbed by the noise, will not be able to bring an action because she does not have a proprietary interest unless she can rely on *Khorasandjian* (above). This is a nuisance causing sensible personal discomfort, and one must investigate the nature of the locality in order to decide whether this amounts to an actionable nuisance.

As Thesiger LJ commented in *Sturges* v *Bridgman* (1879) 11 Ch D 852 'What would be a nuisance in Belgrave Square would not necessarily be so in Bermondsey.' The following factors are relevant in determining whether the interference is unreasonable:

i) the duration and frequency of the noise. In *Moy* v *Stoop* children crying in a day nursery was held not to constitute a nuisance, whereas in *Leeman* v *Montague* [1936] 2 All ER 1677, 750 cockerels crowing between 2.00–7.00 am were held to be a nuisance. Here the gun is sounded at hourly intervals during the day which, in all the circumstances, may not be unreasonable; but the gun does occasionally go off at night, when X forgets to switch it off, and if this happens frequently Y may be able to obtain an injunction to prevent him using the gun at night;

ii) in determining whether there has been an unreasonable interference with the plaintiff's use and enjoyment of land, the court will not take into account abnormal sensitivity on the part of the plaintiff. On the authority of *Heath* v *Mayor of Brighton* (1908) 98 LT 718 and *Robinson* v *Kilvert* (1884) 41 Ch D 88, it seems that no special regard may be held to the special needs of invalids, or to special occupational needs, for there is no redress for damage due to the exceptionally delicate nature of the operations carried on by an injured party.

Consequently no regard would be had to the fact that Y is highly-strung and moody. If, however, it could be established that a reasonable man would have suffered as a result of this unreasonable interference, the damages or injunction will extend to delicate and sensitive operations and, presumably, people (see *McKinnon Industries* v *Walker* [1951] WN 401).

Y will want an injunction here, for he is more concerned with stopping the noise in future than compensation for earlier disturbance.

c) Z's action is founded in public nuisance. This is an unreasonable interference with the exercise of public rights and is primarily a crime for which the remedy is an action by or in the name of the Attorney-General. It consists of an unlawful act or omission to discharge a legal duty which results in danger to the lives, safety and health or comfort of the public generally or some section thereof.

It differs from private nuisance in that:

i) there is certainly no requirement of a proprietary interest;

ii) a single act may constitute a public nuisance;

iii) a plaintiff in public nuisance can certainly recover for personal injuries: *Castle* v *St Augustine's Links*.

In order to bring a civil action in public nuisance an individual must show that he has suffered a greater degree of harm than the public generally or that he has suffered a particular kind of damage such as personal injury, harm to chattels or injury to pecuniary interests.

The facts here suggest that a highway nuisance has been committed. This was defined by Lord Simonds in *Jacobs* v *LCC* [1950] AC 361; [1950] 1 All ER 737 as 'any wrongful act or omission upon or near a highway, whereby the public are prevented from freely, safely and conveniently passing along the highway'.

In *Wringe* v *Cohen* [1940] 1 KB 229 it was held that the occupier of premises on or adjoining a highway was liable in public nuisance to a passer-by who was injured when a part of the premises collapsed due to want of repair. Liability here is strict unless the danger arises from a secret and unobservable operation of nature.

The facts do not state whether Y's farm is adjacent to the highway. If it is he will be liable.

Z may also have a cause of action in negligence. He is owed a duty of care by Y, the owner of the property, under the neighbour principle. Whether or not there is a breach of the duty will depend upon whether a reasonable owner would have taken such steps so as to avoid any injury befalling Z. If the wind which blew the tile off the roof was such that Y could not reasonably have foreseen such an occurrence there will be no liability. There is not sufficient detail to determine this. The damage suffered is, however, reasonably foreseeable. Therefore, provided Z can satisfy the court on the question of the breach in the standard of care expected of the defendant, he will succeed in his negligence claim.

QUESTION THREE

'No precise or universal formula is possible to determine reasonableness (in the sense used in the law of nuisance). Whether an act constitutes a nuisance cannot be determined merely by an abstract consideration of the act itself, but by reference to all the circumstances of the particular case.' (Winfield and Jolowicz)

Discuss.

University of London LLB Examination
(for External Students) Law of Tort June 1987 Q1

Skeleton Solution

Nuisance – scope and extent of the tort – definition showing the concept of reasonableness – elements of nuisance – public and private nuisance – determination of reasonableness and relevant factors – reasonableness in other torts – locality – duration – abnormal sensitivity – malice – utility of the defendant's conduct – whether tort really as inexact as the question implies – balancing of the factors as against their identification.

Suggested Solution

The tort of nuisance consists of two distinct branches: private nuisance and public nuisance. Private nuisance may be described as the unreasonable interference with a person's use or enjoyment of his land or some right in connection with his land. Public nuisance, on the other hand, may be defined as an unreasonable interference with the use or enjoyment of land affecting a section of the public and which has caused special damage to the plaintiff (see *Attorney-General* v *PYA Quarries* [1957] 2 QB 169). It can be seen from these definitions that reasonableness is central to both branches of the tort of nuisance.

Although reasonableness is central to the tort, it is not possible to provide a universally applicable definition of reasonableness. In this sense it is perfectly correct to say that there is no precise or universal formula which is possible to determine reasonableness. Reasonableness is a concept which is very much dependent on the particular factual situation.

Before considering how the courts decide, in a particular case, whether the interference has been unreasonable, it is necessary to consider whether reasonableness, as used in nuisance, differs from reasonableness as used in torts such as negligence. Some confusion was caused by the judgment of Lord Reid in *The Wagon Mound (No 2)* [1967] 1 AC 617 when he said that, although 'negligence' was not essential to the tort of nuisance, 'fault' was almost always necessary and that fault normally involves 'foreseeability'. Although Lord Reid was talking about the standard of liability in both nuisance and negligence and was suggesting that there is a degree of overlap between the two torts it is submitted that he was not suggesting that the

105

standard of liability in nuisance and negligence is the same. As the quotation indicates there is a difference between reasonableness as used in nuisance and reasonableness as used in other torts. In negligence reasonableness is concerned with the foreseeable harm to which a reasonable man would not expose others, while reasonableness in nuisance is concerned with the character of the harm which has been caused to the plaintiff rather than the harm which the reasonable man could foresee. Reasonableness also differs as between the two torts in the sense that it is not necessarily a defence to a nuisance action to show that the defendant took all reasonable case to ensure that the nuisance did not occur. The company which uses all the latest devices to prevent a noxious smell being emitted from its factory may not be liable in the tort of negligence because it has taken all reasonable care to prevent the smell from being emitted but it may still have committed the tort of nuisance on the ground that it is unreasonably interfering with its neighbours' enjoyment of their land.

Although it is not possible to frame a universally applicable definition of reasonableness, it should not be assumed that there are no principles at stake in this area of law and that the solution to a particular case is left to the subjective whim of the individual judge. The courts will, in practice, balance the following factors in considering whether or not the interference with land use has been unreasonable. Although the exact balance will depend very much on the facts of the case, the knowledge that the courts will have regard to these particular factors helps legal advisers to know the principles which will be applied by the courts in a nuisance case.

The first factor is the locality in which the nuisance is alleged to have been committed. In *Sturges* v *Bridgman* (1878) 11 Ch D 852 Thesiger LJ stated that what would constitute a nuisance in Belgravia Square would not necessarily constitute a nuisance in Bermondsey. Thus the person who bought a house in an industrial area of town would find it difficult to show that the noise created by the factories was unreasonable because the courts would have regard to the fact that this was an industrial area in deciding whether or not the noise made by the factories amounted to a nuisance (although see *Roshmer* v *Polsue and Alfieri Ltd* [1906] 1 Ch 234). However it is vital to note that locality is not a relevant factor where the nuisance had caused damage to the property of the plaintiff (*St Helens Smelting* v *Tipping* (1865) 11 HL Cas 642).

The second factor which must be considered is the duration of the activity which is alleged to constitute the nuisance. For example in *Harrison* v *Southwark & Vauxhall Water Co* [1891] 2 Ch 409 it was held that the actions of the defendants in sinking a shaft in the land adjoining the plaintiff's land did not constitute a nuisance because of the temporary nature of the work. However the longer the activity takes place the more likely it is that it will be held to constitute a nuisance.

The third factor concerns the use which the plaintiff is making of the land. Where the plaintiff is making an abnormally sensitive use of his land, as in *Robinson* v *Kilvert* (1884) 41 Ch D 88 and *Heath* v *Mayor of Brighton* (1908) 98 LT 718, then he cannot thereby put a more onerous burden on his neighbour so as to impose liability for what would, apart from his abnormally sensitive use, not constitute a nuisance. Thus in *Robinson* the plaintiff suffered damage because some sensitive paper which he stored on the floor of the flat was damaged because of the heat rising from the defendant's premises underneath. The heat would not ordinarily have interfered with the use of the flat above and it was held that the defendant had not committed the tort of nuisance.

The fourth factor which is relevant is whether or not the defendant was actuated by malice. A good example here is the case of *Hollywood Silver Fox Farm Ltd* v *Emmett* [1936] 2 KB 468. The defendant deliberately caused guns to be fired on the boundary of his own land so that the plaintiffs' silver foxes would be upset during their breeding periods. It was held that the plaintiffs were entitled to an injunction because the defendant was actuated by malice. This case demonstrates the importance of looking to all the factors of the case because, had the defendant not been actuated by malice, the case would probably have been decided differently on the ground that the plaintiffs were making an abnormally sensitive use of their land.

The final factor which is relevant is the utility of the defendant's conduct; the more useful it is the less likely that it will be held to constitute a nuisance. Again, this is merely a factor and not a hard and fast rule – see *Adams* v *Ursell* [1913] 1 Ch 269; *Bellew* v *Cement Co* [1948] Ir R 61.

It can be seen from this brief survey that, as the quotation indicates, reasonableness in the tort of nuisance very much depends upon the facts of each case and there is no substitute for a full blooded analysis of the facts. One jurist, Dean Prosser, has stated that there is no more 'impenetrable jungle' in the whole of the law than that which surrounds the word nuisance. What he means is that the cases are often so dependent upon the facts of the case that it is hard to see any overriding principle at work. However, it is submitted that, although it is correct to say that reasonableness is context dependent, it would be a mistake to jump to the conclusion that there are no principles at all at stake in the tort of nuisance. The courts do consider a relatively limited range of factors and what depends on the facts of the case is the *balancing* of these factors and not the identification of the relevant factors. There are other rules in the tort of nuisance. So it is not true to say that there are no principles in operation at all in the tort of nuisance.

In conclusion it is submitted that Winfield and Jolowicz are correct in saying that it is not possible to frame a universally applicable definition of reasonableness in nuisance and that reasonableness very much depends on the facts of the case, provided that it is recognised that there are identifiable principles at work and that the development of the law is not left to the subjective whim of the individual judge.

QUESTION FOUR

The Mudborough Council have maintained a children's playground on one particular site for some fifty years. It is used by children from all over Mudborough, mainly by children under five during school terms, but also by older children during the holidays. Three years ago a private developer built a number of houses on land adjoining the playground. The purchasers of two of these houses, whose gardens back on to the playground are now complaining of interference from the playground.

One, James, complains that the noise the children make prevents him sleeping in the afternoon. He has to do so as he works on night shifts. The other, Keith, complains that the older children climb on his garden fence so that he and his family have no privacy in their back garden. He also complains that children often come into his garden to retrieve balls which have come over the fence.

Both James and Keith want to get the playground closed. Advise them of their legal rights.

Written by the editor

Suggested Solution

James and Keith would be advised to bring an action in private nuisance and will seek the remedy of a mandatory injunction against the Council so that the playground may be closed.

The essence of the tort of nuisance is unreasonable interference with another's enjoyment of his land. Private nuisance has been defined as being committed when a person is held responsible for an act indirectly causing physical injury to land or substantially interfering with the use or enjoyment of land or of an interest in land, where in the light of all the surrounding circumstances, this injury or interference is held to be unreasonable. (Harry Street 6th Edn *Law of Torts* 1976). The plaintiff's case will be based on the fact that there has been a substantial and unreasonable interference with their enjoyment of their property (see *Walter v Selfe* (1851) 4 De G & S 315).

'Substantial interference' will exclude any interference which is trivial, and although the loss of one night's sleep has been held not to be trivial (*Andreae v Selfridge* [1938] Ch1), the interference suffered by James and Keith must generally not be an isolated incident and it may, however, be a 'state of affairs, however temporary' (per Oliver J in *Bolton v Stone* [1950] 1 KB 201; [1951] AC 850 (HL)).

James claims that he is unable to sleep not at night but in the afternoons and therefore it may be argued that he is an abnormally sensitive plaintiff. However, those cases concerning abnormal sensitivity suggest that the sensitivity lies in the use to which the house is put, rather than personal sensitivity on the part of the plaintiff himself (*Robinson v Kilvert* (1884) 41 Ch D 88).

Unreasonable interference concerns several factors which will apply to both James's and Keith's cases. As the House of Lords in *Sedleigh-Denfield v O'Callaghan* [1940] AC 880 pointed out: 'A balance has to be maintained between the right of the occupier to do what he likes with his own land and the right of the neighbour not to be interfered with. It is impossible to give any precise or universal formula but it may broadly be said that a useful test is perhaps what is reasonable according to the ordinary usages of mankind living in society'.

The character of the neighbourhood is taken into account in assessing what is reasonable (*Bamford v Turnley* (1860) 3 B & S 62), save in cases involving physical damage (*St Helen's Smelting Co v Tipping* (1865) 13 HL Cas 642). At this point, it must be said that in this case, both plaintiffs have come to the nuisance; the nuisance has not come into existence after they have moved in. The playground has been run for 50 years; the houses were built only three years ago. The court would therefore expect greater tolerance by the plaintiffs since they have chosen to live near the playground and may have had some idea of the problems they might have to face. If, however, the nuisance is sufficiently great, the case may be actionable regardless of the locality (*Halsey* v *Esso Petroleum* [1961] 1 WLR 683; [1961] 2 All ER 145). Applying the test used in *Halsey* by Veale J the standard is that of the ordinary and reasonable man who lives in the vicinity of the playground. It is submitted that noise will be expected during the daytime and in school holidays, so that James's claim may fail under this head, although Keith's claim in relation to children climbing over the fence should not be affected by this consideration.

The Council may attempt to set up the defence of prescription (as in *Miller* v *Jackson* [1977] QB 966; [1977] 3 WLR 20) by claiming that they have a right to commit the alleged private nuisance over a period of at least 20 years with continual use and that the plaintiffs (or their predecessors in title) knew of the nuisance. The defence was raised in *Sturges* v *Bridgman* (1879) 11 Ch D 852 but the court held that the defence must fail since the time ran from when the nuisance became apparent. Applying that decision to the facts of the case, the nuisance has only existed for a maximum of three years, so that this defence must fail.

James's claim is arguably doubtful but Keith should have an arguable case. In deciding whether to grant the injunction, the court will have regard to the public interest as opposed to the infringement of the individual's rights. In *Miller* v *Jackson* (supra), the public interest suggested that an injunction should be refused where to hold otherwise would have meant that the playing of cricket would be prevented although this approach was not followed in *Kennaway* v *Thompson* [1981] QB 88; [1980] 3 WLR 361.

Keith may have an alternative action in trespass which involves the 'intentional or negligent entering on or remaining on, or directly causing any physical matter to come into contact with land in the possession of another' (Street). The children have entered Keith's garden clearly without his permission or consent, but the problem here is whom to sue. It would be extremely difficult to bring in the Council as defendants and it may not be worthwhile to bring such an action. Although trespass is actionable per se, many trivial trespassers where no damage is caused to the land are ignored, and this may well be one of those cases.

See also chapter 13 questions 1 to 5 to see how nuisance may come up in a question which is mainly concerned with *Rylands* v *Fletcher*, and see chapter 14 questions 1 and 3 for nuisance cropping up in questions mostly concerning animals.

13 THE RULE IN RYLANDS v FLETCHER AND FIRE

13.1 Introduction

This rule imposes strict, but not absolute, liability on a defendant and was formulated thus by Blackburn J:

'a person who for his own purposes brings on to his lands and collects and keeps there anything likely to do mischief if it escapes, must keep it in at his peril, and, if he does not do so, he is prima facie answerable for all the damage which is the natural consequence of its escape.' (1866) 1 LR 1 Ex 265. This statement was approved by the House of Lords with the addition that the defendant had made a 'non-natural' use of his land (1868) LR 3 HL 330.

13.2 Key points: *Rylands* v *Fletcher*

a) *For his own purposes*

If the thing is brought onto the land for the purpose of someone else the rule does not apply: *Rainham Chemical Works* v *Belvedere Fish Guano Co* [1921] 2 AC 465.

b) *Brings on to his lands*

i)   the rule applies to things brought on to the land, not to things which are naturally on the land: eg

thistles   *Giles* v *Walker* (1890) 24 QBD 656

rainwater *Smith* v *Kenrick* (1849) 7 CB 515

ii) it is an undecided point as to whether the defendant must be in occupation of the land from which the thing escaped, or whether control of the land is sufficient.

c) *Dangerous things*

The rule applies to 'anything likely to do mischief if it escapes'. However, almost anything can do mischief if it escapes, so nowadays there is no requirement that the thing which escapes is dangerous (see *Read* v *Lyons* [1947] AC 156) but the more dangerous a thing is the more likely it will be a non-natural use of land.

d) *Escape*

The thing must escape: *Read* v *Lyons* (above).

e) *Non-natural user*

   i) In *Rylands* v *Fletcher* (above) 'natural' meant something naturally on the land or there by nature.

   ii) Later cases eg *Rickards* v *Lothian* [1913] AC 263 have used 'natural' to mean ordinary or usual, and in *Rickards* it was said that to bring *Rylands* into effect there had to be a special use of land bringing increased danger to others and not ordinary use of land or such use as is proper for the general benefit of the community. However, in *Cambridge Water Co* v *Eastern Counties Leather plc* [1994] 2 WLR 53 this criterion was criticised and the meaning 'something that was there by nature' was preferred.

   iii) In *Mason* v *Levy Auto Parts* [1967] 2 QB 530 special use and increased danger were equated with negligence.

   iv) In *British Celanese* v *Hunt* [1969] 1 WLR 959 it was held that the manufacturing of electrical components on an industrial estate was not a non-natural user of land as that was the very purpose for which the land was designed. However, in *Cambridge Water* (above) the storage of substantial quantities of chemicals on industrial premises was said (obiter) to be a 'classic case of non-natural use'. It thus seems that the original meaning of this phrase is to be preferred.

f) *Foreseeability of damage*

In *Cambridge Water* (above), after an extensive survey of the rule it was held that foreseeability of damage was an essential ingredient of *Rylands*.

g) *Protected interests*

   i) A landowner who suffers property damage on his land can claim: *Rylands* v *Fletcher* (above).

   ii) A landowner who suffers property damage while his property is not on his land (eg car parked on a public road) has been allowed to recover: *Halsey* v *Esso Petroleum* [1961] 1 WLR 683.

   iii) Landowners' personal injuries

Recovery was allowed in *Hale* v *Jennings* [1938] 1 All ER 579, but doubted in *Read* v *Lyons* (above). Again in *Cambridge Water* (above) it was doubted that the rule applies to personal injuries.

   iv) Non-landowners' personal injuries

Held that *Rylands* applied to this category in *Halsey* v *Esso Petroleum* (above) and *Perry* v *Kendrick's Transport* [1956] 1 WLR 85, although *Read* is against recovery. However, all these cases must be reviewed in the light of *Cambridge Water* (above).

v) Economic loss

An undecided point, although *Weller* v *Foot & Mouth Disease Research Institute* [1966] 1 QB 569 is against.

h) *Defences*

i) Act of God

See the definition in *Tennant* v *Earl of Glasgow* (1864) 2 M (HL) 22, and note the only case where it has been successfully pleaded, namely *Nichols* v *Marsland* (1876) 2 Ex D 1.

ii) Fault of the plaintiff

See, for example, *Ponting* v *Noakes* [1894] 2 QB 281.

iii) Plaintiff's consent

Express or implied consent by the plaintiff to the thing being brought onto the defendant's land is a defence: *Kiddle* v *City Business Premises* [1942] 2 All ER 216.

iv) Common benefit

Where the thing is maintained for the common benefit of both plaintiff and defendant, the defendant is not liable in the absence of negligence: *Kiddle* v *City Business Premises* (above).

v) Act of third party

If an independent act of a third party causes the damage, and this act is not foreseeable, the defendant is not liable: *Rickards* v *Lothian* (above); *Perry* v *Kendrick's Transport* (above).

vi) Statutory authority

If the thing is maintained under statutory authority, no liability will arise in the absence of negligence: *Green* v *Chelsea Waterworks* (1894) 70 LT 547.

13.3 Key points: fire

a) *There are three situations at common law in which liability for fires may arise:*

i) In nuisance where the fire interferes with the use or enjoyment of land: *Goldman* v *Hargrave* [1967] 1 AC 645.

ii) In negligence where the defendant failed to take reasonable care: *Musgrove* v *Pandelis* [1919] 2 KB 43; *Ogwo* v *Taylor* [1987] 2 WLR 988.

iii) In an action for fire. In *Mason* v *Levy Auto Parts* (above) it was held that the plaintiff must show:

• the defendant brought on to his land things likely to catch fire and kept them there in such conditions that if they did ignite the fire would be likely to spread to the plaintiff's land

• this was done in the course of some non-natural use

• the things ignited and the fire spread

Note the similarity to *Rylands*.

b) *Common law defences*

Act of a stranger

Act of God

Default of plaintiff

Consent of the plaintiff

Statutory authority

Refer back to the relevant discussions under *Rylands*.

c) *Statutory position*

i) Section 86 Fire Prevention (Metropolis) Act 1774 provides a defendant is not liable for fires which begin accidentally. Accidentally means caused by 'mere chance' or 'incapable of being traced to any cause' – it does not cover negligence: *Filliter* v *Phippard* (1847) 11 QB 347. A fire which is negligently allowed to spread, having been started accidentally, is treated as a separate fire not within the Act: *Musgrove* v *Pandelis* (above); *Goldman* v *Hargrave* (above); *Sochaki* v *Sas* [1947] 1 All ER 344.

ii) Railway statutes

The Railway Fires Acts 1905 and 1923 create and limit liability for fire damage caused by sparks from engines.

13.4 Recent case

Cambridge Water Co v *Eastern Counties Leather Plc* [1994] 2 WLR 53

13.5 Analysis of questions

The rule in *Rylands* v *Fletcher* is a common examination question, sometimes combined with elements of nuisance, animals or negligence.

13.6 Questions

QUESTION ONE

The Veryhazardous Chemical Co owns and operates a large factory close to the fishing port of Codvilla. As part of its normal process of operation it discharges small quantities of highly toxic chemical waste into the sea. It is accepted that such discharges do not cause an unacceptably high level of environmental damage. Last June the safety system at the factory suddenly broke down for some unexplained reason, and this led to a massive discharge of toxic waste into the sea. Officials of the Redpeace Environmental Group were seriously injured when their boat capsized as they were monitoring the discharge. Local fishermen complain that they are unable to fish the area and neighbouring fishmongers also suffer a loss of business.

Advise the Veryhazardous Chemical Co.

How, if at all, would it affect your answer if the discharge had been caused deliberately by an employee of a rival company?

University of London LLB Examination
(for External Students) Law of Tort June 1986 Q9

Skeleton Solution

Rylands v *Fletcher* – Veryhazardous activities 'non-natural' and an escape so the rule applies – damage caused is personal injury and pure economic loss, doubtful as to whether former recoverable, these doubts probably ill founded, latter is certainly not recoverable. Possible defence, if escape due to act of rival employee, under *Rickards* v *Lothian*. Public nuisance – probably no liability to fishermen as no special damage but probably liable to Redpeace officials if personal injury treated as special damage – negligence – case for application of doctrine of res ipsa loquitur.

Suggested Solution

The main causes of action which may be alleged against the Veryhazardous Chemical Co, because of the massive discharge of toxic waste into the sea, are under the rule in *Rylands* v *Fletcher* (1868) LR 3 HL 330; (1866) 1 LR 1 Ex 265, in nuisance and in negligence. For various reasons which are considered below there are a number of weaknesses in these claims if brought by the officials of the Redpeace Environmental Group or the local fishermen and fishmongers. Traditionally, as private nuisance is defined as an unreasonable interference with a person's use or enjoyment of land, it was thought that only persons with an interest in the land affected may sue: *Malone* v *Laskey* [1907] 2 KB 141, although this was recently doubted by the Court of Appeal in *Khorasandjian* v *Bush* [1993] 3 WLR 476. However, in *Khorasandjian* the plaintiff's parents had an interest in the land which the plaintiff occupied and on which the interference occured, whereas there appears to be no legal interest in the sea, so possibly *Khorasandjian* would be distinguished and *Malone* applied here.

The most obvious cause of action against Veryhazardous Chemical Co is under the rule in *Rylands* v *Fletcher* by which there is strict liability for damage caused by an escape of an accumulation of materials brought onto their land which accumulation amounts to non-natural use of the land. For the rule to apply the accumulation must have been brought onto the land voluntarily and not by the effects of nature, such as a natural accumulation of water (see *Smith* v *Kenrick* (1849) 7 CB 515). This requirement appears to be satisfied in respect of the accumulation of toxic waste. The accumulation has to be a non-natural user of the land in the sense that the accumulation was not there by nature: *Cambridge Water Co* v *Eastern Counties Leather plc* [1994] 2 WLR 53. All the circumstances of the case, including time and place, must be considered in deciding if this element is satisfied. In the end 'non-natural' user is a question of fact and the mere fact Veryhazardous Chemical Co got planning permission and provide useful chemicals for the community is not sufficient (see *Dunne* v *N W Gas Board* [1964] 2 QB 806). Thus there seems to be a non-natural user of land in this case. An escape of the non-natural accumulation is necessary and by this is meant an escape from the defendant's land (see *Read* v *Lyons* [1947] AC 156). It does not appear necessary that the escape has to be onto land owned by the plaintiff but merely an escape from the defendant's land causing damage: *Read* v *Lyons* (supra). It would thus appear that all the necessary elements for the application of the rule in *Rylands* v *Fletcher* are present.

The effect of the escape of the toxic waste was to cause personal injuries to the Redpeace officials and to damage the livelihood of fishermen and fishmongers. The damage must be foreseeable: *Cambridge Water*, which seems to give rise to no problems. However, it is debatable if the Redpeace officials can recover damages and not possible for the fishermen and fishmongers to recover. As regards personal injuries, there are dicta in the speech of Lord Macmillan in *Read* v *Lyons* (supra), that these are not recoverable under *Rylands* v *Fletcher*. However, despite these dicta there are a number of cases, some of Court of Appeal authority, where damages were awarded for personal injuries; these include *Schiffman* v *Order of St John* [1936] 1 All ER 557; *Hale* v *Jennings Bros* [1938] 1 All ER 579 and *Perry* v *Kendrick's Transport* [1956] 1 WLR 85. But the tenor of the judgment in *Cambridge Water* is against recovery, although all these dicta were obiter. As for the possible claim by the fishermen and fishmongers this is doomed to failure. It involves pure economic loss and the general rule as to the irrecoverability of such loss in negligence applies to *Rylands* v *Fletcher* cases. This much is evident from the judgment of Blackburn J in *Rylands* v *Fletcher* and also from the decision in *Weller* v *Foot & Mouth Disease Research Institute* [1966] 1 QB 569 in which cattle auctioneers failed in a claim for lost fees as a result of the escape of foot and mouth disease from an experimental station causing the closure of their cattle market. The recovery of economic loss in *Junior Books Ltd* v *Veitchi Co Ltd* [1983] AC 520 would not help here since there is no 'very close proximity' between the parties here, even assuming that such close proximity is ever found by the courts again, which seems unlikely given the restricted interpretation to which *Junior Books* has been subjected.

Veryhazardous Chemical Co may be able to raise a number of defences if the officials of Redpeace should claim damages for personal injuries. If they have special statutory authority to discharge the toxic waste this may assist. Thus, in *Smeaton* v *Ilford Corporation* [1954] Ch 450 the defendants were held to have a complete defence under the Public Health Act 1936 s31 for an escape of sewage. If, as postulated, the escape of toxic waste was caused by an employee of a rival company then it may be possible to plead the defence of act of a stranger: see *Rickards* v *Lothian* (supra). It would seem that in order to succeed in this defence Veryhazardous Chemical Co would have to show that the escape was caused by an unforeseeable act of the stranger without any negligence on their part: see *Perry* v *Kendrick's Transport* (supra)).

An alternative cause of action which may be brought against Veryhazardous Chemical Co is in public nuisance. This is both a tort and a crime (see *R* v *Madden* [1975] 1 WLR 1379). Public nuisance arises where the plaintiff suffers an obstruction, inconvenience or damage in the exercise of a right common to all Her Majesty's subjects (see *A-G* v *PYA Quarries* [1957] 2 QB 169). The Redpeace officials might have been exercising such a right in using their boat in the sea but whether the local fishermen were exercising such a right is more debatable, expecially if they needed licences etc, to fish. As for the local fishmongers, it is difficult to see how they have suffered damage in the exercise of any rights. A claim in public nuisance in tort is only actionable where the plaintiff has suffered some particular or special loss over that suffered by the public at large. There are differing views as to what this means. According to one view it is sufficient if the plaintiff has suffered greater injury or inconvenience than anybody else. This may enable the fishermen to recover provided pure economic loss is recognisable here, a matter which is doubtful. Another view is that the plaintiff must suffer injury different in degree and kind to that suffered by the general public. If this view prevailed the fishermen could not recover (see *Hickey* v *Elec Reduction* (1970) 21 DLR 3d 68). As for the personal injury suffered by the officials of Redpeace this would be recoverable in any event as personal injury appears to be treated as a special loss for these purposes (see *Jacobs* v *LCC* [1950] AC 361).

It would also be possible in any proceedings to allege negligence against Veryhazardous Chemical Co. The facts state that the cause of the incident is unexplained and on this it may be possible for the plaintiffs to invoke the doctrine of res ipsa loquitur. The main conditions for its application are that the toxic waste was in the sole control of the defendant and that the accident was one which would not have occurred without carelessness (see *Ward* v *Tesco Stores* [1976] 1 WLR 810). A plea in negligence would enable the Redpeace officials to recover damages but it is unlikely to be of much value to the fishermen or fishmongers since, as stated above, their losses are purely economic, and in the circumstances are not recoverable in negligence.

QUESTION TWO

Nigel started operating a saw mill in a small village. He has leased the premises for a ten-year period from Michael who had told him to be careful about the noise and dust. To complete a large order, he has had to work late at night for the last month. The noise prevented Joan, the wife of Ken who owns the market garden next to the mill, from getting to sleep at night. Nigel has installed the best wood dust extraction equipment available, but last week the equipment malfunctioned and blew dust over the village. Much of the dust settled on Ken's garden and ruined a large number of sensitive orchids which he was about to send to the flower market. Last night there was a thunder storm and lightning set fire to wood stored in the mill yard. Nigel had not had time to purchase any fire fighting equipment and, because of the way he had stored the wood, the fire quickly got out of control. It spread to Ken's property where it destroyed two tool sheds before the fire brigade brought it under control.

Advise the parties.

University of London LLB Examination
(for External Students) Law of Tort June 1991 Q7

Skeleton Solution

Scope of negligence; nuisance and *Rylands* v *Fletcher* – factual application of tort of nuisance – licensing a nuisance – sensitivity of victim or victim's property distinguished from non-remote damage – liability for escape of fire – defence of Act of God – licensing an escape.

Suggested Solution

The facts involve a number of indirect interferences with neighbouring land and consequently invite discussion of the scope of and relationship between the three relevant torts of negligence, nuisance and *Rylands* v *Fletcher* (1868) LR 3 HL 330 (hereafter *R* v *F*).

The first issue is whether Joan has right of action for her loss of sleep. The tort of *Rylands* is concerned with the escape of tangible things or natural products of tangible things, such as gas or electricity, but not noise, which is not a 'product' in this sense. Further it is doubtful whether noise can be said to 'escape' in the same ways as gas or electricity, fumes, etc.

It seems that Joan may be able to sue in both nuisance and negligence which are overlapping torts. Negligence will require proof of fault so it will be preferable for Joan to sue in nuisance because liability in nuisance is strict: per Lord Simonds in *Read* v *Lyons* [1947] AC 156 HL.

Traditionally to sue in nuisance Joan must first show that she is either legal or equitable owner of the market garden property because the tort of nuisance is confined to the invasion of proprietary rights. As Ken's wife she may have such an interest, although the recent decision of the Court of Appeal in *Khorasandjian* v *Bush* [1993] 3 WLR 476 would allow Joan to sue even if she had no interest in the land. Since she is complaining of interference with her enjoyment of the property a number of factors will be relevant in deciding whether a nuisance was committed. In her favour are the matters of location and duration; industrial noise in a small rural or suburban village is not as acceptable as in an industrial area, and the intensive nature of the activity for something like 30 consecutive nights must render it unreasonable on an objective viewpoint. Nigel was not being malicious in causing the noise, but nevertheless his selfish profit-making motives will not assist him in establishing reasonableness.

The only factor which may count against Joan is the question of why Ken did not also complain about loss of sleep, because if Joan had special problems about getting to sleep and a normal person would have been untroubled by the noise, then nuisance is not established: *Robinson* v *Kilvert* (1884) 41 Ch D 88 CA. But, assuming the point in her favour, it seems she will succeed in proving a substantial interference with her enjoyment of land because for this purpose the loss of just one night's sleep is a serious and substantial matter: per Lord Greene in *Andreae* v *Selfridge* [1938] Ch 1 CA.

Joan may sue Nigel, as creator of the nuisance, and also Michael, who leased the premises to Nigel knowing that noise is a natural consequence of using a saw-mill; licensors are liable for such permitted use and consequences: *Tetley* v *Chitty* [1986] 1 All ER 633. It might have been different if Michael had insisted on undertakings from Nigel not to use the mill at night since licensors cannot be expected to supervise the daily activities of licensees or prevent unauthorised activities: *Smith* v *Scott* [1973] 3 All ER 645.

If Joan can establish injury to her health as a result of the loss of sleep she will be entitled to damages; she will be entitled to an injunction preventing Nigel from using the saw-mill at night. The second issue is whether Ken can sue in respect of the damaged orchids. In addition to the actions in nuisance and negligence an action under the rule in *Rylands* may also be relevant as the escape involved a natural product of sawn wood which Nigel had accumulated on his land.

In regard to negligence Ken would have difficulty proving fault because Nigel took reasonable care to prevent the escape of dust by installing the 'best wood dust extraction equipment available'; it may well be that Nigel was not responsible for the malfunction. Hence Ken is advised to sue in nuisance and/or *Rylands*, where liability is strict.

In regard to whether the escape of the dust was a nuisance, an isolated or one-off escape may constitute a nuisance if it arises from a state of affairs, such as a factory site, and it is irrelevant that the escape was of limited duration if the state of affairs is continuing and not temporary: *Matania* v *National Provincial Bank* [1936] 2 All ER 633. Further, the sensitivity of Ken's orchids is not relevant to establishing the nuisance which existed by the time the orchids were covered in dust (dust had blown over the whole village): *McKinnon* v *Walker* (1951) 3 DLR 577 (also involving orchids!). This is in contrast to Joan's claim where any special sensitivity of Joan to noise was relevant to establish the existence of nuisance.

It follows that since the damage to the orchids was the non-remote consequence of the nuisance Ken will be entitled to compensation for such damage, but not for loss of prospective profits from their sale, which was uncertain and not reasonably foreseeable. The principles of remoteness in the tort of negligence apply equally to actions in nuisance: dicta in the *Wagon Mound (No 2)* [1966] 2 All ER 709 PC and *Cambridge Water Co* v *Eastern Counties Leather plc* [1994] 2 WLR 53. Ken can sue both Nigel and Michael. Ken can also sue under *Rylands* (considered below), though the choice of action will make no difference to assessment of loss. The third issue is whether Ken can sue for the damage to the tool sheds caused by the escape of fire. Special rules have developed in regard to fire, which today is best dealt with under the tort of *Rylands* which imposes strict liability for non-natural use of land involving the escape onto neighbouring property of things likely to do harm. (Hence the escape of wood dust is also caught by the rule.) It is a defence under the Fire Prevention Act 1774 to show that a fire had accidentally begun on a person's premises but it had been held that this defence does not apply to claims under the rule in *Rylands*: *Musgrove* v *Pandelis* [1919] 2 KB 43 CA. It is debatable whether today the defence of Act of God covers a common, predictable event such as a thunderstorm but even if it does the defence is lost if negligence also contributed to the escape of the fire: *Goldman* v *Hargrave* [1967] 1 AC 645 PC. On the facts Nigel was negligent for the way he stored the wood and the lack of fire-fighting equipment. It is advised that Ken can sue Nigel under *Rylands* or in negligence, but that he cannot sue Michael under *Rylands* because licensors are regarded as having insufficient direct control over the occupier's acts or omissions which have given rise to the escape: per Pennycuick V-C in *Smith* v *Scott* (though there are earlier conflicting authorities which have allowed licensors to be sued for an escape in the same way as being sued for licensing a nuisance; on balance the modern authority of Pennycuick V-C is preferred here).

QUESTION THREE

Giles has a very large oil storage tank on his farm. He uses the oil to run the central heating system in his farmhouse, in his glasshouses in which he grows vegetables and in the building in which he houses a thousand battery chickens. Giles allows his barn to be used each week by the local Boy Scout troop. One evening a scout wanders away from the barn and accidentally turns the drain tap of the tank. The oil spills out and on to the land of Giles's neighbour, Ham, where it destroys his crop of brussels sprouts which were at a very delicate stage of development. While rushing to attempt to stop the oil after he has seen it cover his sprouts Ham slips on the oil, falls and cuts open his head.

Advise Ham.

Written by the editor

Suggested Solution

In this problem, there are several causes of action on which Ham may base his claim, and they are *Rylands* v *Fletcher*, private nuisance and negligence in respect of the damage to his property and his personal injury respectively.

The rule in *Rylands* v *Fletcher* imposes strict liability on a defendant for the escape from land under his control of things brought on to his land in the course of a non-natural user of the land, where those things are such that they are 'likely to do damage if they escape' and damage is foreseeable: *Cambridge Water Co* v *Eastern Counties Leather plc* [1994] 2 WLR 53. The first question is therefore whether the large oil storage tank which Giles has on his land constitutes a 'non-natural user'.

'Non-natural' for this purpose does not simply mean artificial, but imparts some element of risk or danger (*Read* v *Lyons* [1947] AC 156). In *Mason* v *Levy Auto Parts of England Ltd* [1967] 2 QB 530, MacKenna J considered that the relevant factors were:

i)   the quantities of material (in *Mason*, combustible material) which the defendants brought onto the land:

ii)   the way in which they were stored;

iii) the character of the neighbourhood.

Lord Moulton in *Rickards* v *Lothian* [1913] AC 263 said that the use must not merely be the ordinary use of the land or such a use as is proper for the general benefit of the community. This classic formulation of the test was criticised by the House of Lords in *Cambridge Water* where the simple test 'there by nature' was preferred.

While it may be argued that since Giles has chosen oil central heating, he should be allowed to store the oil on his own land, the fact remains that the oil has escaped from his land to the land of another. Similar substances which have been held to be non-natural user have been gas (*North Western Utilities Ltd* v *London Guarantee & Accident Co* [1936] AC 108), electricity (*National Telephone Co* v *Baker* (1933)) and petrol (*Musgrove* v *Pandelis* [1919] 2 KB 43), although this decision is doubtful).

On the facts of this case, the large quantity of oil stored on Giles' land, suggests a non-natural user; this is re-inforced by the fact that the neighbourhood is predominantly rural, rather than industrial.

Giles must have brought the oil on to the land for his own use, which he has, and the oil has escaped. The oil is dangerous because of its flammability, and, as in this case, because of its contaminating qualities giving rise to foreseeable damage.

On this analysis there is a prima facie case against Giles and he will be liable for the damage suffered by Ham unless he can plead as a defence that the escape was caused by the act of a stranger. This act must be independent in the sense that Giles must have had no control over the boy scout (*Perry* v *Kendrick's Transport Ltd* [1956] 1 WLR 85; [1956] 1 All ER 154), and it must be such that Giles could not reasonably have foreseen it and therefore guarded against it.

Giles, it is submitted, clearly has some degree of control over the boy scouts since he has permitted them to be on his land and presumably he has the right to ask them to leave at any time. In addition to this, he allows them to use the barn each week and it is reasonably foreseeable that some of them may wander about the farm. He should, therefore, take precautions by making any potentially dangerous structure or substance on the farm inaccessible to them. This he has clearly failed to do, and should therefore be liable.

Under the rule in *Rylands* v *Fletcher*, compensation for damage to property has always been recoverable, so that Ham will be entitled to damages for the loss of his brussels sprouts and, if applicable, their loss of profit. There is some doubt as to whether personal injuries damages are recoverable under the rule because its origins are in nuisance and trespass to land where only property damage is recoverable (*Read* v *Lyons* [1947] AC 156; [1946] 2 All ER 471).

Certain authorities do allow recovery for personal injuries: one such case is *Hale* v *Jennings Bros* [1938] 1 All ER 579, where the successful plaintiff was a bare licensee who did not have an interest in land. The Court of Appeal in *Perry* v *Kendrick's* left the point open, but did not rule out the possibility of the recovery of damages for personal injury, and damages were also awarded in *Schiffman* v *Order of St John* [1936] 1 All ER 557. The House of Lords in *Read* v *Lyons* seemed to suggest such damages were irrecoverable, as they did in the recent *Cambridge Water* case.

He may also have a claim in private nuisance, for which he must have an interest in land, which he seems to have on the facts. He must show an interference by Giles with Ham's use of his land or his enjoyment of that land. It is not impossible for a nuisance consisting of one event to be actionable, despite Oliver J's dictum in *Bolton* v *Stone* [1951] AC 850; [1951] 1 All ER 1078 that a nuisance must be 'a state of affairs, however temporary and not merely an isolated happening'. In *Midwood* v *Mayor of Manchester* [1905] 2 KB 597 the plaintiff succeeded in a nuisance action where a gas main exploded on the grounds that the nuisance consisted not only of the explosion but also of the pre-existing state of affairs during which the gas was accumulating on the defendant's premises. This reasoning may be applied to Ham's case to render Giles' interference with Ham's land unreasonable.

Against, there is some uncertainty in the law of nuisance as to whether damages for personal injury are recoverable since the tort is designed to protect property rather than the person. *Malone* v *Laskey* [1907] 2 KB 141 suggests that such damages are recoverable.

The better course of action may be for Ham to rely on negligence in relation to his personal injury claim. Under Lord Atkin's neighbour principle in *Donoghue* v *Stevenson* [1932] AC 562, Giles, as a neighbouring landowner should reasonably foresee that by his negligent acts or omissions he may cause harm or injury to Ham, therefore, he owes him a duty of care. Although the damage is caused by a third party, he has a right of control over the boy scout (*Home Office* v *Dorset Yacht Co* [1970] AC 1004; [1970] 2 WLR 1140) and a reasonable man would, in the circumstances have guarded against interference with the oil storage tank. Certainly, the damage to Ham's land is reasonably foreseeable and Ham stands a good chance of recovering damages in negligence.

QUESTION FOUR

Andrew, Basil and Clive each leases premises on an industrial estate. Andrew has recently greatly increased the use of his premises and often overloads the drains and sewage system. There is frequently an unpleasant smell hanging over the other workshops and both Basil and Clive find that there is sometimes a flow back of sewage into their systems.

Basil uses his premises for his photography business. He has chemicals stored in his basement. These are kept in accordance with the manufacturers' instructions. However water has seeped into the basement from Andrew's overflowing sewage system and this results one evening in a violent explosion. Bricks and glass shower down on Clive's premises damaging some goods stored there and Daphne, who was walking past in the street, was showered with broken glass.

Discuss the issues of liability in tort raised by these facts.

University of London LLB Examination
(for External Students) Law of Tort June 1993 Q8

Skeleton Solution

Private nuisance: factors to consider – public nuisance – the elements of *Rylands* v *Fletcher* – negligence and the question of remoteness.

Suggested Solution

This question is concerned with property being used in such a way that it annoys or damages other people. It is therefore concerned with the torts of private and public nuisance and the rule in *Rylands* v *Fletcher* (1866) LR 1 Ex 265 as well as with negligence.

The first problem to deal with is the smell hanging over other workshops owing to A overloading the drains and sewage system. Any action would be in private nuisance, which can be defined as unlawful interference with a person's use and enjoyment of land. An unpleasant smell is sufficient to constitute a nuisance (eg *Rapier* v *London Tramways Co* [1893] 2 Ch 588).

B and C are both leaseholders and therefore have sufficient interest in the land to sue in nuisance (*Inchbald* v *Robinson* (1869) LR 4 Ch 388). They can sue A because presumably he or his servants or agents created the nuisance. The damage is not tangible and has not caused material damage, therefore one has to consider a number of factors to decide whether or not A acted unreasonably and created a smell which constitutes a nuisance.

One of these factors is the nature of the locality. As was memorably stated by Thesiger LJ in *Sturges* v *Bridgman* (1879) 11 Ch D 852, 'What would be a nuisance in Belgrave Square would not necessarily be so in Bermondsey'. A, B and C all lease properties on an industrial estate, therefore it might be felt that unpleasant smells are a hazard of such places. However, it is submitted that the fact the smell emanates from overloading the drains and sewage systems, rather than from the proper use of the premises, makes the nature of the location less relevant. Smells from drains are equally unpleasant everywhere.

It may be that A is involved in some activity of general benefit, which would be a factor in his favour, although in the Irish case of *Bellew* v *Cement Co* [1948] Ir R 61 the court forbade a nuisance even though it meant closing the only cement factory in Ireland. In A's case, whatever the activity, he has overloaded the system which would surely negate the mitigating effect of social utility.

The court would not take account of any abnormal sensitivity on the part of A or B (eg *Heath* v *Mayor of Brighton* (1908) 98 LT 718). On the other hand, the fact that the smell is frequent is important for the success of the action, since a temporary or occasional smell would probably be insufficient (eg *Bolton* v *Stone* [1951] AC 850).

These are the issues of liability with regard to the smell and, on the facts, it seems likely that B & C's action in private nuisance would succeed. The remedy they would be seeking would be an injunction to bring the nuisance to an end.

What has been said about the smell will also apply to the flow back of sewage into B and C's systems with regard to an action in private nuisance, although if the flowback has caused material damage, the additional factors become less relevant, since the nuisance is tangible. The remedy would be in damages.

Is there an action in public nuisance? The smell is a nuisance which materially affect the reasonable comfort and convenience of a class of Her Majesty's subjects, namely the occupants of the industrial estate. It arises from A overloading the drains and sewage system. B and C have also suffered additional, particular damage – the flow back of sewage – beyond the general inconvenience caused by A's behaviour. Therefore they could sue in public nuisance also.

Turning to B, he has brought chemicals onto his premises. Since these have been kept in accordance with manufacturers' instructions, it does not appear that he has acted negligently, unless it could be argued that it was negligent to keep them there in the first place. Nevertheless, they have come into contact with water and exploded, causing damage to C's premises and personal injury to D. The action that one is looking at here is under the rule in *Rylands* v *Fletcher*.

The rule as stated by Blackburn J is this: a person who for his own purposes brings on his lands and collects and keeps there anything likely to do mischief if it escapes, must keep it at his peril, and, if he does not do so, is prima facie answerable for all the damage which is the natural consequence of its escape. This rule was somewhat tempered by Lord Cairns LC in the House of Lords when he relied upon the 'non-natural use' of the land to uphold the decision. Subsequent case law has similarly relied upon this additional element, which has weakened the strict liability that would otherwise apply. (Indeed, were this not the case, then B and C might have been helped by one of Blackburn J's examples, that of the person whose cellar is invaded by the filth of his neighbour's privy!)

Applying the rule to the facts of this case: the rule in *Rylands* v *Fletcher* has been applied to explosions (*Miles* v *Forest Rock Co* (1918) 34 TLR 500). The chemicals have been accumulated on B's land for his own purposes, in other words for his own benefit. There has been an escape, in that the explosion has extended beyond B's land (see the House of Lords' decision in *Read* v *Lyons* [1947] AC 156). Keeping combustible chemicals carries with it inherent risks and it is submitted that this is non-natural use of the land. See the dicta of Lord Goff in *Cambridge Water Co* v *Eastern Counties Leather plc* [1994] 2 WLR 53.

The risk is B's and, subject to any defences, he is therefore liable under the rule. While C could certainly recover damages for property damage, there has been some uncertainty over recovery for personal injury. Although the House of Lords in *Read* v *Lyons* doubted whether there could be recovery for personal injury, given the context of the original decision in *Rylands* v *Fletcher*, there have been decisions in which damages for personal injuries were allowed (eg *Perry* v *Kendrick's Transport Ltd* [1956] 1 WLR 85), although such recovery was doubted in *Cambridge Water*.

B will argue, in his defence, that the explosion was caused not by him, but by A and that A's act was an unforeseeable one. He will say that he has followed the manufacturers' instructions and has not been negligent and, if he can prove this and that the seeping water was unforeseeable, he has a defence to the claim. From the facts, this may seem to be the case.

Finally, there is the issue of A's negligence. He owes a duty of care to B and C as well as to D, the passer-by, not to injure them by his negligent acts. He has breached this duty by unreasonably unloading the drains and sewage system. This breach may have caused damage to B and C's sewage systems, in which case they can sue him for damages. It has also caused the damage to C's premises and to D, since 'but for' A's negligence, the explosion would not have occurred (*Barnett* v *Chelsea and Kensington Hospital Management Committee* [1969] 1 QB 428).

However, it is arguable whether it is foreseeable that overloading one's drains will lead to an explosion and therefore A will argue that the damage to C and D is too remote. The test of foreseeability is contained in *The Wagon Mound (No 1)* [1961] AC 388, namely that the damage is too remote if a reasonable man would not have foreseen the consequences.

See also chapter 14 questions 1 and 3 to see how *Rylands* v *Fletcher* can occur in a question predominantly set on animals.

14 ANIMALS

14.1 Introduction

14.2 Key points

14.3 Recent cases and statute

14.4 Analysis of questions

14.5 Questions

14.1 Introduction

Liability for animals exists at both common law and under statute, particularly the Animals Act 1971. Section 2 of this Act is particularly important and its contents should be studied and understood, together with s6, before any question on animals is attempted.

14.2 Key points

a) *Common law position*

Liability may arise under normal tortious principles for acts done through the agency of an animal, eg

i) nuisance

- allowing an animal to block the highway: *Cunningham* v *Whelan* (1917) 52 Ir LT 67

- noisy animals: *Leeman* v *Montague* [1936] 2 All ER 1677

ii) battery

- setting a dog on another

iii) trespass

- allowing an animal to trespass: *League Against Cruel Sports* v *Scott* [1985] 2 All ER 489

iv) negligence

- failure to prevent dogs escaping: *Draper* v *Hodder* [1972] 2 QB 556

b) *Animals Act 1971*

i) Dangerous animals

By s2(1) Animals Act 1971 'where any damage is caused by an animal which belongs to a dangerous species, any person who is a keeper of the animal is liable for the damages, except as otherwise provided by this Act.'

Note:

- the definition of keeper in s6(3)
- the definition of dangerous species: s6(2) 'not commonly domesticated in the British Islands and whose fully grown animals normally have such characteristics that they are likely, unless restrained, to cause severe damage or that any damage that they may cause is likely to be severe.'
- it is the species which must be dangerous and not the particular animal, so it is no defence to show that the animal in question was tame.

ii) Non-dangerous animals

Note the complex wording of s2(2):

'Where damage is caused by an animal which does not belong to a dangerous species, a keeper of the animal is liable for the damage ... if

- the damage is of a kind which the animal, unless restrained, was likely to cause or which, if caused by the animal, was likely to be severe; and
- the likelihood of the damage or of its being severe was due to characteristics of the animal which are not normally so found in animals of the same species or are not normally found except at particular times or in particular circumstances; and
- these characteristics were known to that keeper .... etc.'

    - Regarding s2(2)(b) in *Wallace* v *Newton* [1982] 1 WLR 375 it was held that the animal need not have a vicious tendency to attack others, merely that it possessed characteristics not normally found in that species.
    - See *Kite* v *Napp* (1982) The Times 1 June; *Cummings* v *Grainger* [1977] QB 397 and *Curtis* v *Betts* [1990] 1 All ER 769 for examples of such characteristics, and note that the comparison is with animals of the same breed rather than with animals of that type generally: *Hunt* v *Wallis* (1991) The Times 10 May.
    - See *Curtis* v *Betts* (above) for the correct interpretation of s2(2)(b) and *Smith* v *Ainger* (1990) The Times 5 June for the correct interpretation of s2(2)(a).
    - See *Cummings* v *Grainger* (above) and *Curtis* v *Betts* (above) for examples of all the requirements of s2(2) being met.
    - See *Smith* v *Ainger* (above) for a wide interpretation of s2(2)(a).

iii) Defences

See s5 1971 Act.

- damage wholly due to the fault of the plaintiff: s5(1)
- volenti: s5(2) (but not for an employee of the keeper – s6(5))
- against trespassers if

    - the animal was not kept for the protection of persons or property or
    - if it was then keeping it for that purpose was reasonable: s5(3).

Note in *Cummings* v *Grainger* (above) although the plaintiff made out a case under s2(2), she failed because the defendant could rely on s5(2) and s5(3).

Finally, note that neither an act of God nor an act of a stranger is a defence to s2.

iv) Straying livestock

Section 4 1971 Act imposes liability for animals which stray on to another's land and cause damage or expense, and s7 allows an occupier onto whose land livestock has strayed to sell the livestock to recover for damage to his property and expenses caused, subject to the closely defined conditions in s7(3).

By s5(5) there is no liability where the livestock stray from a lawful use of the highway: *Tillet* v *Ward* (1882) 10 QBD 17; *Matthews* v *Wicks* (1987) The Times 25 May.

v) Animals straying on to the highway

Liability arises if animals stray on to the highway: s8(1), but note the defence in s8(2).

vi) Protection of livestock against dogs

Section 3 imposes strict liability when dogs kill or injure livestock, and s9 allows a defendant to kill or injure a dog to protect livestock.

c) *Guard Dogs Act 1975*

Section 1 of this Act provides that a person shall not use, or permit the use of, a guard dog on any premises unless a competent handler is present and a warning notice is exhibited at the entrance to the premises. However, breach of s1 is a criminal offence only, and s5(1) of this Act expressly provides that breach shall not confer a civil right of action.

14.3 Recent cases and statute

Curtis v *Betts* [1990] 1 All ER 769

Smith v *Ainger* (1990) The Times 5 June

Hunt v *Wallis* (1991) The Times 10 May

Dangerous Dogs Act 1991

14.4 Analysis of questions

Questions on animals are popular with the examiner, either as an entire question or as part of a question involving (say) occupiers' liability or nuisance. It is most important for students to understand particularly s2(2)(a)–(c) as exemplified by *Cummings* v *Grainger*, *Curtis* v *Betts* and *Smith* v *Ainger*.

14.5 Questions

QUESTION ONE

Adam is an amateur biologist. In order to house his very large collection of rats and mice, he built a series of cages in his garden. These were built on top of a disused trench whose existence had been forgotten and was not discovered while the cages were being built. A few weeks later the trench gave way under the weight of the cages and large numbers of rats and mice escaped. Many of them made their way into Brian's house next door where they frightened his wife and children. A colony of the rats have established themselves in an overgrown garden belonging to Cecil, an elderly recluse. These attract cats to Cecil's garden which adjoins Brian's where their howling during the night keeps Brian and his family awake. Brian has started retaliating by using electrical equipment at times when he knows that it will interfere with the reception of wild life television programmes which Adam likes to watch.

Discuss the rights and liabilities of the parties in tort.

University of London LLB Examination
(for External Students) Law of Tort June 1988 Q3

Skeleton Solution

Animals Act – s2(2)(b) – damage – fright – *Rylands* – does it apply to animals? – defences – nuisance – who is liable? – remoteness – *Sedleigh-Denfield* – malice – television and recreational interests.

Suggested Solution

This question raises a number of issues. The basic problem is identifying the cause of action. The first issue relates to the escape of the rats and mice from Adam's garden. The rats and mice have escaped and frightened Brian's wife and children. The first possibility is a cause of action under the Animals Act 1971 but such an action would experience considerable difficulties. Rats and mice are not dangerous animals (s2(1)) but they may be non-dangerous animals under s2(2) of the Act. The damage which a rat or a mouse may cause by a bite is arguably likely to be severe but the problem is that the likelihood of the damage being severe must be due to characteristics of the rats or the mice which are not normally found in rats or mice or are not normally found except at particular times or in particular circumstances. This requirement does not appear to have been met here unless the rats or mice are being used by Adam, who is an amateur biologist, for some unusual purposes and this characteristic has caused them to escape and do damage. If, however, it is held that the rats and mice are covered by s2(2) then Adam, as the keeper of the rats and mice, will be liable for the damage which they cause. Damage is defined in s11 as including injury to any person, which for this purpose includes impairment of a mental condition. Therefore Brian's wife and children may not be able to recover if they have suffered mere fright; they must show that some mental condition of theirs has been impaired. Liability under the 1971 Act is strict and there do not seem to be any other defences which Adam could invoke under the Act.

There could also be liability under the rule in *Rylands* v *Fletcher* (1868) LR 3 HL 330 if collecting rats in his house is held to be a non-natural user of land. The test to be applied is whether there is some special use of the land by Adam bringing with it increased danger to others (*Rickards* v *Lothian* [1931] AC 263). There is certainly an accumulation as the rats and mice appear to have been brought on to the land and there has also been an escape. The most difficult question here is whether the rule in *Rylands* applies to the escape of animals. In *Behrens* v *Bertram Mills Circus Ltd* [1957] 2 QB 1 it was held that it was possible that such an action

127

could be taken under the rule in *Rylands*, but an example given of the type of case in which it was thought it might be applicable was the escape of a tiger, and rats and mice are nowhere near as dangerous as tigers. On the other hand if one asks the question whether rats and mice are likely to do mischief if they escape the answer might well be 'yes' so as to bring them within the scope of the rule. Once again it is unclear whether Brian's wife and children will be able to recover in respect of their fright. It depends on whether or not their 'fright' is a medically recognised psychiatric illness. An additional problem is created by the dicta of Lord MacMillan in *Read v Lyons* [1947] AC 156 that damages in a *Rylands* action are not recoverable for personal injury. Recovery was allowed in *Perry v Kendrick's Transport Ltd* [1956] 1 WLR 85 and *Hale v Jennings* [1938] 1 All ER 579, but the tenor of the judgment is *Cambridge Water Co v Eastern Counties Leather plc* [1994] 2 WLR 53 is against recovery. Adam may rely upon the defence of act of a stranger or an act of God by suggesting that the cause of the damage was the collapse of the trench which enabled the rats to escape. The difficulty here is that the weight of the cages is a factor which contributes towards the collapse and it is unlikely that he will be able to establish either of these defences.

Alternatively the entrance of the rats on to the land of Brian and Cecil may constitute the tort of trespass to land. The plaintiff in a trespass to land case must show that he has possession of the land and that there has been interference with his possession. Trespass can be committed where an animal belonging to the defendant trespasses on the plaintiff's land. Trespass is a tort of intention in the sense that the defendant must have intended to enter upon the land where the trespass was committed. It remains unclear whether trespass to land can be committed negligently and this issue is crucial here because the trespass of the rats is not intentional. A useful case here is *League Against Cruel Sports Ltd v Scott* [1985] 2 All ER 489. The plaintiffs, who were opposed to blood sports, owned a sanctuary for wild deer and refused the defendant permission to come on their land during a local hunt. Despite this fact the hunt strayed on to the plaintiffs' land on seven occasions and the master of the hunt was held to be liable in trespass if he knew that there was a real risk of hounds entering on to the plaintiffs' land and if he intentionally or negligently permitted the hounds to enter the plaintiffs' land. An application of this reasoning here would lead to the conclusion that Adam may be liable to Brian and Cecil in the tort of trespass to land if it can be shown that he was negligent in permitting the rats to escape and this will turn on whether he should have known of the existence of the trench under his garden.

The howling of the cats during the night may constitute a nuisance. Nuisance may be defined as the unlawful interference with a person's use or enjoyment of his land. Formerly only persons having an interest in land could sue in private nuisance: *Malone v Laskey* [1907] 2 KB 141, but this rule was recetly relaxed by the Court of Appeal who held that members of a houseowner's family had a cause of action in nuisance: *Khorasandjian v Bush* [1993] 3 WLR 476. Hence, following *Khorasandjian* both Brian and the members of his family may sue in private nuisance. In considering whether the howling constitutes a nuisance the court will have regard to the duration of the nuisance, the fact that it is at night, the character of the locality (apparently residential), the utility of the defendant's conduct (none) and any abnormal sensitivity of the plaintiff (trying to get some sleep at night could not be described as abnormally sensitive use).

Thus the howling appears to be a nuisance but the problem arises as to who is liable for the nuisance. The howling of the cats at night is likely to be too remote a consequence of any tort committed by Adam. The nuisance takes place on Cecil's land. It is clear that the occupier of the land may be liable where he has created the nuisance but Cecil has not created the nuisance. However in *Sedleigh-Denfield* v *O'Callaghan* [1940] AC 880 the House of Lords held that the occupier could be liable for the nuisance of a trespasser if he continued or adopted the nuisance. Here it is submitted that the presence of the cats is analagous to the position of the trespassers. Here it cannot be said that Cecil has adopted the nuisance but he could have continued it. A person continues a nuisance if, with knowledge or presumed knowledge of the existence of the nuisance, he fails to take reasonable means to bring it to an end, although he had ample time to do so. Cecil is an elderly recluse but we are not told that he is deaf so he must have knowledge of the howling and the only question is: has he failed to take reasonable steps to bring it to an end? Much here depends on the standard which is expected of an elderly recluse.

Adam may have a cause of action against Brian in nuisance in respect of the interference with his television programmes. Two particular points are relevant here. The first is that Brian is actuated by malice and his activities are similar to those of the defendant in *Christie* v *Davey* [1893] 1 Ch 316 where the defendant resorted to beating on trays, whistling and shrieking in an effort to disrupt the piano lessons which the plaintiff was giving next door. It was held that the defendant had committed the tort of nuisance. This would suggest that Brian is committing the tort of nuisance and that Adam may be entitled to an injunction to restrain the nuisance. In *Bridlington Relay Ltd* v *Yorkshire Electricity Board* [1965] Ch 436 Buckley J refused to grant an injunction to the plaintiffs when the defendants' power line interfered with the reception on the plaintiffs' television broadcasting system. However, in the recent case of *Hunter* v *Canary Wharf* (1994) The Independent 20 December it was held that such interference could constitute an actionable nuisance. So it is submitted that the tort of nuisance has been committed by Brian and that Adam will be entitled to an injunction restraining the commission of the nuisance.

QUESTION TWO

Plum was exercising his alsatian dog, Terror, in the park when he saw Grape trying to steal the handbag of a young woman wheeling a pram. Plum released the dog from its lead and said, 'Get him, Terror.' Terror pounced on Grape and brought him to the ground. Grape hurt his back when he fell and was also bitten in the face. Grape was a drug addict and therefore could not be given the normal treatment for the bite and for his other injuries. As a result his treatment was delayed and he was in hospital for six months. At the time of his injury he had just been asked to join a new pop group, the Soft Fruits, which has now had a number of successful concerts. Grape's place was taken by another instrumentalist and he is now unemployed.

Advise Grape.

University of London LLB Examination
(for External Students) Law of Tort June 1987 Q7

Skeleton Solution

Plum – sets Terror on Grape – Animals Act 1971 – dangerous or non-dangerous species – *Cummings* – negligence – trespass to the person – assault by words – battery – remoteness in intentional torts – causation – ex turpi causa – effect of defence.

Suggested Solution

Grape may have a remedy against Plum under the Animals Act 1971 and at common law for the torts of negligence, assault and battery. In all cases, however, Plum may have available to him the defence of ex turpi causa.

Dealing firstly with Grape's claim under the Animals Act 1971, Plum is clearly the keeper of Terror under s6(3) of the Act because he owns Terror and so will be liable for the acts of Terror if they fall within the ambit of the Act. The 1971 Act draws a distinction between dangerous and non-dangerous species and so it is important to consider the category, if any, into which Terror falls. The position of alsatian dogs was considered by the Court of Appeal in *Cummings* v *Grainger* [1977] QB 397. To constitute a dangerous species it must be shown under s6(2) that an alsatian dog is not commonly domesticated in the British Islands (which is not the case here) and that a fully grown alsatian dog normally has such characteristics that it is likely, unless restrained, to cause severe damage or that any damage which it may cause is likely to be severe. Hence an alsatian is not a member of a dangerous species and Plum is liable for its acts under s2(2) of the Act. Three conditions must be satisfied before Plum can be held liable under s2(2). In the first place it must be shown that the alsatian dog was likely, unless restrained, to cause damage or that, if it caused damage, that damage was likely to be severe. The damage done by a bite from an alsatian dog is likely to be severe. Secondly it must be shown that the likelihood of damage or of its being severe was due to characteristics which are not normally found in alsatians or are not normally found except at particular times or in particular circumstances. This hurdle was overcome in *Cummings* because it was held that alsatian dogs were not normally vicious except in the 'particular circumstances' of their being kept as guard dogs. Here it could be argued that the attack by Terror was simply a normal characteristic of an alsatian when it is released in such circumstances by its owner. If this was the case then Grape could not proceed against Plum under s2(2). Lastly it must be shown that these characteristics were known to the keeper. Here it could be shown that Plum was aware of the characteristics because he told Terror to get Grape, showing that he was aware of Terror's potential to attack people.

If Grape was unable to satisfy the second of these conditions then he may have to resort to a common law negligence action. If the damage done by Terror was a foreseeable consequence of the release of Terror then Plum may be liable in the tort of negligence (see *Draper* v *Hodder* [1972] 2 QB 556).

Plum may however have a defence to Grape's action under the 1971 Act. He may argue that, under s5(1), the damage was caused 'wholly by the fault of the person suffering the damage', namely Grape. This, however, involves a rather strained construction of s5(1) in that it requires the court to hold that in attempting to steal the woman's handbag Grape had, by that act, brought about the attack by Terror. It is submitted that a court would not accept such a strained construction of the section. Difficulty would also be caused in relation to s5(1) by the fact that it was Plum's exhortation which was the factor which was the immediate cause of the attack by Terror.

A more likely defence is the defence of ex turpi causa. This defence is essentially one based upon public policy so that a cause of action in tort may be denied to a person who was committing a criminal act at the time at which the tort was alleged to have been committed. See the recent House of Lords' decision in *Tinsley* v *Milligan* [1993] 3 WLR 126 for a discussion of the scope and basis for this defence. It must be shown that there is a causal connection between the offence and the damage which the plaintiff has suffered (see *Ashton* v *Turner* [1981] QB 137). Thus in *Cummings* v *Grainger* (above) Lord Denning stated that a burglar who was bitten by a guard dog may be met by a plea of ex turpi causa. Therefore it can be argued that, as Grape was in the course of a criminal act, Plum's response was a legitimate one and that therefore Grape will be unable to recover from Plum.

Alternatively Grape may argue that Plum has committed the torts of assault and battery. An assault is committed where the defendant by his threat puts the plaintiff in a state of reasonable apprehension of immediate physical contact with his person. Here an assault would appear to have been committed when Plum shouted 'Get him, Terror' and released the dog from its lead. This would certainly put Grape in reasonable apprehension of immediate contact with his person. Once again, however, Plum may have available to him the defence of ex turpi causa.

The attack by Terror at the instigation of Plum could constitute the tort of battery. A battery consists of a direct act of the defendant which has the effect of causing contact with the person of the plaintiff, without the latter's consent. The difficulty here may lie in establishing whether the attack by Terror was a 'direct act of the defendant'. However, it does not seem to matter that Plum used an animate object to injure Grape. In *Dodwell* v *Burford* (1670) 1 Mod 24 the defendant smacked the plaintiff's horse causing it to bolt and throw and injure the plaintiff. It was held that a battery had been committed. It is likely that here the act of Plum is a direct one because there is no intervening act between him releasing Terror and Terror's attack on Grape. Once again, however, Grape may be met with the defence of ex turpi causa. The defence was invoked in the case of *Murphy* v *Culhane* [1977] QB 94, where the plaintiff's husband was killed by the defendant during the course of criminal conduct instigated by the plaintiff's husband. Lord Denning held that the deceased would have been unable to maintain an action in battery because of the defence of ex turpi causa. Lord Denning did, however, hold that the defence would not be applicable where the act of the defendant was out of all proportion to the occasion. It is unlikely to be the case here that Plum's action was out of all proportion to the occasion as he was simply attempting to prevent Grape from escaping with the proceeds of the theft.

Assuming, however, that the defence of ex turpi causa was not made out and that Grape was entitled to recover damages, a difficult issue then arises as to the damage which Grape has suffered. Grape has suffered both personal injury and consequential loss of earnings. Grape's physical injuries have been made worse by the fact that he is a drug addict and so cannot have the normal treatment for the bites. However, the rule in tort is that you must take your victim as you find him (see *Smith* v *Leech, Brain* [1962] 2 QB 405). It is not the case here that Grape has unreasonably refused to undergo treatment; it is simply the case that by virtue of the fact that he *is* a drug addict that he is *unable* to undergo the treatment. This, therefore, is the classic type of case to which the eggshell skull rule is applicable and it is submitted that Plum would be liable for the damage suffered by Grape.

The loss of earnings as a pop group instrumentalist poses more difficulty. It is well settled that loss of earnings caused by negligently inflicted personal injury are recoverable, but here there is difficulty over the issues of remoteness and causation. Once again it is clear that the fact that the tortfeasor injures a high income earner is no defence to an action in tort and so the loss is not too remote. However, Winfield and Jolowicz argue, relying upon the decision of the Court of Appeal in *The Arpad* [1934] P 189, that a musician may not be able to recover for the losses which he suffers as a result of being disabled by the defendant from being able to perform particular contracts. However, it is submitted that this is incorrect and that there is no reason why Grape should not be able to recover for his loss of earnings. The fact that he earns his income by performing contracts to play music should not bar him from recovering in respect of his loss of earnings.

One further problem remains, however, and that is that Grape had not accepted the offer to join the group at the time of the accident. Thus, he may find it difficult to prove that the attack by Terror caused him any loss. For example, Plum might argue that the pop group could have withdrawn the offer or that Grape might not have joined the group anyway. However, it is submitted that Plum would have to prove that one of these two possibilities was what would, in fact, have happened. Having caused the loss it would not lie in the mouth of Plum to argue that Grape would not have joined the group. So it is submitted that, unless Plum was able to prove one of these two points, Grape would be able to recover for his loss of earnings, subject to a deduction for the unemployment benefits received to the date of trial.

QUESTION THREE

Sally, an animal lover, lives in a home with a garden on the outskirts of a village. She keeps a large number of animals and also is in the habit of looking after sick and wounded wild animals which are brought to her. Other residents in the village complain of the noise and smell, particularly Tracey, who lives next door to Sally, and is frightened of all animals.

Una, a village girl who helps out at Sally's house, allowed a ferret which Sally was treating to escape from its cage. It ran into Tracey's garden where Victor, her two-year old son, was playing. Victor thought it was a cat and tried to play with it, but the ferret bit him. Tracey heard his screams and struggling to overcome her fears beat away the ferret. Victor was not seriously hurt, but the strain on Tracey was such that she has been suffering from nervous illness ever since.

Discuss the rights and liabilities of the parties in tort.

University of London LLB Examination
(for External Students) Law of Tort June 1985 Q6

Skeleton Solution

Private and public nuisance – Animals Act 1971, liability and defences – *Rylands* v *Fletcher* – negligence.

Suggested Solution

This problem concerns potential liability for a number of torts. The residents and Tracey may consider bringing an action in nuisance against Sally for the noise and smell of the animals. If sufficient members of the community (*A-G* v *PYA Quarries* [1957] 2 QB 169) are affected, then an action may be brought in public nuisance, either by the Attorney-General as a relator action or by Tracey as a member of the community who has suffered damage over and above the rest. Otherwise Tracey and any other residents affected may bring an action in private nuisance by showing that Sally has interfered with the use and enjoyment of their land, here by way of personal inconvenience rather than actual damage, and since the recent decision of the Court of Appeal in *Khorasandjian* v *Bush* [1993] 3 WLR 476 it will not be necessary for any potential plaintiffs to have an interest in land and so all the residents could sue in private nuisance.

The law expects give and take between neighbours and, to strike a balance between a plaintiff's quiet enjoyment of his land as against the defendant's right to do what he likes on his land, the defendant must be acting unreasonably. In cases involving inconvenience, the nature of the locality is taken into account (*St Helen's Smelting Co* v *Tipping* (1865) 11 HLC Cas 642; *Sturges* v *Bridgman* (1879) 11 Ch D 852), and the courts have also taken the view that the inconvenience must not be trifling (*Halsey* v *Esso Petroleum* [1961] 1 WLR 683). It must generally be a continuing state of affairs, rather than an isolated event (*Bolton* v *Stone* [1951] AC 850). Compensation has been awarded for smells from animals (*Bone* v *Seale* [1975] 1 All ER 787), and, as long as the inconvenience is more trifling, it is submitted that on the facts of this case, the above criteria are satisfied. However, abnormal sensitivity on the part of the plaintiffs may destroy their claim (*Robinson* v *Kilvert* (1884) 41 Ch D 88); *Whycer* v *Urry* [1956] JPL 365 CA), and while the courts may have some regard to the social utility of the defendant's conduct, it is by no means conclusive if, as here, the defendant is doing something which may indirectly benefit the community (*Adams* v *Ursell* [1913] 1 Ch 269).

On balance, therefore, if the inconvenience is sufficiently grave, there is an actionable nuisance against Sally by the residents and possibly also by Tracey, as her fear would not then constitute abnormal sensitivity.

As far as the escape of the ferret is concerned, there may be liability under the Animals Act 1971. The first point to consider is whether a ferret is a dangerous or non-dangerous species. Under s6(2), a dangerous species is one which is not commonly domesticated in the British Isles and whose fully grown animals normally have such characteristics that they are likely, unless restrained, to cause severe damage or that any damage they cause is likely to be severe (liability under this section is strict). Alternatively, under s2(2) there are three criteria for liability for non-dangerous animals. It is submitted that the latter is the category into which the ferret would fall since it does not fit within the ambit of s6(2).

Before considering s2(2) in detail, the keeper must be ascertained; by virtue of s6(3), a person is the keeper if he owns the animal or has it in his possession or if he is the head of a household of which a member under the age of sixteen owns the animal. From this definition, Sally will be the keeper as opposed to Una, since the animal is in Sally's overall possession or control, although s6(4) states that where an animal is in a person's possession in order to restore it to its owner, that person is not the keeper; however, as the ferret here is a wild animal one assumes it will not be restored to its owner as such.

Under s2(2) Sally will be liable for the injury to Victor if it is the kind of damage which the animal unless restrained is likely to cause or which if caused by the animal is likely to be severe. Injury by biting is, it is submitted, damage which ferrets are likely to cause. Section 2(2)(b) is more difficult to ascertain; possibly it may be argued that the likelihood of the damage only occurs at particular times or in particular circumstances in ferrets (perhaps expert evidence is needed here), and those characteristics must be known to Sally, or Una as the keeper's servant. None of the defences under s5 apply in this case, and it must be pointed out that Tracey's nervous illness is possibly not a likely type of damage under s2(2)(a).

An alternative cause of action for both Tracey and Victor in view of the uncertainties outlined above is negligence, which may be brought against Sally and possibly Una. Sally may be liable for insufficient fencing around the garden, and Una for her lack of care in allowing the ferret to escape (subject to her age). Tracey will wish to recover for nervous shock, defined as mental injury or psychiatric illness (*Brice* v *Brown* [1984] 1 All ER 997), but in order to do so, she must prove that Sally or Una owed her a duty of care. The question here is whether nervous shock is a reasonably foreseeable consequence of Sally's negligence in not establishing adequate fencing etc, or of Una's negligence in allowing the animal to escape. It is submitted that both parties will owe a duty of care to neighbouring householders not to allow animals to escape since injury of some kind is reasonably foreseeable. As regards Tracey's nevous shock, Tracy would appear to be able to satisfy the criteria required by *Alcock* v *Chief Constable of South Yorkshire Police* [1991] 4 All ER 907 is that Tracey's relationship to the primary victim (Victor) is sufficiently close that it is reasonably foreseeable that Tracey might suffer nervous shock; Tracey's proximity to the accident is sufficiently proximate in both time and space; and Tracey suffered nervous shock through seeing and hearing the accident. In the absence of further details, it would appear from the facts that both Sally and Una are in breach of duty from which damage has resulted both to Victor and to Tracey.

Tracey and Victor may also consider an action in *Rylands* v *Fletcher* (1868) LR 3 HL 330, so long as the rule could extend to the escape of an animal; by analogy, *Rylands* has been held applicable to the escape of people (*A-G* v *Corke* [1933] Ch 82) but this case has met considerable criticism. Otherwise, there has been an escape of an animal that is dangerous but one must question whether this constitutes a non-natural user of land. Sally's use of the land may be a special use if there is a sufficiently large number of animals on it. Personal injuries have been held to be actionable under *Rylands* (*Perry* v *Kendrick's* [1956] 1 WLR 85; *Hale* v *Jennings* [1938] 1 All ER 579), although this is currently an area of considerable doubt: *Read* v *Lyons* [1947] AC 156; *Cambridge Water Co* v *Eastern Counties Leather plc* [1994] 2 WLR 53. And there do not appear to be any defences appropriate to Sally's case; she could not plead that Tracey has impliedly consented to the source of the danger since it may well be that Sally has acted negligently (*A-G* v *Cory Bros* [1921] 1 AC 521). There is unlikely to be an action in nuisance for the escape of the ferret, since it is an isolated event, and as such is not actionable unless it has been preceded by such a state of affairs as existed in *Midwood* v *Mayor of Manchester* [1905] 2 KB 597, or unless the damage is sufficiently serious, which it is submitted is not the case here.

In conclusion, therefore, the villagers and Tracey may have an action against Sally in nuisance and possibly in *Rylands* v *Fletcher* (vide supra); Tracey and Victor will have a case in negligence against Sally and Una; and Victor may have an arguable case under the Animals Act.

QUESTION FOUR

'The enactment of the Animals Act 1971 was a job half done. Its provisions are inadequate as a statutory basis for liability in respect of damage done by animals.'

Discuss.

Written by the editor

Skeleton Solution

Background to Act – distinction between dangerous and non-dangerous animals drafting of s2(2) – not comprehensive – Guard Dogs Act 1975 – strict liability – s4 – suitability of tort law for statutory regulation.

Suggested Solution

The law of tort has always made separate provision for the liability of animals. Prior to the Animals Act 1971 there was an old form of action which was specifically applicable to damage caused by animals. This was an action on the case for damage done by a savage or dangerous animal and was known as the 'scienter' action. To establish liability the plaintiff had to show that the defendant, who was the keeper of the animal, knew or ought to have known that the animal was of a dangerous character. For this purpose a distinction was drawn between two different types of animals; dangerous animals (ferae naturae) and non-dangerous animals (mansuetae naturae). Once it was shown that the animal belonged to one or other category the liability which was imposed on the defendant was strict.

The Animals Act 1971 was introduced in an effort to codify the law relating to the liability for the acts of animals and to bring it up to date. The Act was introduced after extensive consideration of the law by the Law Commission but has nevertheless been subjected to considerable criticism.

The Act abolishes the old scienter action and replaces it with a statutory code enacted in s2. The abolition of the old form of action was a useful step to take because one of the problems which is sometimes caused by legislation in the area of tort law is that the old forms of action are retained and the legislation is superimposed on the existing common law. This can cause problems in seeking to marry together the common law and the statute. However, the Act is not an exhaustive statement of the range of liability for damage caused by animals. A plaintiff may elect to bring an action in negligence, trespass to the person or defamation where the damage, defamatory statement or attack is carried out by an animal belonging to the defendant. Thus a problem still remains in ascertaining the relationship between the common law and statute law because a plaintiff can still try to use the common law to evade the statutory restrictions. Even the statutory provisions are not complete because in 1975 the Guard Dogs Act was enacted to make further provision for the use of guard dogs. Thus the Act may be said to be a job half-done because it is not a complete statement of the liability for damage done by animals because a considerable body of law still lies outside the ambit of the Act in the common law.

Section 2 of the 1971 Act retains a distinction between dangerous and non-dangerous species. A dangerous species is a species which is not commonly domesticated in the British Islands and whose fully grown animals normally have such characteristics that they are likely, unless restrained, to cause severe damage or that any damage which they may cause is likely to be severe (s6(2)). The keeper (defined in s6(3)) of such a dangerous species is liable, subject to certain defences, for the damage caused by the animal (s2(1)). In relation to non-dangerous species the keeper of an animal is liable where the damage is of a kind which the animal, unless restrained, was likely to cause or which, if caused by the animal, was likely to be severe (s2(2)(a)), the likelihood of the damage or of its being severe was due to characteristics of the animal which are not normally so found in animals of the same species or are not normally found except at particular times or in particular circumstances (s2(2)(b)) and these characteristics were known to the keeper (s2(2)(c)). The drafting of s2(2) is not entirely satisfactory. Difficulties arise in giving a meaning to s2(2)(b) because it is not entirely clear what was meant by the phrase 'characteristics of the animal which are not normally so found in animals of the same species'. In *Kite* v *Napp* (1982) The Times 1 June it was held that a dog was caught by s2(2)(b) because it had a propensity to attack people carrying bags. But, had it not been for such an unusual propensity, it is doubtful whether the dog would have been caught by the Act. See *Hunt* v *Wallis* (1991) The Times 10 May where it was held that in deciding whether a dog had characteristics not normally found in animals of the same species, the relevant comparison was with dogs of the same breed rather than with dogs generally. This would appear to admit the defence that all members of that species are bad-tempered. In an Act which was supposed to clarify the law one could have hoped for better drafting than this. The drafting of s2(2)(b) was subjected to criticism by the Court of Appeal in *Cummings* v *Grainger* [1977] QB 397. It is also submitted that the retention of the distinction between dangerous and non-dangerous animals was less than satisfactory because animals come in many different shapes and sizes and it is not clear what useful purpose is served by trying to compress them within two groups.

The Act is also unsatisfactory in that it makes no provision for a test for remoteness of damage. Is the test established in *Wagon Mound (No 1)* [1961] AC 388 to be applied or the directness test applied in *Rylands* v *Fletcher* (1868) LR 3 HL 330? Once again one would have thought that the Act would have some provision for this situation.

Section 4 of the Act makes provision for the liability for damage caused by straying livestock. The section is badly drafted because it is not entirely clear whether it applies to personal injury. But it appears that the intention was to provide a remedy for property damage only and it is submitted that the omission of protection for personal injury is rather unusual because the law of tort usually accords greater protection to a person's interest in his personal security than in his property.

However, it is submitted that the Animals Act is generally a satisfactory piece of legislation. It has a number of defects which we have noted, principally the fact that it is not comprehensive and the rather poor drafting of s2(2)(b). But it is suggested that it would be going too far to suggest that the Act was 'a job half-done'. Rather the

Act underlines the difficulty of legislating in the area of tort law. Tort law, by its very nature, is open textured and it is difficult to tie liability down within precise boundaries. The same problem can be seen in both the Occupiers' Liability Acts. Seen in this light, the Animals Act does not appear inadequate as a piece of legislation, but it is an open question whether it would have been preferable to refuse to legislate and to allow the courts to develop the common law in a more flexible manner.

15 DEFAMATION

15.1 Introduction

Defamation is a major topic in tort, and students must not only have a good grasp of the elements of liability (which are relatively straightforward), but also of the defences, especially those of qualified privilege and fair comment.

15.2 Key points

a) *Libel and slander*

 i) A defendant's statement in permanent form is libel.

 ii) Television and radio broadcasts are treated as libel: ss1 and 16 Defamation Act 1952, as are theatre performances: s4 Theatres Act 1968.

 iii) A defendant's statement in transient form is slander.

 iv) A statement can include pictures, cartoons or a wax effigy: *Monson* v *Tussauds* [1894] 1 QB 671

 v) Libel is actionable per se; slander requires proof of special damage.

 vi) However, slander is actionable per se where:

 • it imputes a crime punishable by imprisonment

 • it imputes certain contagious and infectious diseases, eg VD, plague, leprosy

 • it imputes unchastity in a woman: Slander of Women Act 1891

 • it is calculated to disparage the plaintiff in any office, profession, calling, trade or business held or carried on by him at the time of the publication: s2 Defamation Act 1952.

b) *Plaintiff*

Only a living person may sue in defamation. This includes companies: *Metropolitan Saloon Omnibus* v *Hawkins* (1859) 4 H & N 87, but not trade unions: *EETPU* v *Times Newspapers* [1980] QB 585. In *Derbyshire County Council* v *Times Newspapers* [1993] 2 WLR 449 the House of Lords held that a local authority could not sue for libel in respect of its governmental and administrative functions.

c) *Elements of defamation*

The plaintiff must prove

i)   a defamatory statement

ii)   which refers to the plaintiff

iii)   was published to a third party

d) *Defamatory statement*

i)   test: does the statement tend to lower the plaintiff in the estimation of right thinking members of society generally? *Sim* v *Stretch* [1936] 2 All ER 1237, or expose the plaintiff to hatred, ridicule or contempt? *Parmiter* v *Coupland* (1840) 6 M & W 105.

ii)   the standard is objective – what would right thinking members of society think, not the plaintiff's friends? *Byrne* v *Deane* [1937] 1 KB 818.

In *Hartt* v *Newspaper Publishing plc* (1989) The Times 9 November the Court of Appeal held that in determining the meaning of the words the approach adopted should be that of the hypothetical ordinary reader who was neither naive not unduly suspicious, but who might read between the lines and be capable of loose thinking.

In *Charleston* v *News Group Newspapers* [1995] 2 WLR 450 the House of Lords re-emphasised that the statement or article must be considered in its entirety.

iii)   for slander only, note the special rule that abuse or insult is not defamation: *Parkins* v *Scott* (1862) 1 H & C 153; *Lane* v *Holloway* [1968] 1 QB 379.

iv)   if the statement is not prima facie defamatory but only by implication the plaintiff will have to plead an innuendo.

v)   a true innuendo involves the existence of extraneous facts which the plaintiff must prove: *Tolley* v *Fry* [1931] AC 333; *Cassidy* v *Daily Mirror* [1929] 2 KB 331.

vi)   a false innuendo arises where the words have a secondary meaning, either because the words have several meanings or a slang meaning: *Allsop* v *Church of England Newspaper* [1972] 2 QB 161; *Winyard* v *Tatler Publishing* (1991) The Independent 16 August

e) *Reference to the plaintiff*

i)   The statement must reasonably be understood to refer to the plaintiff (judge to decide) and be so understood by reasonable people (jury to decide).

ii)   The defendant need not intend to refer to the plaintiff: *Hulton* v *Jones* [1910] AC 20; *Cassidy* v *Daily Mirror* (above).

iii)   It is no defence that the defendant intended to refer to another person: *Newstead* v *London Express Newspapers* [1940] 1 KB 377.

iv)   There is no requirement that the defendant expressly refer to the plaintiff: *Morgan* v *Odhams Press* [1971] 1 WLR 1239; *Cassidy* v *Daily Mirror* (above).

v)   Statements regarding a class will not be taken to refer to an individual member of that class unless the class is so small that the statement must necessarily refer to each member of it, or the words point particularly to the plaintiff: *Knupffer* v *London Express Newspapers* [1944] AC 116.

f) *Publication*

   i) means the act of making the statement known to someone other than the plaintiff

   ii) Publication to the defendant's spouse is insufficient: *Wennhak* v *Morgan* (1888) 20 QBD 635, but to the plaintiff's spouse is sufficient: *Wenman* v *Ash* (1853) 13 CB 836.

   iii) Publication must be made to a person who understands the defamatory nature of the statement and its reference to the plaintiff: *Sadgrove* v *Hole* [1901] 2 KB 1.

   iv) Publication need not be intentional – negligent publication is enough: *Theaker* v *Richardson* [1962] 1 WLR 151.

   v) Each repetition of the statement constitutes a fresh publication, and a fresh cause of action arises: *Cutler* v *McPhail* [1962] 2 QB 292.

   vi) A republisher (eg bookseller, newsvendor) is not liable if he can prove that he did not know the matter he distributed contained a libel and could not reasonably be expected to know this: *Sun Life Assurance Co of Canada* v *W H Smith* (1934) 150 LT 211.

   See also the recent case of *Slipper* v *BBC* [1991] 1 All ER 165 on liability for republication.

g) *Defences*

   i) Consent, eg *Chapman* v *Lord Ellesmere* [1932] 2 KB 431

   ii) Justification or truth

   • the defendant must prove that the statement is true in substance rather than in each and every respect: *Alexander* v *North Eastern Railway* (1865) 6 B & S 340.

   By s5 Defamation Act 1952, if the words contain two or more distinct charges, a defence of justification will not fail merely because the truth of every charge is not proved if the words not proved to be true do not materially affect the plaintiff's reputation, having regard to the true charges.

   • By s13 Civil Evidence Act 1968 a conviction in a criminal court is conclusive proof that the convicted person committed the crime.

   • By s8 Rehabilitation of Offenders Act 1974, a spent conviction may be used for justification, fair comment or qualified privilege in the absence of malice.

   • the defendant may plead a less defamatory meaning than that alleged by the plaintiff and that in this lesser sense the statement is true. The defendant may also widen the meaning of the words by arguing that they impute general dishonesty rather than dishonesty in a particular matter: *Williams* v *Reason* [1988] 1 All ER 262, and he may plead justification of any alternative meaning of the words: *Prager* v *Times Newspapers* [1988] 1 All ER 300.

- the defendant must particularise the meaning of the words he alleges are justified: *Lucas-Box* v *News Group Newspapers* [1986] 1 WLR 147, and this must be done clearly so that the plaintiff and the court are aware of precisely what meaning the defendant intends to justify: *Morrell* v *International Thomson Publishing* [1989] 3 All ER 733.

iii) Fair comment

ie the statement is fair comment based on true facts made in good faith on a matter of public interest.

- public interest is interpreted widely: see Lord Denning's comments in *London Artists* v *Littler* [1969] 2 QB 375.
- the comment must be based on true facts which must be either stated in the comment or be capable of being inferred from the comment: *Kemsley* v *Foot* [1952] AC 345. If not all the facts are true note the effect of s6 Defamation Act 1952. If the fair comment is based on an untrue statement made on a privileged occasion note that the report of the statement must be fair and accurate: *Brent Walker* v *Time Out* [1991] 2 WLR 772.
- the statement must be one of opinion and not of fact, although it may be difficult to distinguish between these: *Dakhyl* v *Labouchere* [1908] 2 KB 325.
- by fair is meant that the defendant must have honestly believed the opinion expressed: *Slim* v *Daily Telegraph* [1968] 2 QB 157, and not that a reasonable person would agree with the opinion: *Silkin* v *Beaverbrook Newspapers* [1958] 1 WLR 743.

Note the situation where the allegation is that the plaintiff had a corrupt or dishonest motive: *Campbell* v *Spottiswoode* (1863) 3 B & S 769.

- the defence may be rebutted by showing the defendant was acting out of malice, ie spite, ill-will or improper motive: *Thomas* v *Bradbury Agnew* [1906] 2 KB 627. Note that the plaintiff must prove malice: *Telnikoff* v *Matusevich* [1991] 3 WLR 952. However, if the author of the statement acts maliciously and the publisher does not, the publisher is not tainted with the author's malice: *Lyon* v *Daily Telegraph* [1943] KB 746.

iv) Absolute privilege

No action will lie for any defamatory statement, no matter how false or malicious, made in:

- parliamentary proceedings
- official reports of parliamentary proceedings
- state communications
- judicial proceedings
- fair, accurate and contemporaneous newspaper or broadcast reports of judicial proceedings
- reports of the Parliamentary Commissioner
- husband and wife communications

v) Qualified privilege

The defence can be destroyed by showing that the defendant was actuated by malice. Malice means the defendant had no honest belief in the truth of his statement: *Horrocks* v *Lowe* [1975] AC 135.

The defence applies to:

- fair and accurate reports of judicial and parliamentary proceedings (no need to be contemporaneous or in a newspaper).
- newspaper reports covered by s7 Defamation Act 1952. Note the categories carrying the right of explanation or contradiction and those categories which do not.
- statements made under a duty, ie a statement made by A to B concerning C where:

  - A is under a legal, social or moral duty to make the statement to B and B has a corresponding interest to receive it: *Watt* v *Longsden* [1930] 1 KB 130.

  - A has an interest to be protected and B is under a duty to protect that interest: *Osborne* v *Boulter* [1930] 2 KB 226.

  - A and B have a common interest in the statement: *Watt* v *Longsden* (above); *Bryanston Finance* v *De Vries* [1975] QB 703.

Note that it is possible to sidestep the defence of qualified privilege by framing an action in negligent misstatement. *Lawton* v *BOC Transhield* [1987] 2 All ER 608; *Spring* v *Guardian Assurance* [1994] 3 WLR 354 which held that the writer of a reference owed a duty of care to the *subject* of the reference.

vi) Apology

A newspaper or periodical may plead apology as a defence if the statement was published without malice and without gross negligence, and an apology was published as soon as possible; a payment into court by way of amends must also be made: Libel Acts 1843 and 1845.

vii) Unintentional defamation

A defence is given by s4 Defamation Act 1952 to words which are published innocently, ie:

- where the publisher did not intend them to refer to the plaintiff and did not know of any circumstances whereby they might be understood to do so (eg *Hulton* v *Jones* (above)); or
- where the words were not defamatory on the face of them and the publisher did not know of circumstances whereby they might be understood to be defamatory (eg *Cassidy* v *Daily Mirror* (above)); and
- in either case the publisher was not negligent.

In such situations the publisher may make an offer of amends, involving publishing a correction, an apology and informing persons to whom the statement was published that it is alleged to be defamatory.

If the offer is accepted no action lies.

If the offer is not accepted, the publisher has a defence if he can prove that:

- the words were published innocently (ie as above)
- the offer was made as soon as practicable and has not been withdrawn
- the author wrote the words without malice.

h) *Remedies*

Usually damages, decided by a jury. In *Rantzen* v *Mirror Group Newspapers* [1993] NLJ 507 the Court of Appeal held that the test of whether damages awarded are excessive is whether a reasonable jury could have thought that the award was necessary to compensate the plaintiff and to re-establish his reputation. If not the Court of Appeal may order a new trial under s8(1) Courts and Legal Services Act 1990 or substitute a sum under s8(2) of the 1990 Act. A jury may be referred to previous such awards by the Court of Appeal, but not to previous jury awards. In the meantime juries should be told to consider the purchasing power of any award, as in *Sutcliffe* v *Pressdram* [1990] 1 All ER 269.

The plaintiff may seek an interlocutory injunction, but this is rarely granted where the defence is one of justification, fair comment or qualified privilege: *Bestobell Paints* v *Bigg* (1975) 119 SJ 678.

15.3 Recent cases and statute

Sutcliffe v *Pressdram* [1990] 1 All ER 269

Hartt v *Newspaper Publishing plc* (1989) The Times 9 November

Telnikoff v *Matusevich* [1991] 3 WLR 952

Slipper v *BBC* [1991] 1 All ER 165

Winyard v *Tatler Publishing* (1991) The Independent 16 August

Brent Walker Group v *Time Out* [1991] 2 ALL ER 753

Rantzen v *Mirror Group Newspapers* [1993] NLJ 507

Derbyshire County Council v *Times Newspapers* [1993] 2 WLR 449

Spring v *Guardian Assurance plc* [1994] 3 WLR 354

Charleston v *News Group Newspapers* [1995] 2 WLR 450

Section 8 Courts and Legal Services Act 1990

15.4 Analysis of questions

A question is set on defamation each year, and often it involves a consideration of what is defamatory and the defences, with fair comment and qualified privilege being especially favoured by the examiner.

15.5 Questions

QUESTION ONE

Harriet established a fund to award a substantial prize each year for the best work of art submitted for consideration by an artist under thirty. Two of the six trustees of the fund are Jeremy and Kenneth. One of the candidates for the prize in 1990 was Lionel. In his report to the other trustees, Jeremy stated that 'Lionel's work is devoid of all artistic originality'. Lionel has recently been divorced by Jeremy's daughter. Kenneth's report stated, 'I hear from various sources that Lionel was concerned in a recent scandal involving the production of artistic fakes. It would be better not to consider him until the position is clear.' Kenneth had his report typed by his wife, Molly, who is the secretary to the director of an art gallery. She used the word-processor in her office and did not immediately delete the document in case it required corrections. Before she could do so, her employer, in searching for another document, came upon Kenneth's report. He abandoned plans to hold an exhibition of Lionel's work.

Advise Lionel.

University of London LLB Examination
(for External Students) Law of Tort June 1990 Q6

Suggested Solution

We must consider whether Lionel has been defamed by Jeremy, Kenneth or Molly.

The reports by Jeremy and Kenneth are in permanent form and so any defamation that has occurred will take the form of libel. As regards Molly's use of the wordprocessor, this would also appear to be a communication in permanent form (as indeed it lasted long enough for her employer to see it), so this would also be libel if it were defamatory. In fact, as the allegation in the word processor imputes a crime punishable by imprisonment, and also would tend to disparage the plaintiff in any business or calling, if it were to be slander it would be actionable per se and require no proof of special damage (see s2 Defamation Act 1952) which from Lionel's point of view is the most important difference between the statement being held to be slander rather than libel.

To succeed in an action for defamation Lionel must prove that the statement complained of was defamatory; that it could reasonably be understood to refer to Lionel; and that it was published to a third party.

The usual test of a statement being defamatory is that it tends to lower the plaintiff in the estimation of right thinking members of society generally: *Sim* v *Stretch* [1936] 2 All ER 1237 or which expose him to hatred, contempt and ridicule: *Parmiter* v *Coupland* (1840) 6 M & W 105.

Jeremy's statement is prima facie defamatory as it would tend to lower Lionel in the estimation of right thinking members of society, and the fact that Jeremy did not intend to defame Lionel is irrelevant: *Cassidy* v *Daily Mirror Newspapers* [1929] 2 KB 331.

As regards Kenneth's statement the situation is a little more complex. In *Lewis* v *Daily Telegraph* [1964] AC 234 it was held that to say a person was being investigated

144

for fraud was not the same as saying that he was guilty of fraud. However, Kenneth has stated that he has heard that Lionel was concerned with fakes rather than being investigated for fakes; Kenneth might argue that his recommendation to delay a decision rather than to refuse Lionel the prize is implying that he is not claiming that the allegation is true, but is rather awaiting clarification of the situation. In *Hartt* v *Newspaper Publishing* (1989) The Times 9 November the Court of Appeal held that the approach to adopt was that of the ordinary hypothetical reader who was neither naive nor unduly suspicious but who might read between the lines and be capable of loose thinking. Ultimately it would be a question for the jury to decide, but we shall continue the discussion on the assumption that the statement is prima facie defamatory.

Lionel must also prove that the statements refer to him and have been published to a third party. As regards both Jeremy and Kenneth there is no problem here as Lionel is mentioned by name and Jeremy has sent his report to the other trustees. I assume that Kenneth has also sent his report to the other trustees, but if he has not the fact that Molly's employer has seen it is sufficient publication.

We must now consider Molly. Assuming that Kenneth's statement is defamatory, and it clearly refers to Lionel, there has been a publication by Molly to her employer as every repetition of the statement constitutes a fresh publication and gives rise to a fresh cause of action: *Cutler* v *McPhail* [1962] 2 QB 292. The publication need not be intentional, negligent publication is sufficient: *Theaker* v *Richardson* [1962] 1 WLR 151. Hence prima facie Molly has defamed Lionel.

Let us now turn to any defences which are available to the defendants.

One defence that is available to all defendants is justification ie truth of the statement concerned, but the facts of the problem do not tell us whether this is so and we shall assume that a plea of justification will fail.

Jeremy may seek to rely on the defence of qualified privilege on the grounds that he has a legal, social or moral duty to make the statement to the other trustees and that they have a corresponding interest to receive it: *Watt* v *Longsden* [1930] 1 KB 130. It seems clear from the facts of the problem that such a duty exists on both sides and would provide a defence to Jeremy. However, the defence of qualified privilege can be destroyed by showing that the defendant was actuated by malice, and as Lionel has recently been divorced by Jeremy's daughter, Jeremy may have made the statement with a malicious motive. By malicious is meant that Jeremy has no honest belief in the truth of his statement: *Horrocks* v *Lowe* [1975] AC 135. If Jeremy honestly believes his statement, malice cannot be inferred merely because Jeremy's belief is unreasonable or unfair: *Horrocks* v *Lowe*; lack of honest belief is essential.

Jeremy may also claim that his statement is fair comment based on true facts made in good faith on a matter of public interest. The courts tend to define public interest widely: *London Artists* v *Littler* [1969] 2 QB 375, and the award in question would be a matter of public interest. The comment must be fair in the sense that the defendant honestly believed the opinion stated: *Slim* v *Daily Telegraph* [1968] 2 QB 157. However, the question arises, has there been a comment based on facts or has Jeremy merely made a statement of fact? It seems that Jeremy has merely made a statement of fact and not opinion, there being no sub-stratum of fact as in *Kemsley* v *Foot* [1952] AC 345. Again the presence of malice will destroy this defence: *Thomas* v *Bradbury, Agnew* [1906] 2 KB 627.

Kenneth may seek to rely on the defence of qualified privilege as regards publication to the other trustees, and as with Jeremy the duty to make and to receive the statement exists and there is no reason to impute malice to Kenneth.

As regards the publication by Kenneth to Molly, as this is a husband and wife communication it attracts absolute privilege and no action will lie in respect of it. The publication would also be covered by qualified privilege: *Bryanston Finance* v *De Vries* [1975] QB 703.

Considering the publication by Molly to her employer, Molly cannot use the defence of qualified privilege as although her employer may have an interest in receiving the statement, Molly appears to have no interest in making the statement to her employer: *Watt* v *Longsden*. Molly may seek to rely on the defence that she is an innocent republisher and as such she will not be liable if she did not know the statement contained a libel and could not reasonably be expected to know this: *Sun Life Assurance Co of Canada* v *W H Smith* (1934) 150 LT 211.

Thus Lionel should be advised to sue Jeremy, Kenneth and Molly although of these Kenneth would appear to have the best defence.

QUESTION TWO

The Arctic TV Company broadcast a news item during a spell of exceptionally cold weather about problems facing the old in such conditions. The film first showed a number of old people shopping in a supermarket, one of whom was Lucy. The commentary on the film said: 'Old people, often frail and forgetful, with their life savings gone, have a hard struggle making ends meet in this bitter weather.' The commentary continued: 'Even worse is the plight of Maisie, 85 years old and unable to get out in the cold, but afraid of the heating bills which will follow if she tries to stay warm at home.' The film shows Maisie climbing into bed wearing a winter coat and scarf and holding two hot water bottles.

Lucy is very fit and mentally alert and proud that she has enough money saved to preserve her independence; she did not know that she was being filmed until she saw herself on television. Maisie had agreed to be filmed at the request of the social services department of her local council, which is campaigning against the government's treatment of the elderly; Maisie is in fact visited every day by her daughter Nora, who pays all her heating bills. Nora works as a volunteer for charities concerned with old people.

Has Lucy or Nora a cause of action in defamation?

University of London LLB Examination
(for External Students) Law of Tort June 1987 Q4

Skeleton Solution

Lucy – visual association with commentary – whether defamatory – is it libel? – defences – justification – fair comment.

Nora – innuendo that mother left and uncared for – libel? – defences – consent (to what?) – justification – fair comment – s4 of the Defamation Act 1952.

Suggested Solution

Lucy and Nora may both have a cause of action against the Arctic TV Company as the result of this particular broadcast. As their claims raise different issues in the tort of defamation they will be dealt with separately. There is, however, one issue which is common to both claims and that is whether the claim is for libel or slander. Libel is a defamatory statement which is contained in a permanent form, such as writing, whereas slander is not contained in a permanent form. In *Youssoupoff* v *Metro-Goldwyn-Mayer* (1934) 50 TLR 581 it was held that a defamatory statement contained in a film was libel. This was because the photographic part of the film was contained in a permanent form and the speech part of it was merely ancillary to the film and so the cause of action lay in libel (see also s1 and s16 Defamation Act 1952). So both Lucy and Nora would bring their action in libel.

Dealing now with Lucy's claim, the first difficulty which she will experience is in showing that the statements which she alleges were made about herself were defamatory. Lucy is complaining that she has been associated with the commentary in the film about old people, in particular the comments about forgetfulness and an inability to support oneself. In considering whether or not this statement is defamatory the test to be applied is whether the words would tend to lower Lucy in the eyes of right thinking members of society, or otherwise cause Lucy to be shunned or avoided (*Sim* v *Stretch* [1936] 2 All ER 1237 and *Youssoupoff* v *Metro-Goldwyn-Mayer* (above)).

It does seem that the film was defamatory of Lucy. The film shot of her at the same time as the commentary links her with the comments 'often frail and forgetful' and 'have a hard struggle making ends meet'. Although Lucy is only one of a number of old people who is in the film at the time, it seems clear that she is associated with the commentary. The allegations seem tantamount to implying that Lucy is both senile and a drain on national resources. If this interpretation is the one which the jury accepts then it would clearly be defamatory. It seems that the defamatory material has been published to third parties when the film was broadcast and so there is no problem in satisfying this element of the tort.

Arctic may however seek to rely on a number of defences to Lucy's action. The first may be that the statements were not referring to Lucy herself but to 'the old people of our society'. Arctic could argue that Lucy was only one of a number of people in the film and that the commentary should not be associated with her.

However Lucy does not have to show that Arctic intended that the statement be understood as referring to her. It is sufficient if the statement can impliedly be understood as referring to her (*Le Fanu* v *Malcolmson* (1848) 1 HL Cas 637). It is submitted that Lucy could clearly establish that the broadcast impliedly referred to her.

Arctic may also claim that their statement was fair comment. To establish such a defence Arctic would have to establish that there was a basis of fact for their comment, that the comment was fair and that it was in the public interest. It is likely that this would be held to be a matter of public interest because this is a matter in which the public are legitimately interested (*London Artists Ltd* v *Littler* [1969] 2 QB 375). However Arctic are likely to flounder when it comes to showing that their statement of opinion was based upon facts which are true. In *London Artists Ltd* Lord Denning said that the person making the comment must get his basic facts right. Here Arctic have manifestly failed to get their basic facts right. Lucy is very fit and mentally alert and has enough money to preserve her independence and so Arctic could not rely on a defence of fair comment.

Turning now to the case of Nora, she was not referred to in the broadcast and so it is more difficult for her to succeed in her action against Arctic. She must show firstly that the statement was defamatory of her and secondly that the statement referred to her. On the first issue, the fact that Arctic did not intend to defame Nora is irrelevant to the question whether or not their statement was defamatory. This can be seen from the case of *Cassidy* v *Daily Mirror Newspapers Ltd* [1929] 2 KB 331. The picture of the plaintiff's husband with another woman, above the caption 'Engaged to be married', gave rise to the implication that the plaintiff slept with a man to whom she was not married. It was held that the plaintiff was entitled to succeed in her defamation action. Russell LJ stated that it was the fact of defamation which was important and not the intention of the defamer. In the same way Nora can argue that the fact that she is Maisie's daughter and that her mother is stated to lead such an impoverished life implies that she did not care for her own mother. Thus the implication would clearly be that Nora does not look after her own mother and to someone who is concerned with the care of the elderly such an implication is clearly defamatory.

Nora could also argue that, even if it is held that the broadcast is not on the face of it defamatory of her, it is defamatory when combined with some extrinsic facts known to the watchers of the broadcast. Such was the case in *Tolley* v *JS Fry & Sons Ltd* [1931] AC 333 when a picture of the plaintiff, who was an amateur golfer, on an advertising poster belonging to the defendants, was held to be defamatory because it gave rise to an innuendo that the plaintiff had flouted his amateur status by agreeing to appear in the advertisement for financial reward. Applying this reasoning here it could be argued that the broadcast was defamatory because watchers would think that Nora, who was supposedly concerned with the welfare of old people, did not look after her own mother.

Secondly Nora must show that Arctic's defamatory statement referred to her. It is clear that the plaintiff does not need to be expressly referred to in the statement, but that it can be implied that the broadcast referred to her. Such was the case in *Morgan* v *Odhams Press Ltd* [1971] 1 WLR 1239 where the House of Lords held that there was sufficient evidence to go to the jury because the ordinary reader who had special knowledge of the circumstances would conclude that the article referred to the plaintiff. Applying such a test here the ordinary watcher who knew of the circumstances of Maisie and Nora would conclude that the broadcast referred to Nora.

There are, however, a number of defences which may be relied upon by Arctic. The first is that Maisie consented to appearing in the film. It is not clear, however, that that consent is relevant to Nora's action for damages. Nora in no way consented to the broadcast. Even if it was held to be the case that Maisie's consent was relevant, it is necessary to examine what it was that Maisie consented to. Her consent was made at the request of the council who were campaigning against the government's treatment of old people. She did not consent to anything else. In *Chapman* v *Lord Ellesmere* [1932] 2 KB 431 the consent was held to be limited to publication in the 'Racing Calendar' and that it did not extend to publication in 'The Times'. Here it can be argued that Maisie consented to being filmed, but she did not consent to any defamation of her daughter nor indeed was she able to do so.

The other defence which may be open to Arctic is the defence of justification or fair comment. However both defences are likely to fail because there was insufficient basis of fact for the statements made by Arctic. It was not true to say that Maisie was afraid of the heating bills because Nora paid for all her heating bills. Therefore they could not rely upon either of these defences.

However Arctic may be able to rely upon s4 of the Defamation Act 1952. Section 4 applies to any defamatory words which are innocently published and where either the publisher did not know of the circumstances whereby the words may be understood as referring to the plaintiff or where the words are not on the face of them defamatory and the publisher did not know of the circumstances by virtue of which they might be understood to be defamatory of the plaintiff. It seems that Arctic may well be able to rely upon s4 because they did not know of the circumstances by which the broadcast might be understood as referring to Nora. If s4 does apply then Arctic can avoid liability to Nora by offering to publish a suitable apology and correction and by taking reasonable steps to notify the distributors. If Nora accepted this apology and offer of amends then she would have no action against Arctic in libel. If she did not accept the apology then Arctic would still have a defence under s4 to her libel action provided that the apology and offer of amends were made as soon as possible and not withdrawn.

QUESTION THREE

Rupert is a general medical practitioner. He asks Fanny, his secretary, to type out some rough hand-written notes of remarks he proposes to make at a public meeting, which has been called to discuss the closure of a number of national health service hospitals in the area. These remarks include criticisms of Humphrey, a local councillor who is chairman of the area health authority, alleging that he is not concerned about the cutbacks since he arranges private medical care for himself and his family. Rupert also dictates a letter to Fanny containing the same criticisms and intended for publication in a local newspaper. He uses the notes as the basis for his speech at the meeting but in the end decides not to send the letter to the newspaper. In fact Humphrey has only on two occasions sought private medical treatment, on both of them for his wife who had been taken suddenly ill on holiday.

Advise Humphrey.

University of London LLB Examination
(for External Students) Law of Tort June 1986 Q7

Skeleton Solution

Defamation – speech wrongly accusing public health authority chairman of taking private medicine – libel rather than slander. Letter and notes to same effect given to typist for typing both libel as publication of these to typist – Defence available –

qualified privilege probably available in respect of publication to typist but unlikely to be available in respect of speech – Defences of truth or justification and fair comment not available as allegations untrue.

Suggested Solution

Humphrey may bring proceedings against Rupert in defamation, more particularly in libel, in respect of the remarks made by Rupert at the meeting and in respect of the contents of his handwritten notes and the letter intended for publication which were handed to Fanny, his secretary, for typing. Whether proceedings against Rupert would be successful depends on if he can successfully raise any defences.

As stated this is a case of libel, because all of the matters which are actionable fall to be treated as libellous rather than slanderous. Libel generally arises where a defamatory statement or material is in a permanent form and, possibly, also visible and slander where it is in a non-permanent form. The handwritten notes and the draft letter given by Rupert to Fanny would clearly be in a permanent form. But, the speech at the meeting by Rupert raises more complicated issues. In *Forrester* v *Tyrrell* (1893) 9 TLR 257 the Court of Appeal treated the reading aloud of a defamatory script to an audience as libel. The reasoning behind this decision is difficult to ascertain mainly because the judgments are inadequately reported. It may be that this was a case of libel because the audience knew that the defamatory material was being read from a script so that there was publication of a statement in a permanent form. If so, then the case would be one of slander if they were not aware of this but believed the statement was being made extempore. On the facts of the present case it is unclear if the audience at the meeting knew Rupert was reading from his notes or giving an extempore speech. In the long run the matter may be academic for the purposes of this case since the real importance of treating Rupert's speech as libellous is that libel is actionable per se, ie without proof of special damage, whereas, as a general rule, slander is not. However, there are a number of exceptions to this general rule concerning slander. One of these is that under s2 of the Defamation Act 1952 a slanderous statement calculated to disparage the plaintiff in any office, profession, calling, trade or business is actionable per se. It is highly likely that Humphrey could rely on this, if necessary, on the ground that the remarks made by Rupert in his speech disparaged him in his office as chairman of the area health authority.

The remarks made by Rupert about Humphrey giving his family the benefit of private health care whilst chairman of the local area health authority are, in my view, defamatory. In order that a statement may be treated as defamatory as a matter of law it must be shown that the words used were capable of being treated as defamatory; that they referred to Humphrey and that they were published. A statement is treated as defamatory if it tends to lower the plaintiff in the estimation of right thinking members of society generally. See *Sim* v *Stretch* [1936] 2 All ER 1237; or, where they were calculated to bring the plaintiff 'into hatred, contempt or ridicule'. See *Parmiter* v *Coupland* (1840) 6 M & W 105. The effect of the remarks made by Rupert were to show Humphrey as quite unworthy to hold the office of chairman of the area health authority as he did not think its services worthy to provide medical treatment for his own family. Further, he may be viewed as a hypocrite quite unfit to hold that office by reason of his family taking private medical treatment: see *Tolley* v *J S Fry & Sons Ltd* [1931] AC 333. There is little doubt that the remarks referred to Humphrey, the facts appear to indicate direct references to him by name. In any event this is not essential because so long as the remarks are such as could be understood by a reasonable man as referring to Humphrey, this will be sufficient: see *Lewis* v *Daily Telegraph* [1964] AC 234. There was publication of the remarks also. They appear to have been made to an audience at the meeting at which Rupert spoke and the giving of the notes and the letter to Fanny for typing constituted publication. For the purposes of defamation publication means communication of the remarks to a third party, that is, someone other than the maker thereof and the person to whom they refer: see *Pullman* v *W Hill & Co Ltd* [1891] 1 QB 524.

Thus, as stated, Humphrey could prove that the statements were prima facie, defamatory. But, it is open to Rupert to raise defences negativing any successful cause of action by Humphrey. As regards the handing of the notes and the letter to Fanny, this was, as stated above, a publication of defamatory material. However, Rupert could plead qualified privilege here, ie that the communication of the material to Fanny for typing was privileged. In *Bryanston Finance Ltd* v *De Vries* [1975] QB 703 Lord Denning MR held that the privilege applied to a case of dictation of a letter to a secretary by a businessman because of a common interest in getting the letter written. There appears to be no good reason for not applying this to a case, as here, where handwritten material is given to a secretary for typing as there is a common interest in having the material typed. But, it will also be necessary to show that there was no malice involved on the part of Rupert, since this defeats qualified privilege: see *Horrocks* v *Lowe* [1975] AC 135. Malice includes where the defendant, ie Rupert, did not honestly believe in the truth of what he said. It is not clear whether Rupert would be deprived of the defence of privilege because of malice. In determining this matter the court will seek to discover if Rupert acted 'honestly' even though in arriving at his conclusion he may have been careless, impulsive, irrational or prejudiced: see *Horrocks* v *Lowe*.

The only defence that might be available to Rupert in respect of the remarks made in his speech is that of qualified privilege. He could not plead justification or truth since the statement he made was untrue: see *Walkey* v *Cooke* (1849) 4 Exch 511. A defence of fair comment is not available even though the matter might have been in the public interest because the fair comment must be upon facts which are true: see *London Artists Ltd* v *Littler* [1969] 2 QB 375. It is true that Humphrey did get private medical treatment for his family when they suddenly took ill on holiday but Rupert's statement is a general assertion that infers Humphrey invariably gives his family private medical treatment. This statement is not, in itself, true. Even if this were not accepted then fair comment is arguably not available because the defence concerns the comments made upon facts. Rupert merely asserted, incorrectly, a matter of fact and did not make a comment thereon, it is submitted. The problem of distinguishing fact from comment is not always easy but, it is difficult to see how the remarks made by Rupert could be regarded as comment: see *Kemsley* v *Foot* [1952] AC 345. As to the defence of qualified privilege in relation to Rupert's speech, this might be available on the basis that Rupert had a moral or social duty to communicate the matter to his audience at the meeting since it was expressly called to discuss the closure of some national health hospitals in the area. This defence must be rather weak in the light of the decision in *Watt* v *Longsden* [1930] 1 KB 130 where it was held that a stranger was not privileged to communicate to a wife matters concerning the integrity and moral behaviour of her husband. It is nevertheless arguable that Rupert had a social duty to speak as he did since the matter concerned Humphrey's fitness to continue as chairman of the area health authority.

The appropriate remedy for Humphrey, should he succeed in his action against Rupert, will be damages.

QUESTION FOUR

a) Discuss the scope of the defence of fair comment to an action in defamation.

b) Sarah Siddons is a stage actress who is equally well known for her acting ability and for her strongly held and expressed political views. She is engaged to play a leading role in a play written by a young author. The play and Miss Siddons are well received by the first night audience. However on the following morning the Daily Globe newspaper published a review by its influential drama critic, Doreen Knock, which contained the passage: 'This young playwright shows signs of promise but he will need care and understanding from those who produce his works. For me this play was ruined by the strident acting of Miss Siddons and her abject failure to portray an innocent young girl. Innocence is a quality which Miss Siddons, who will not see 45 again, lost long ago. It is high time she realised she is an ugly old cow who should choose her roles with greater regard to her audience's sensitivities.' Other daily papers carried reviews highly critical of the themes and structure of the play but giving some praise to Miss Siddons. The play which has been expected to run for at least three months closed after three nights. Its promoters lost money and Miss Siddons had to wait for six weeks before obtaining another role in a different play which unexpectedly ran for one year in London. Doreen Knock is known to hold political views strongly opposed to those of Miss Siddons.

Advise Miss Siddons.

University of London LLB Examination
Mid-sessional, 1989

Skeleton Solution

a) Fair comment – public interest – statement of opinion – must get basic facts right – *London Artists* v *Littler* – fairness – absence of malice – importance to newspapers and freedom of the press.

b) Libel – publication – referred to the plaintiff – defamatory – *Sim* v *Stretch* – defences – justification – fair comment – Defamation Act 1952 – apology and amends – measure of damages.

Suggested Solution

a) The defence of fair comment is an important one and it is frequently invoked by the newspapers in the courts. It is, however, available only within certain narrow confines. There are four distinct elements to the defence.

The first factor which must be established is that the defendant's statement was made on a matter of public interest. This question of what is in the public interest is a question for the court but it has been interpreted fairly widely by the courts. It may be satisfied by showing that the public either have a legitimate interest or a legitimate concern in the issues. A legitimate interest would encompass such matters as the 'goings on' in the theatre and the show business world (*London Artists Ltd v Littler* [1969] 2 QB 375). A legitimate concern, on the other hand, would encompass a statement that the cottages which were owned by a major mining company and which were the major source of housing in a particular village were in an insanitary condition (*South Hetton Coal Co Ltd v North-Eastern News Association Ltd* [1894] 1 QB 133).

The second factor is that the defendant's statement must be a statement of opinion and not one of fact. The difficulty for defendants here is that it has been held that the opinion must be stated upon the basis of facts which are true. In *London Artists Ltd v Littler* (above) Lord Denning said that the defendants must get their basic facts right. This makes it difficult for the press to invoke the defence. However the position has been alleviated somewhat by s6 of the Defamation Act 1952 which states that the defence of fair comment shall not fail because the truth of every allegation of fact is not proved if the statement of opinion is fair having regard to such of the facts alleged as are proved to be true.

Thirdly, it must be shown that the statement was, in all the circumstances, a fair one to make. One of the crucial issues here is the motive with which the statement was made. If it was made with a dishonest motive then it will be more difficult for the defendant to invoke the defence (*Campbell v Spottiswoode* (1863) 3 B & S 769).

Fourthly, the defendant must not be actuated by malice. It is for the plaintiff to show that the defendant was actuated by malice (see *Telnikoff v Matusevich* [1991] 3 WLR 952). The burden of proof is an extremely important practical consideration and, in putting the onus of proof on the plaintiff, it makes it easier for the defence to be invoked and for comment to be made on matters of public interest.

The defence of fair comment is a vital defence if free speech is to be maintained on matters of public interest. However, at the same time the law must seek to protect the interest of individuals in ensuring that untrue defamatory statements are not published about them. It is submitted that the defence of fair comment, as amended by s6 of the Defamation Act 1952, provides a suitable compromise for these competing interests.

b) Miss Siddons will wish to bring a libel action against the Daily Globe newspaper and its drama critic Doreen Knock. It would constitute a libel because the allegedly defamatory statement is contained in a permanent form. To establish that the tort has been committed Miss Siddons must establish three things. The first is that she must show that the defamatory statement was published. This is clearly satisfied because the review was printed in the newspaper. The second thing which she must establish is that the defamatory statement referred to her. Once again there is no difficulty with this point as Miss Siddons is expressly referred to in the review. The third thing which Miss Siddons must establish is that the statement was defamatory of her. The test here is whether the statement would tend to lower her in the estimation of right thinking members of society generally (*Sim v Stretch* [1936] 2 All ER 1237). The review states that she 'ruined' the play, that her portrayal of the character was an 'abject failure' and that she was 'an ugly old cow' who lost her innocence many years ago. It is submitted that such statements would tend to lower Miss Siddons in the estimation of right thinking members of society and that the review is therefore defamatory.

Doreen Knock may however wish to rely on a number of defences to Miss Siddons' action in libel. The first defence which she may wish to invoke is justification; that is to say that the review was true. It would be for Doreen Knock to show that her statement was true. The difficulty is that the play was well received by the first night audience and that Miss Siddons' performance was given some praise by other reviews. So it would be difficult for Miss Knock to invoke the defence. If Miss Knock can prove that parts of her review are true then she may be able to invoke s5 of the Defamation Act 1952 which states that the defence of justification shall not fail if the words not proved to be true do not materially injure Miss Siddons' reputation having regard to the truth of the remaining charges.

Doreen Knock may also wish to invoke the defence of fair comment. The matter is certainly one of public interest (*London Artists Ltd* v *Littler* [1969] 2 QB 375). The difficulty may arise in showing that Doreen Knock got her basic facts right. It may also be possible for Miss Siddons to show that Doreen Knock was actuated by malice. We are told that Miss Siddons is equally well known for her strongly held political views and that Doreen Knock holds political views strongly opposed to those of Miss Siddons. If Miss Siddons can show that Doreen Knock was actuated by malice then Doreen Knock will be unable to rely on the defence of fair comment. *Thomas* v *Bradbury Agnew* [1906] 2 KB 627; *Telnikoff* v *Matusevich* [1990] 3 All ER 865.

Finally, if all else fails, Doreen Knock can apologise for the defamatory statement which she has made and pay a sum of money into court by way of amends. The effect of the apology would be to mitigate the damages for which she would otherwise be liable.

The final difficulty would be in establishing the measure of damages to which Miss Siddons is entitled. Libel is actionable per se. But Miss Siddons has obtained a role in a play which has run for a year in London. In *Cornwell* v *Myskow* [1987] 1 WLR 631 the Court of Appeal accepted that a defendant could lead evidence of an undiminished reputation at the date of trial in order to show that the publication had caused the plaintiff no real damage. So it is submitted that the damages awarded to Miss Siddons will reflect the fact that she appears to have suffered no real damage as a result of the publication.

QUESTION FIVE

A chain of local newspapers (including the *Westtown Gazette*) carries a syndicated column under the heading 'Dr Healwell Answers'. This gives advice to parents who write in with problems on the health and upbringing of children. Dr Healwell is not a real person and the column is written by several people. A few months ago, in response to an enquiry, 'Dr Healwell' recommended that parents should not worry about truancy and that children who were reluctant to go to school would learn more if they were taken on country outings.

A Dr Healwell, who had practised as a children's doctor in Australia, had retired a few years ago and settled in Westtown. He had not seen the column but had noticed that he had not recently been asked, as he often had in the past, to speak in local schools. He had also been invited to serve as a governor of Westtown Academy, but the invitation had been withdrawn. He has now learned about the column and has also learned that the headmaster of the academy had written to all the governors, saying, 'I have enough problems as it is without that lunatic Healwell breathing down my neck'.

Advise Dr Healwell whether he has a cause of action in defamation.

University of London LLB Examination
(for External Students) Law of Tort June 1993 Q4

Skeleton Solution

Is the statement defamatory? – does it refer to the plaintiff? – was it published? – are there any defences applicable?

Suggested Solution

Defamation is concerned with the protection of reputations and Dr Healwell's reputation has been threatened in two ways: by the association of his name with the newspaper column and by the local headmaster's letter.

Dealing first with the syndicated column: this purports to carry the recommendations of Dr Healwell. First, are the words themselves defamatory? Many definitions have been given of what constitutes a defamatory statement, but Lord Atkin's dictum in *Sim* v *Stretch* [1936] 2 All ER 1237 is apposite here: 'Would the words tend to lower the plaintiff in the estimation of right-thinking members of society generally?' Clearly, taken at face value, the purported words of Dr Healwell are not defamatory.

In order for them to be construed as defamatory, the plaintiff, Dr Healwell, will have to show that persons having knowledge of particular facts would attach a defamatory meaning to the words. This is an innuendo. In the well-known case of *Tolley* v *JS Fry & Sons Ltd* [1931] AC 333, the plaintiff, a well-known golfer, was caricatured by the defendants – without his knowledge – in an advertisement. He alleged that the suggestion was that he had consented to taking part in the advertisement and this called into question his integrity as an amateur golfer. The same would apply in this case: Dr Healwell would allege in his innuendo that the statement would be taken as coming from him and expressing his sentiments and the idiocy of the statement would call into question his professional competence. The extrinsic facts upon which he would rely to support his innuendo are that he is a doctor who lives in the town, his practice used to be as a children's doctor and that he would not hold such far-fetched views.

Even though the words apparently emanate from Dr Healwell, they in fact are part of a column written by several people and the columnist Dr Healwell does not exist. Therefore the next question is whether the statement refers to the plaintiff. The intention of the writers is immaterial; the test is whether reasonable people would think the reference was to the plaintiff (*Hulton & Co* v *Jones* [1910] AC 20). It is submitted that the test would be satisfied in this problem.

The third essential that the plaintiff must prove is that the words were published. Publication means the communication of the words to at least one other person than the person defamed (*Bata* v *Bata* [1948] WN 366). The column has obviously been published. What is interesting here is the syndication of the column since every repetition of defamatory words is a fresh publication and creates a fresh cause of action. However, for the innuendo to succeed, the plaintiff is relying upon local knowledge, so it is suggested that only an action against the local newspaper will succeed. The potential defendants are the writer of the column, the editor, as well as the publisher.

The defamatory statement is a libel, rather than slander, because it is contained in written form. Therefore it is actionable per se, that is to say, without the plaintiff having to prove special damage.

What defences are there? If the words were published innocently, then the defendants can avail themselves of the Defamation Act 1952, s4. This allows a complete defence on the basis that the words were not defamatory on the face of them and the writers and publishers did not know of circumstances by virtue of which they might be understood to be defamatory of the plaintiff. The defendants would have to publish an apology in the *Westtown Gazette* and pay the plaintiff's costs and expenses reasonably incurred as a result of the publication. None of the other defences – justification, fair comment, privilege – apply here.

Therefore, in terms of the column, the plaintiff may have an action but there would seem to be a statutory defence if those responsible for the column were unaware of the real Dr Healwell's existence.

Turning to the local headmaster: he has written to all the governors of Westtown Academy and therefore, again, one is dealing with libel rather than slander. Are the words defamatory? It is often said that mere abuse is not defamation. As Mansfield CJ said in *Thorley* v *Kerry* (1812) 4 Taunt 355, 'For mere general abuse spoken, no action lies'. However, the word 'spoken' is relevant here. If this were slander and these were words spoken on the heat of the moment then they might not be defamatory. Where the words are written down, as in this case, there has been time for reflection and the abuse takes on a more permanent and damaging meaning. Therefore it is suggested that these words are indeed capable of being defamatory.

It is worth noting here that if this matter came to trial it would be for the judge to decide whether no reasonable man could regard the words as defamatory, and if so, he must withdraw the case from the jury. If he decided to leave the case to the jury, then they would decide whether the words were, in fact, defamatory.

The statement refers to 'that lunatic Healwell' and reasonable people would, given the facts of the case, assume that the letters referred to the plaintiff. There is similarly no difficulty over publication.

Does the headmaster have any defences? Again, a mistake has been made. The headmaster has unintentionally defamed the plaintiff because of the views mistakenly attributed to him. In that sense the words are published innocently and he may avail himself of the Defamation Act defence discussed above.

In all, Dr Healwell does have a cause of action in defamation but he is advised that both defendants might rely on defences to escape liability.

16 TRESPASS TO THE PERSON AND TO LAND

16.1 Introduction

16.2 Key points

16.3 Recent cases

16.4 Analysis of questions

16.5 Questions

16.1 Introduction

Trespass to the person includes the torts of battery, assault and false imprisonment, and like trespass to land it is actionable per se.

16.2 Key points

a) *Battery*

  i) Definition

   A direct act of the defendant which causes contact with the plaintiff's body without the plaintiff's consent.

  ii) Elements

   • the act must be direct; see *Scott* v *Shepherd* [1733] 2 W Bl 892 for the effect of intervening acts.

   • the act must be intentional. It is clear that the tort cannot be committed in the absence of intent: *Stanley* v *Powell* [1891] 1 QB 86, and it cannot be committed negligently: *Letang* v *Cooper* [1965] 1 QB 232; *Miller* v *Jackson* [1977] QB 966; *Wilson* v *Pringle* [1987] QB 237, ie there is no overlap between the torts of battery and negligence. See *Stubbings* v *Webb* [1993] 2 WLR 120 where the House of Lords emphasised the distinct and separate nature of these two torts.

   • the act must be hostile: *Wilson* v *Pringle* (above).

   • there must be active contact with the person of the plaintiff, however slight: *Cole* v *Turner* (1704) 6 Mod 149.

  iii) Defences

   • consent

   eg a medical operation, playing sport in accordance with the rules, but if the defendant steps outside the rules an action in battery may lie: *R* v *Billinghurst* [1978] Crim LR 553. Note that the rationale of consent for everyday jostlings in *Cole* v *Turner* (above) and *Collins* v *Wilcock* [1984] 3 All ER 374 was rejected by the Court of Appeal in *Wilson* v *Pringle* (above).

- self defence

  providing that the steps taken are not out of proportion to the harm threatened: *Lane* v *Holloway* [1968] 1 QB 379.

- contributory negligence

  held to be applicable in *Barnes* v *Nayer* (1986) The Times 19 December

- lawful arrest

- parental authority

b) *Assault*

  i) Definition

  A threat to apply force to another whereby that other is reasonably put in fear of immediate physical contact.

  ii) Elements

  - a threat is sufficient. If actual physical contact occurs the tort of battery is committed

  - the essence of the tort is fear. It now seems that words alone are sufficient: *R* v *Wilson* [1955] 1 WLR 493

  - words may accompany an act and prevent it from being an assault: *Turberville* v *Savage* (1669) 1 Mod Rep 3

  - if the defendant is restrained from physical contact by a third party, the tort of assault is still committed because the plaintiff was in fear of immediate physical contact: *Stephens* v *Myers* (1830) 4 C & P 349.

c) *False imprisonment*

  i) Definition

  The total deprivation of the freedom of another, for any period, however short, without lawful justification.

  ii) Elements

  - the restraint may be physical, eg placing the plaintiff in a locked room, or practical, eg surrounding the plaintiff by threatening persons

  - the restraint must be total. If the plaintiff has a reasonable means of exit no imprisonment has taken place merely because he is inconvenienced: *Bird* v *Jones* (1845) 7 QB 742

  - the restraint must be unlawful; if a condition or restriction on leaving premises is reasonably imposed and the plaintiff chooses not to comply with this, there is no false imprisonment: *Robinson* v *Balmain Ferry* [1910] AC 295

  - there is no obligation to assist another to obtain his freedom: *Herd* v *Weardale Steel Coal & Coke* [1915] AC 67

  - the tort is committed even if the plaintiff is unaware of the restriction on his liberty: *Meering* v *Grahame-White Aviation* (1919) 122 LT 44; *Murray* v *Ministry of Defence* [1988] 2 All ER 521, although this may affect the quantum of damages

- note that a prisoner cannot sue for false imprisonment as regards deprivation of his residual liberty. *Weldon* v *Home Office*; *R* v *Deputy Governor of Parkhurst Prison, ex parte Hague* [1991] 3 WLR 341, although in *Pritchard* v *Ministry of Defence* (1995) The Times 27 January it was held that unlawfully requiring a person to serve in the armed forces could constitute false imprisonment.

iii) Defences

- consent
- lawful arrest; see ss24 and 25 Police and Criminal Evidence Act 1984 and note the trap in *Walters* v *WH Smith* [1914] 1 KB 595 and its recent application in *R* v *Self* [1992] 1 WLR 657
- lawful imprisonment: see s12(1) Prison Act 1952

d) *Intentional infliction of nervous shock*

It was held in *Wilkinson* v *Downton* [1897] 2 QB 57 that where the defendant wilfully does an act calculated to cause physical damage to the plaintiff, and has in fact caused harm, a cause of action arises. See also *Janvier* v *Sweeney* [1919] 2 KB 316.

e) *Trespass to land*

i) Definition

A direct interference with the possession of another's land, without lawful justification.

ii) Elements

- Possession

Possession not ownership gives the right to sue

  - so a landlord can only sue where damage is to his reversion: *Jones* v *Llanrwst UDC* [1911] 1 Ch 393
  - but where a tortfeasor claims possession, the courts are willing to hold that any action by the owner which shows an intent to take possession is sufficient to give the right to sue in trespass: *Ocean Estates* v *Pinder* [1969] 2 AC 19.

- Interference

Must be direct and immediate, eg entry or placing something on land, including resting a ladder on the plaintiff's wall: *Westripp* v *Baldock* [1938] 2 All ER 799.

If a person abuses permission to be on land or refuses to leave when asked he becomes a trespasser: *Robson* v *Hallett* [1967] 2 QB 393.

If the trespass is continuing, a new cause of action arises each day the trespass lasts: *Holmes* v *Wilson* (1839) 10 Ad & El 503.

Some interferences have given rise to problems:

     – highway

Where the highway is used for a purpose which is not reasonably incidental to the purpose of passage, a trespass can be committed against the person in possession of the highway: *Hickman* v *Maisey* [1900] 1 QB 572; *Harrison* v *Duke of Rutland* [1893] 1 QB 142.

     – subsoil

Trespass can be committed against the owner of the subsoil: *Cox* v *Moulsey* (1848) 5 CB 533.

     – airspace

There is no need for contact with the plaintiff's land; an intrusion into the plaintiff's airspace is sufficient: *Kelsen* v *Imperial Tobacco* [1957] 2 QB 334.

However, the intrusion must be at a height which interferes with the property: *Lord Bernstein* v *Skyviews* [1978] QB 479, where it was held that the plaintiff could not sue in respect of an overflying aircraft.

But in *Anchor Brewhouse Developments* v *Berkley House* [1987] 2 EGLR 173 it was held that *Bernstein* was confined to the specific issue of overflying aircraft, so the plaintiff could obtain an injunction to prevent the trespass of the boom of a crane into their airspace despite the considerable cost of complying.

     – trespass ab initio

Where the defendant enters land with the authority of law (rather than of the plaintiff) and later abuses that right he becomes a trespasser ab initio: *The Six Carpenters' Case* (1610) 8 Co Rep 146a; *Cinnamond* v *British Airports Authority* [1980] 2 All ER 368.

iii) Intent

The defendant must have intended to enter the land, but need not have intended to trespass. Hence it is no defence to show that the defendant was unaware the land belonged to someone else: *Conway* v *Wimpey* [1951] 2 KB 266, but it is a defence to show he had no intention of entering the land: *Smith* v *Stone* (1647) Style 65.

iv) Defences

    • licence

There is no trespass where there is express or implied consent; only when the consent is exceeded or revoked can a trespass occur: *Robson* v *Hallett* (above).

    • lawful authority

eg police; to abate a nuisance; public right of way

    • necessity

It was held in *Rigby* v *Chief Constable of Northamptonshire* [1985] 1 WLR 1242 that necessity was a defence to trespass to land, providing that the defendant had not negligently contributed to the necessity.

v) Remedies

* damages

Only nominal damages will be awarded for a trivial trespass.

If the land is damaged, the measure is the loss in value of the land.

* injunction

This is particularly useful where the trespass is continuing or threatened.

* re-entry

A person entitled to possession may re-enter and use reasonable force to eject the trespasser: *Hemmings* v *Stoke Poges Golf Club* [1920] 1 KB 720.

* mesne profits

The plaintiff may sue for profits the defendant has made from his occupation, and for damages for deterioration and costs of obtaining possession.

* ejection

The plaintiff may bring an action for ejectment where he has an immediate right to possession.

* distress damage feasant

Where his land is damaged by a chattel, the plaintiff may retain the chattel until the owner pays compensation. The plaintiff has no right to sell or use the chattel.

* self redress

In clear and simple cases or in an emergency: *Burton* v *Winters* [1993] 1 WLR 1077.

16.3 Recent cases

Weldon v *Home Office* [1991] 3 WLR 341

R v *Deputy Governor of Parkhurst Prison, ex parte Hague* [1991] 3 WLR 341

Stubbings v *Webb* [1993] 2 WLR 120

R v *Self* [1992] 1 WLR 657

Burton v *Winters* [1993] 1 WLR 1077

Pritchard v *Ministry of Defence* (1995) The Times 27 January

16.4 Analysis of questions

A few questions have been set solely on these topics, but trespass often occurs in occupiers' liability questions and as part of a question. However, in view of the recent developments in the law, such as hostile touching, trespass to airspace and false imprisonment of prisoners, these topics may gain popularity with the examiner.

16.5 Questions

QUESTION ONE

Keith is a lecturer in law at the University of Slumsville. One of his duties is to organise moots and mock trials. He arranged with Lucy, a mathematics student, and Mark, a law student, that they would stage an incident which would be the basis of a mock trial. In accordance with the arrangement, as Lucy walked into a mathematics lecture, Mark seized her from behind, tore her shoulder bag from her and rushed from the room. Lucy collapsed and another student, Noel, sprang from his seat and tackled Mark. In the ensuing scuffle, Mark suffered a dislocated shoulder and Noel lost several teeth.

Lucy suffered from a rare medical condition and the incident caused a spasm which constricted her throat and she died of asphyxiation. Neither Lucy nor anyone else had known that she suffered from this condition, but the evidence now is that she could have died at any time if she suffered severe shock. Mark's shoulder injury did not respond to treatment and he is likely to have a permanent disability. He was so distressed by learning of Lucy's death that he suffered a complete nervous breakdown and is unlikely to be able to resume his studies.

Advise Mark, Noel and Lucy's father as to any possible claims in tort.

University of London LLB Examination
(for External Students) Law of Tort June 1990 Q3

Suggested Solution

As regards the incident between Lucy and Mark and its consequences, as Mark's act is intentional we must consider trespass to the person and in particular the tort of battery which consists of the intentional and direct application of force to another person. In *Letang* v *Cooper* [1965] 1 QB 232 it was held that where the act which caused the damage was intentional the cause of action lies in trespass to the person, and this was accepted by the Court of Appeal in *Wilson* v *Pringle* [1987] QB 237. Thus it would appear that there is no overlap between the torts of trespass to the person and negligence, and this view was accepted by the House of Lords in *Stubbings* v *Webb* [1993] 2 WLR 120.

Clearly Mark's actions constitute an intentional and direct application of force to Lucy. However, Lucy has a problem in establishing liability in that in *Wilson* v *Pringle* it was held that the act of touching the plaintiff had to be a 'hostile touching'. In view of Lucy's agreement with Mark to stage the incident the touching would appear to be non-hostile. A further problem for Lucy is that she has consented to the physical contact by Mark and volenti would provide a complete defence to Mark. Even if Lucy was unaware of the exact incident, providing she was aware in general terms of what was to happen this would be enough to support the defence of volenti: *Chatterton* v *Gerson* [1980] 3 WLR 1003; [1981] QB 432.

Noel has committed a battery on Mark as Noel's actions were direct and intentional. Noel would seek to raise the defence of acting in support of the law as he thought that Mark had stolen Lucy's property. By s24(4) Police and Criminal Evidence Act 1984 a person may arrest without warrant any person who is, or who he suspects with reasonable cause to be, in the act of committing an arrestable offence. Section 24(5) also allows any person who has reasonable cause to believe that a person is guilty of an arrestable offence to arrest that person without warrant if that arrestable offence has in fact been committed. Thus Noel has fallen foul of the trap in *Walters* v *W H Smith* [1914] 1 KB 595 in that he must prove that an offence has actually been committed, and it is no defence to show there were reasonable grounds for believing the person arrested to be guilty. Hence Noel cannot rely on the defence that he was acting in support of the law and is liable to Mark in battery. Noel will be prima facie liable for the damage to Mark's shoulder and as regards Noel's lost teeth, he will be regarded as the author of his own misfortune.

Noel could also attempt to justify his attack on Mark on the grounds that Mark was a trespasser in so far as Mark is a law student and the lecture was a mathematics lecture. However, as Noel is not the occupier of the lecture theatre he will have to show that he has the authority of the occupier to eject a trespasser, which seems unlikely. Noel would also have to show that Mark was requested to leave the premises, had a reasonable opportunity to do so, and failed to leave. As no request was made for Mark to leave Noel cannot raise this defence.

As regards the injury to Mark's shoulder, as Noel intended to inflict harm on Mark no question of remoteness of damage will arise: *Quinn* v *Leatham* [1901] AC 495; *Doyle* v *Olby (Ironmongers) Ltd* [1969] 2 QB 158 and Noel will be liable for the damage to Mark's shoulder. As regards Mark's nervous breakdown the question of causation arises, ie what event caused the breakdown. We are told that it was caused by Mark's distress at Lucy's death. Turning to Lucy's death we are told Lucy collapsed after Mark removed her shoulder bag and that Noel attacked Mark after this occurrence. I assume that the 'incident' referred to in the problem which caused the spasm was therefore the removal of the bag by Mark. As Mark intended to harm Lucy then again no question of remoteness of damage would arise and Mark would be liable to Lucy's death, but as we have seen Lucy's consent will provide a total defence to Mark's actions.

Thus we should advise Mark that he can sue Noel in respect of his dislocated shoulder, but that he has no remedy for the nervous breakdown he has suffered. We should advise Noel that he is liable to Mark for Mark's shoulder injury, but has no remedy as regards his lost teeth. We should advise Lucy's father that he has no claim.

We could also consider whether Keith is vicariously liable for the actions of Lucy or Mark. Keith is not the employer of Lucy or Mark but we should consider whether an ad hoc agency has arisen as in *Ormrod* v *Crossville Motor Services* [1953] 1 WLR 1120 where Keith is the principal and Lucy and Mark are his agents acting on his behalf. If so, then the University of Slumsville would be liable for Keith's acts as they are his employer, Keith is their employee and Keith was organising the incident in connection with a mock trial and so was acting in the course of his employment. However, this would not affect the liabilities of the parties as described above.

QUESTION TWO

Arthur has agreed with Bertram to use his front room on the day following the Cup Final in order to watch the local team return triumphant or otherwise, with the Cup. He agrees to pay five pounds for this. On the morning of the day in question Arthur arrives with several friends, some of whom appear to be still intoxicated after the celebrations of the previous night, Bertram says: 'The deal's off. Take this mob away.'

Arthur says: 'You can't do this. We agreed. Let me through.'

He pushes Bertram aside and sits down in the room. Bertram fetches his friend Bruce who throws Arthur out onto the road and injures his back. Arthur's friends who have retreated out of the house in some disarray throw bottles through the windows of Bertram's house.

Advise Bertram.

Written by the editor

Suggested Solution

When Arthur agrees with Bertram to use his front room in return for £5, he is given a contractual licence to enter the premises. Arthur's friends, however, are not part of the agreement, and when they walk up Bertram's path to his house, they have merely an implied gratuitous licence.

Both contractual and gratuitous licences are 'bare licences' and should be distinguished from a licence coupled with a grant where the licensee is granted a proprietary interest in the land to which the licence is ancillary to enable the licensee to enjoy the grant. A bare licence can be revoked at will, subject to the payment of compensation in the case of a contractual licence, whereas a licence coupled with a grant cannot be revoked arbitrarily. Therefore, when Bertram says, 'The deal is off. Take this mob away', he is withdrawing Arthur's contractual licence in respect of which Arthur may be able to claim compensation (although it could be an implied term of the agreement that he would be in a condition suitable to entering the premises) and Arthur's friends' gratuitous licence.

When Arthur pushes Bertram aside and enters the house, there is an assault if Bertram apprehended fear of battery, and a battery since Arthur has intentionally applied force to Bertram. The lightest touch of a person is actionable: *Cole* v *Turner* (1704) 6 Mod 149. Both torts are actionable per se, ie without proof of damage although, if no damage is established, Bertram's entitlement is to nominal damages only, ie a few pounds in recognition that the plaintiff's rights have been infringed.

When Arthur sits down in the front room, he also commits a trespass to land because he has entered without lawful authority or the permission of Bertram, the person in possession. Again, this tort is actionable per se.

When Bertram's friend, Bruce, throws Arthur out of the house and injures his back, he is ejecting a trespasser. If a trespasser enters forcibly the occupier may use reasonable force to eject him without a prior request to leave. Third parties may intervene only as agents of the occupier, and the force used may only be such as is necessary to remove the trespasser; it may not be used as chastisement.

Here Bruce is acting as Bertram's agent, but the force used, if excessive, may be both an assault and a battery and, since injuries were sustained, if Arthur is successful he will recover substantial, as opposed to nominal, damages. The question of whether the force employed was reasonable is a question of fact to be decided by the court in all the circumstances.

Throwing bottles through Bertram's window is an act of criminal damage by Arthur's friends. If Bertram was in the room at the time, it is an assault and battery. The acts also amount to a trespass to land, for this tort can be committed by putting things on to the land: *Turner* v *Thorne and Thorne* (1959) 21 DLR (2d) 29; *Gregory* v *Piper* (1829) 9 B & C 591. This is actionable at the suit of Bertram, the person in possession.

QUESTION THREE

Minos owns a large detached house in its own grounds. It adjoins a park owned by the Cnossos District Council. Visitors frequently go to the park to fly kites, which often blow at some height over Minos's house and garden and occasionally become entangled in his trees or in parts of the house.

One day Icarus, aged 14, went to the park with his father, Daedalus, to fly his kite. A strong wind was blowing towards Minos's house and the kite was blown out of the park and became fouled on the telephone wires attached to the chimney breast of the house. Icarus rang the front door bell to ask for permission to retrieve his kite but received no reply. He took a ladder which he found in the garden and climbed on to the roof. Minos returned home at that point and, seeing Icarus, lost his temper and removed the ladder, locking it away and telling Icarus that he could stay on the roof all night. Daedalus, who had remained in the park, now came into Minos's garden, advanced threateningly and told him that, if he did not replace the ladder, he would give him a thrashing that he would remember for the rest of his life. Minos tried to strike Daedalus with a spade, but Daedalus was able to avoid it and to punch Minos, leaving him lying winded. He then helped Icarus down and they left. Minos later cut down the kite but refuses to give it back to Icarus.

Advise Minos (i) as to whether he can stop the activities of the kite flyers and (ii) as to his rights and liabilities in respect of the incident involving Icarus and Daedalus.

University of London LLB Examination
(for External Students) Law of Tort June 1986 Q4

Skeleton Solution

Nuisance in kites flying over Minos's house – injunction appropriate remedy to stop this and should be sought against the Council – availability of such an injunction and factors considered in granting it. Trespass to land – Icarus not trespasser in merely recovering his kite but, quaere, if so when he climbed onto roof of house. Daedalus a trespasser in entering Minos's property in threatening manner. Assault and battery – Minos could sue Daedalus in assault and battery and Daedalus could sue Minos for assault. False imprisonment – Icarus appears to have a good cause of action for this against Minos. Conversion – Icarus may be able to sue for conversion in respect of his kite.

Suggested Solution

If Minos wishes to stop kites flying over his house and garden from the park owned by Cnossos District Council then he must seek an injunction against the Council. In order to obtain this injunction he must show that the Council is liable in nuisance. This is a case of nuisance rather than trespass to land because the activities of kite-flyers are not a direct interference but only a consequential interference with the use or enjoyment of his property. It may be added that whether an interference is direct or consequential is often a matter of judicial opinion and, as the judgments of the Court of Appeal and speeches in the House of Lords in *Southport Corporation* v *Esso Petroleum Co Ltd* [1956] AC 218; [1954] 2 QB 182 indicate these opinions may differ sharply. Further, in order for a case in trespass to succeed it must be shown that there was an intentional interference with the rights of Minos. The facts of this case do not suggest such on the part of the Council. See *Smith* v *Stone* (1647) Style 65.

As regards an action in nuisance, Minos has an interest in the land affected: *Malone* v *Laskey* [1907] 2 KB 141 (although the need for such an interest was doubted in the Court of Appeal in *Khorasandjian* v *Bush* [1992] 3 WLR 476). Minos appears to satisfy this. The Council is the appropriate defendant in this action because it is the occupier of the park and it seems that as a matter of procedure a nuisance action must be brought against the occupier from whose premises the nuisance emanates: see *Smith* v *Scott* [1973] 1 Ch 314. There should be no difficulty in holding the Council liable in nuisance. The case law strongly suggests that where an occupier of land allows a person onto his premises, whose activities he is in a position to regulate or control, and that person commits a nuisance, then the occupier is liable. See *Matania* v *National Provincial Bank Ltd* [1936] 2 All ER 633. Thus, an occupier is liable for a nuisance committed by an independent contractor whom he invites to his premises and also for the activities of gypsies whom he permits to take up residence on his premises: see *A-G* v *Corke* [1933] Ch 82. Therefore, as the kite-flyers were only visitors to the park whose activities could be regulated or even stopped by the Council, they are accordingly liable for the nuisance caused by them.

The mere fact that a case in nuisance is made out against the Council does not necessarily mean that Minos will get an injunction to prevent kite flying in the future: see *Miller* v *Jackson* [1977] QB 966. This equitable remedy, like all equitable remedies, is discretionary and may only be granted in cases of nuisance, it seems, if on balance the social and other merits of the defendant's conduct are outweighed by plaintiff's right to an injunction. In *Miller* v *Jackson* the Court of Appeal would not have granted an injunction to stop the playing of cricket, even if a nuisance, because socially it was a good thing and, furthermore, account was taken of the fact that the plaintiff had come to the nuisance knowing of it, ie purchasing a house in that case which was next to the cricket ground. This decision has caused some difficulty in that it appears to go against earlier decisions such as *Shelfer* v *City of London Electric Lighting Co* [1895] 1 Ch 287 where the defendant's conduct in operating a power station was stopped because it caused vibrations in the plaintiff's premises even though this was socially useful. The court in that case pointed out that no matter how beneficial a defendant's activity might be if it amounted to a nuisance then, the court would not let him 'buy the right to commit it'. In more recent cases the courts appear to be more inclined to grant an injunction unless it would be unworkable in the circumstances. In *Kennaway* v *Thompson* [1981] QB 88 the plaintiff got an injunction to restrict power boat racing on a lake next to her house. The fact she came to build her house there knowing that such activities took place on the lake was considered but did not prevent the court granting the injunction so as to restrict the increase in the size, noise and frequency of such boats on the lake. In *Tetley* v *Chitty* [1986] 1 All ER 663 an injunction was granted to prevent go-kart racing near the plaintiff's house and the social utility of this activity was given little weight.

In the light of these decisions Minos would appear to have a good prospect of obtaining an injunction. Damages would be of little value to him if he is being constantly bothered by kites becoming entangled in his trees or parts of his house and the consequent trespass by kite-flyers to retrieve them. The Council could easily take steps to forbid kite-flying in the park or, alternatively restrict it to areas of the park where such interference with Minos would not occur. But it may be added that if the number of times kites actually fall on Minos's premises is small he may be refused relief. I doubt if a court would grant an injunction to stop mere kite flying over Minos's premises if the kites were so high as not to interfere with ordinary user by Minos. However, much must depend on the facts for it is one thing to expect him to put up with the occasional kite but quite another to expect him to put up with hundreds of them regularly.

In respect of the incident involving Icarus and Daedalus, Minos may bring proceedings on the basis of trespass to land and assault and battery. But he may also be liable to Icarus for false imprisonment, and trespass to goods, and to Daedalus for assault.

Minos may sue for trespass to land in respect of the kite landing on his property, in respect of Icarus's entry to retrieve it especially by climbing on the roof of his house, and in respect of Daedalus's entry to his garden in a threatening manner. As regards the claim concerning the kite, whether this is trespass depends on whether it is regarded as a 'direct' or a 'consequential' interference with Minos's land. As stated earlier there is some difficulty in the case law over this distinction. The decision in *Gregory* v *Piper* (1829) 9 B & C 591 and some of the judgments in *Southport Corporation* v *Esso Petroleum* suggested that if the defendant intentionally initiated a force which directly caused the kite to land in Minos's land this would be sufficient. Other judgments in the Esso case suggest that this would not be anything but 'consequential' and not actionable in trespass. If the entry of the kite was a trespass then there would have been a 'continuing trespass' for as long as it remained there. See *Konskier* v *Goodman* [1928] 1 KB 421. Icarus would have a duty to remove it and for this purpose he would have a licence to enter onto Minos's land to recover it. In doing this he would not be a trespasser, but it may be otherwise regarding his climbing onto the roof of the house. Further, if the entry of the kite was not of itself a trespass, a similar licence would be inferred so no trespass would arise. See *Anthony* v *Heney* (1832) 8 Bing 186. It may be noted that legal authority on these points is thin and there is little beyond the case cited. So far as Daedalus is concerned his entry onto Minos's land appears to have been made for the purpose of securing the release of Icarus but it was also to threaten Minos. In view of the latter it is difficult to see how Daedalus's entry onto Minos's land could be treated as anything other than an act of trespass. See *Anthony* v *Heney* (above).

Minos may also bring proceedings against Daedalus for assault and battery. Two incidents are relevant here, first the threats which Daedalus made while advancing towards Minos and, second, the punch Daedalus delivered winding Minos. The first incident amounted to an assault since its object was to create an apprehension of imminent harmful or offensive conduct. The words used would have aroused fear in the mind of a reasonable person in the circumstances: see *Read* v *Coker* (1853) 13 CB 850. The second incident amounted to a battery only as it does not appear to have been preceded by any threats by Daedalus: see *Cole* v *Turner* (1704) 6 Mod 149. Daedalus may seek to raise a defence of self-defence in respect of this incident but it is unlikely to succeed if Minos was in no position to hit him with the spade when he delivered his punch. Self-defence only permits the use of such force as is reasonable in the circumstances and, thus, it is also arguable that a punch which left Minos winded was excessive: see *Lane* v *Holloway* [1968] 1 QB 379.

Icarus may have a claim against Minos in false imprisonment in respect of the removal of the ladder so as to leave him stranded on the roof. It may be that he was a trespasser in going onto the roof to retrieve his kite but this does not permit false imprisonment. This tort consists of restricting a person's freedom through actual confinement or preventing him from leaving a place in which he is: see *Balmain New Ferry* v *Robertson* (1906) 4 CLR 379. If Icarus was stranded on the roof without a reasonable means of escape then the elements of the tort are satisfied, see *Meering* v *Graham-White Aviation* (1919)122 LT 44. It is irrelevant that the roof may be spacious or pleasant since the real issue is whether he was prevented from leaving the place: see *Bird* v *Jones* (1845) 7 QB 742. Whether Minos has any defence here is debatable since he appears to have been aware of the reason for Icarus's presence on the roof. But, matters may have been different if he had reasonably believed him to be a burglar and took the action he did in order to confine him so that he could call the police, see *Alderson* v *Booth* [1969] 2 QB 216.

Icarus may also have a claim against Minos for conversion because of the refusal of the latter to give him back the kite: see *Howard Perry* v *British Railways Board* [1980] 1 WLR 1375. Against this claim Minos may be able to allege distress damage feasant in defence, ie that he is entitled to retain the kite until any damage to his property caused by it is compensated.

Daedalus may have a claim against Minos for assault in respect of the incident where the latter attempted to hit him with the spade. The necessary conditions for assault, referred to above, appear to be satisfied.

QUESTION FOUR

Alan is an old age pensioner living with Brian, his nephew, in Stoketon. Brian treats Alan badly, threatening to punch him if he leaves his room without permission. Alan is too frightened to disobey. Their neighbour, Clive, suspects that Alan is badly treated and tells Diane, the Stoketon social services supervisor. Diane tells Clive that social services will arrange a visit but they fail to do so and simply pass on the information to a local pensioner support group. Edward, a volunteer from the group, calls but fails to recognise the signs of age abuse which would be obvious to a professional. Alan becomes so depressed that he tries to commit suicide by jumping out of his window. He breaks his leg and is taken to Stoketon Hospital where Fiona, an experienced medical student working in casualty, fails to recognise the problems that can be caused by bone fractures in the elderly. As a result, Alan does not receive proper treatment and will always have to walk with the aid of a stick. If Alan had received proper treatment, he would have had a reasonable chance of making a full recovery.

Advise Alan.

University of London LLB Examination
(for External Students) Law of Tort June 1991 Q5

Skeleton Solution

Alan v *Brian*: ingredients of torts of assault and false imprisonment.

Alan v *Stoketon Council*: vicarious liability for Diane; the law on omissions: is there a duty to rescue? the special rules for public authorities; causation; prevention of suicide attempts; 'novus actus interveniens'.

Alan v *Edward*: standard of care from a volunteer.

Alan v *Stoketon Hospital*: direct and vicarious liability for hospital staff; standard of care; inexperienced staff; causation; balance of probabilities test; is loss of a chance recoverable in tort?

Suggested Solution

A number of possible claims arise out of the facts given and it will be convenient to consider them separately, although in some claims there will be similar or overlapping issues (such as causation).

Alan v Brian (A v B)

A may sue B for assault. Assault is any act (including words) which causes another person to apprehend the infliction of immediate unlawful force: *Wilson* v *Pringle* [1987] QB 237 CA. B's threat to punch A falls within this definition.

A may also sue B for false imprisonment, which involves the unlawful imposition of constraint on one's freedom of movement from a particular place: *Wilson* v *Pringle*. B's confinement of A to his room under duress falls within this definition.

Both torts are actionable per se.

Alan v Stoketon Council

If Diane was negligent the Council will be vicariously liable as her employer for acts or omissions occurring during the course of her employment.

The first difficulty is in establishing that the Council owed A a duty of care. The failure to arrange the promised visit by the social services department is an example of a pure omission and the law of tort does not impose a positive duty to act (here, effectively, a duty to rescue) unless there is a special relationship between the parties in which one exercises control and the other is dependent on the controlling party.

Mere status does not imply control or duty to rescue; there must be also practical ability to control the particular situation, such as in the case of a lifeguard on the lookout for swimmers in distress: example given by Bowman and Bailey in (1984) Public Law at p277.

The courts are especially reluctant to impose positive duties on public authorities which may be faced with limited resources and difficult operational decisions, eg it has been held that the police are not under a duty to answer a burglar alarm or 999 emergency call in the absence of a contract or other special relationship with the plaintiff: *Alexandrou* v *Oxford* [1993] 4 All ER 328; *Hill* v *Chief Constable of West Yorkshire* [1988] 2 All ER 238 HL.

However, in the present problem Diane had promised to investigate A's circumstances and such assumption of responsibility might be enough to give rise to the duty of care. If so, it is advised that the Council were in breach of that duty by 'passing the buck' to an unprofessional organisation.

The next issue is one of causation. If A had suffered further abuse from B as a result of the failure to investigate, there would be little doubt as to the Council's liability. However, A's actual damage is the broken leg caused by a suicide attempt at a time when he was depressed. Although the Council were under a duty to exercise supervision, it would be going too far to suggest that they were under a duty to prevent a suicide attempt, because they did not have sufficient degree of control over Alan's hour-by-hour movements. Even if they had had such control (eg, if A had been transferred into their custody) a suicide attempt would be unforeseeable in the absence of direct knowledge of A's clinical depression and suicidal tendencies.

For those reasons the present facts are distinguishable from *Kirkham* v *Chief Constable of Greater Manchester Police* [1990] 2 WLR 987 where the police had known of such tendencies in a remand prisoner but had failed to alert the hospital wing which would otherwise have taken protective action. The prisoner's widow was successful in suing the police for negligence (defences of 'ex turpi causa', and 'volenti' were rejected, and the plea of contributory negligence was also regarded as unavailable).

Hence, although the Council were in breach of their duty of general supervision, A cannot sue them for the damage to his leg, which was not caused by such breach of duty. The suicide attempt could be described as a 'novus actus interveniens' breaking the chain of causation leading from the breach of duty to the actual damage sustained.

Alan v *Edward (A* v *E)*

On the existence of a duty of care it has been said that if a person undertakes to perform a voluntary act he is liable if he performs it improperly: per Willes J in *Skelton* v *L & NW Ry* (1867) LR 2 CP 631. Hence the issue here is whether Edward was in breach of the duty he undertook to investigate A's circumstances. The standard of care expected from him was that which would be expected from a member of a 'pensioner support group'. Since the objectives of such a group are wide-ranging and involve activities of a political nature rather than medical or quasi-medical the law would not impose on its members the standards expected from a professional social services worker. Since the facts indicate that the signs of A's age abuse were not obvious to a non-professional such as Edward, he was not in breach of his duty to A. Even if there were a breach of the duty of care, E would not be liable because of the causation issue, which would apply in the same way as in A's claim against the Council (above).

A v *Stoketon Hospital*

If Fiona was negligent Stoketon Hospital (SH) would be liable, either directly for failure to provide competent medical staff or vicariously for the individual act of negligence committed by an employee in the course of employment: *Cassidy* v *Ministry of Health* [1951] 1 All ER 574 CA.

On the issue of medical negligence the test will be whether Fiona failed to diagnose a problem which would have been diagnosed by a responsible body of medical practitioners: *Bolam*'s case [1957] 2 All ER 118. On that test Fiona is in breach of her duty of care to A and her inexperience will not affect her liability because a uniform standard of care is required from all those who undertook the practice of medicine in the casualty unit of the hospital, be they doctors of 30 years' experience or, like Fiona, a student 'learning on the job': *Wilsher* v *Essex Area Health Authority* [1988] 1 All ER 871 HL; [1986] 3 All ER 801 CA. In the law of tort the duty is tailored to the act being performed and not to the actor performing it: *Nettleship* v *Weston* [1971] 2 QB 691 CA (driving a car: learner-driver under same standard of care as qualified driver).

However, even though Fiona was in breach of her duty of care, the issue of causation remains: did her breach cause A's permanent disability? If it can be shown that it was more probable than not that A would have been permanently disabled in any event as a result of the suicide attempt, that will conclude the issue in the hospital's favour, because evidence that D's conduct may have caused or contributed to P's injury will only result in a finding that it did cause that injury if there is no or inadequate evidence of any other causal factor which on the balance of probabilities resulted in the injury: see *Hotson* v *East Berkshire Area Health Authority* [1987] 2 All ER 909 HL where it was found that there was a 25 per cent chance that the delay in diagnosis contributed to the development of D's condition but a 75 per cent chance that it would have happened anyway as a result of established other causes. It was held that the delay in diagnosis was not a cause of the injury on the civil standard of probabilities and so the hospital escaped liability. It was left open whether a lost chance of recovery which could be proved to result from a breach of duty could be compensated in tort, as it clearly is in contract law (*Chaplin* v *Hicks* [1911] 2 KB 786 CA: see further, article Hill (1991) Modern Law Review at p511).

In the present case the facts would seem to suggest that it was Fiona's negligence which prevented A's complete recovery and therefore A may have at least an arguable case for compensation on the basis of his lost chance of complete recovery.

See also chapter 14 question 2 for an example of trespass as part of an examination question.

17 DECEIT, MALICIOUS FALSEHOOD, PASSING OFF

17.1 Introduction

These torts cover the infliction of economic harm, but for historical reasons they are not classed with the economic torts (see chapter 18).

17.2 Key points

a) *Deceit*

i) Definition

The wilful and reckless making of a false statement to another with the intent that the other shall act on reliance upon the statement and that other relies to his injury: *Pasley* v *Freeman* (1789) 3 TR 51.

Note the similarity and the differences between this tort and the tort of negligent misrepresentation; deceit is, in fact, the tort of fraudulent misrepresentation.

ii) Elements

• false statement

The representation must be false and there must be a representation either by speech or conduct: *R* v *Barnard* (1837) 7 C & P 784. Liability may also arise from a failure to speak where:

– an initially true representation becomes false to the knowledge of the maker: *With* v *O'Flanagan* [1936] Ch 575

– the representation is a misleading half-truth: *Nottingham Brick* v *Butler* (1886) 16 QBD 778

– there is a uberrimae fidei contract

– there is a fiduciary relationship between the parties

• representation of existing fact, not:

– mere puff: *Dimmock* v *Hallett* (1866) LR 2 Ch App 21

– opinion: *Bisset* v *Wilkinson* [1927] AC 177 unless the maker had special knowledge: *Brown* v *Raphael* [1958] Ch 636 or the statement was not his true opinion: *Smith* v *Land & House Property Corpn* (1884) 28 Ch D 7

– intention; unless a present intention is misrepresented: *Edgington* v *Fitzmaurice* (1885) 29 Ch D 459

– law

• knowledge of falsity

The false statement must be made knowingly, or without belief in its truth, or recklessly careless whether it be true or false: *Derry* v *Peek* (1889) 14 App Cas 337.

• intention

The defendant must intend that his statement is acted on. No problem arises where the statement is made to the plaintiff directly, but difficulties can arise where the statement is made to a class of persons; compare *Peek* v *Gurney* (1873) LR 6 HL 377 with *Andrews* v *Mockford* [1896] 1 QB 372.

• plaintiff must act on the statement

But the statement need not be the decisive factor as regards the plaintiff's decision: *Edgington* v *Fitzmaurice* (above). If the plaintiff was unaware of the misrepresentation: *Horsfall* v *Thomas* (1862) 1 H & C 90, or regarded it as unimportant: *Smith* v *Chadwick* (1884) 9 App Cas 187, or relied on his own investigations: *Attwood* v *Small* (1838) 6 Cl & Fin 232, reliance will not be present. However, the fact that the plaintiff could have found that the defendant's statement was false will not negate reliance: *Redgrave* v *Hurd* (1881) 20 Ch D 1.

• damage

The plaintiff must show that he has suffered damage from the statement and can recover for all loss, whether or not it was reasonably foreseeable: *Doyle* v *Olby (Ironmongers) Ltd* [1969] 2 QB 158.

b) *Malicious falsehood (or injurious falsehood)*

i) Definition

The making of a false statement, with malice, to a person other than the plaintiff which causes damage to the plaintiff, as in eg *Ratcliffe* v *Evans* [1892] 2 QB 524.

Note the distinction between deceit, malicious falsehood and defamation, namely: in deceit the false statement must be made to the plaintiff; in malicious falsehood it is made to a third party.

Defamation is an attack on the plaintiff's reputation; malicious falsehood is typically an attack on the plaintiff's business or property, although there can be an overlap with defamation: *Joyce* v *Sengupta* [1993] 1 WLR 337.

ii) Elements

• false statement

As in deceit there must be a statement of fact, not puff, opinion, etc. Compare *White* v *Mellin* [1895] AC 154 and *De Beers* v *Electric Co of New York* [1975] 1 WLR 972 for the difference between a trader boosting his own goods and denigrating the plaintiff's goods.

- malice

  ie an improper motive such as spite or a wish to injure the plaintiff. If the defendant knows his statement is false, or is reckless whether it be true or false, then malice is present. An honest belief in the truth of the statement, or absence of intent to injure the plaintiff, shows an absence of malice: *Balden* v *Shorter* [1933] Ch 247.

- damage

  The plaintiff must suffer damage from the statement. Proof of general loss of business is sufficient: *Ratcliffe* v *Evans* (above), and note s3 Defamation Act 1952 and its application in *Kaye* v *Robertson* [1991] FSR 62.

c) *Passing off*

  i) Definition

  There must be 'a misrepresentation, made by a trader in the course of trade, to a prospective customer of his or ultimate consumer of goods or services supplied to him, which is calculated to injure the business or goodwill of another trader (in the sense that this is a reasonably foreseeable consequence) and which causes actual damage to a business or goodwill of the trader by whom the action is brought or will probably do so' per Lord Diplock in *Erven Warnink* v *Townend* [1979] AC 731.

  As the elements are self-explanatory we shall look at the ways in which the tort may be committed:

  ii) Methods of passing off

  - direct statement that goods belonging to the plaintiff belong to the defendant, as in *Lord Byron* v *Johnson* (1816) 2 Mer 29
  - imitating the appearance of the plaintiff's goods, eg *White Hudson* v *Asian Organisation* [1964] 1 WLR 1466; *Reckitt & Coleman Products* v *Borden Inc* [1990] 1 All ER 873. Note the extension of this concept to advertising campaigns: *Cadbury-Schweppes* v *Pub Squash* [1981] 1 WLR 193.
  - using a similar name for goods eg *Reddaway* v *Banham* [1896] AC 199; *Bollinger* v *Costa Brava Wine* [1960] Ch 262; *Erven Warnick* v *Townend* (above); *Mothercare* v *Penguin Books* (1987) The Times 8 July, but note that the plaintiff cannot protect the name of a class of goods: *British Vacuum Cleaner* v *New Vacuum Cleaner* [1907] 2 Ch 312.
  - using the plaintiff's name, ie the use of the plaintiff's name as opposed to the name of the plaintiff's goods: *Maxim's Ltd* v *Dye* [1977] 1 WLR 1155.
  - using the defendant's name. The defendant may not use his own name if that would mislead the public: *Parker-Knoll* v *Knoll International* [1962] RPC 265.

  Note that if the parties are not in the same trade it is more difficult for the plaintiff to prove that the public will be misled: *Granada* v *Ford Motor Co* [1972] FSR 103; *McCullough* v *May* [1947] 2 All ER 845. Similarly where the product is only bought by professionals who would not be misled by any attempted deception: *Hodgkinson & Corby* v *Wards Mobility Services* [1994] 1 WLR 1564.

Note also the relevance of the perception of the public and the effect of a disclaimer: *Associated Newspapers* v *Insert Media* [1991] 3 All ER 535. Finally note that the mere copying, however deliberate or provocative, of the name or style which another trader had used for his goods or services is not necessarily sufficient to found an action in passing off: *County Sound* v *Ocean Sound* (1979) The Times 7 November.

iii) Remedies

Injunction and/or damages or the profits of the passing off.

17.3 Recent cases

Associated Newspapers v *Insert Media* [1991] 3 All ER 535

Kaye v *Robertson* [1991] FSR 62

Reckitt & Coleman Products v *Borden Inc* [1990] 1 All ER 873

Joyce v *Sengupta* [1993] 1 WLR 337

Taittinger v *Allbev Ltd* [1993] 4 All ER 75

Hodgkinson & Corby v *Wards Mobility Services* [1994] 1 WLR 1564

17.4 Analysis of questions

No questions have been set on the above topics in recent years, but they may occur in questions set primarily on the economic torts. See, for example, Chapter 18, question 1.

18 THE ECONOMIC TORTS

18.1   Introduction

18.2   Key points

18.3   Recent cases

18.4   Analysis of questions

18.5   Questions

18.1 Introduction

Here we are concerned with the intentional, as opposed to negligent infliction of harm on another. Many of the cases are concerned with industrial action and alleged unlawful competition, and this area is still being developed by the courts. There are, however, limitations to this development as there is no common law requirement that parties must trade fairly: *Associated Newspapers* v *Insert Media* [1988] 1 WLR 509. Note that this is not the position in European Community law: in *Akzo Chemie* v *Commission of the European Communities* (1991) The Times 7 October (Case C–62/86) the European Court held that Article 86 of the Treaty of Rome prohibited a dominant undertaking from eliminating a competitior by means other than competition on merit and that not all price competition was legitimate.

18.2 Key points

a) *Background*

In *Mogul Steamship* v *McGregor, Gow* [1892] AC 25 the House of Lords held that conspiracy to injure the plaintiff was not actionable as the defendant had not committed an unlawful act vis-à-vis the plaintiff. Similarly, in *Allen* v *Flood* [1898] AC 1 it was again held that the plaintiff could not sue the defendant in the absence of an unlawful act. But in *Quinn* v *Leatham* [1901] AC 495 it was held that the defendants had conspired unjustifiably to inflict harm on the plaintiff and so were liable. The difference between *Quinn* and *Mogul* and *Allen* is that in *Quinn* there was more than one defendant, and the rule that a number of persons acting together can make a lawful act actionable is confined to conspiracy to injure and is not to be extended: *Lonrho* v *Shell Petroleum Co (No 2)* [1982] AC 173.

We shall now consider the various economic torts.

b) *Conspiracy*

i) Definition

The agreement of two or more persons to do an unlawful act or a lawful act by unlawful means: *Mulcahy* v *R* (1868) LR 3 HL 306, 317. The second part of this definition covers the anomalous tort in *Quinn* v *Leatham* (above).

In *Lonrho* v *Fayed* [1991] 3 WLR 188; [1991] 3 All ER 303 the House of

Lords held that the tort of conspiracy to injure could be established either by showing that an intention to injure the plaintiff in his business was the predominant purpose, even though the means used were lawful and would not have been actionable if carried out by an individual, or by showing that unlawful means were used. But where there was intent to injure the plaintiff and unlawful means were used it was no defence to show that their predominant purpose was to protect their own interests; it was sufficient that they had used unlawful means to constitute the tort.

ii) Common elements

- two or more persons. Note that a company can conspire with its directors, and a husband and wife can conspire with each other.
- parties combine. No contractual agreement is required, merely that the parties combine for a common purpose.
- damage to the plaintiff is required.

iii) Unlawful act conspiracy

This includes conspiracy to commit a crime or tort and probably a breach of contract.

iv) Lawful act by unlawful means conspiracy

Because it is anomalous (see (a) above) the scope of this tort has been restricted. In *Crofter Hand Woven Harris Tweed* v *Veitch* [1942] AC 435 it was held that no action would lie where the predominant purpose of the defendants was not to injure the plaintiff but rather to defend their own interests, *providing no unlawful means were used*. The defendants may not avail themselves of this defence if they are motivated by spite: *Huntley* v *Thornton* [1957] 1 WLR 321.

c) *Inducing a breach of contract*

This is the most developed of the economic torts and dates back to *Lumley* v *Gye* (1853) 2 El & Bl 216.

i) Forms of the tort

In *Thomson* v *Deakin* [1952] Ch 646 three forms were identified:

- direct persuasion to break a contract eg *Lumley* v *Gye* (1853) 2 El & Bl 216
- defendant prevents performance by direct and unlawful means
- defendant induces third party to break his contract with his employer so that the employer is unable to peform his contract with the plaintiff. For this third form there are four elements: the defendant must have known of the contract between the plaintiff and the employer; the defendant must have intended to breach this contract; the employees must have broken their contracts of employment; the breach between the employer and the plaintiff must have been a necessary consequence of the breach by the employees of their contracts of employment. Note the application of these criteria in *Thomson* v *Deakin* (above) and its application in *Middlebrook Mushrooms* v *Transport and General Workers Union* (1993) The Times 18 January. It may

be difficult in particular cases to decide which form of the tort has occurred: *Stratford* v *Lindley* [1965] AC 269.

- in *Law Debenture Trust Corpn* v *Ural Caspian Oil Corpn* [1994] 3 WLR 1221 it was held that the tort did not cover a situation where the right violated was a secondary right to a remedy arising out of the inducement of a breach.

ii) Knowledge and intention

The defendant must have knowledge of the contract broken and have intended to bring about a breach of contract; the tort cannot be committed negligently.

The exact nature of the breach need not be known; in *Merkur Island Shipping* v *Laughton* [1983] 2 AC 570 it was held that trade union officials must be deemed to know that industrial action would lead to a breach of contract. Recklessness is sufficient intent: *Emerald Construction* v *Lowthian* [1966] 1 WLR 691.

iii) Breach

Actual breach is not required; it is sufficient if the performance of the contract is interfered with: *Torquay Hotel Co* v *Cousins* [1969] 2 Ch 106.

iv) Damage

Damage to the plaintiff is essential, but the courts are willing to infer that a breach of contract has caused damage.

v) Justification

Self-interest: *South Wales Miners' Federation* v *Glamorgan Coal* [1905] AC 239 or altruistic motives: *Greig* v *Insole* [1978] 1 WLR 302 is not justification. The defence was reviewed in *Edwin Hill* v *First National Finance* [1989] 3 All ER 801 where the possession of an equal or superior right to the plaintiff was held to constitute justification, as was a moral duty to intervene: *Brimelow* v *Casson* [1924] 1 Ch 302, or the fact that the contract interfered with was inconsistent with a previous contract with the interferer: *Smithies* v *National Association of Operative Plasterers* [1909] 1 KB 310.

d) *Intimidation*

The modern law here dates from *Rookes* v *Barnard* [1964] AC 1129.

i) Definition

Consists of threats by the defendant to a third party that the defendant will use unlawful means against the third party unless the third party does or refrains from some act and the plaintiff suffers loss as a result.

ii) Elements

- threat

The defendant must threaten or put pressure on the third party, and the courts distinguish between a threat and a warning.

- unlawful means or act

  The threat must be of some unlawful means or act, which includes a crime, tort or breach of contract: *Rookes* v *Barnard* (above).

- submission to threat

  The third party must submit to the defendant's threat.

- damage

  The plaintiff must suffer damage.

- justification

  It is unclear whether justification exists as a defence.

See *Godwin* v *Uzoigwe* (1992) The Times 19 June for a recent example of this tort.

e) *Interference with trade by unlawful means*

This has only recently been recognised as a separate tort in *Merkur Island Shipping* v *Laughton* (above) and *Hadmor Productions* v *Hamilton* [1983] 1 AC 191; [1982]) 2 WLR 322.

Unlawful means includes a crime, tort or breach of contract, but in *Lonrho* v *Shell Petroleum Co (No 2)* (above) the defendants were in breach of a penal statute and the breach interfered with the plaintiff's business, but the plaintiff could not recover. Also in *Chapman* v *Honig* [1963] 2 QB 502 it was held there was no action in tort in respect of a contempt of court, whereas in *Acrow* v *Rex Chainbelt* [1971] 1 WLR 1676 a contempt of court was held to be unlawful means when the plaintiff suffered loss thereby.

In *Lonrho* v *Fayed* [1989] 2 All ER 65 the Court of Appeal held that it was not an essential element that the predominant purpose was to injure the victim rather than to further the defendant's own interest. Nor was it necessary to prove the existence of a complete tort between the tortfeasor and the person against whom the wrong was committed. However, it was necessary to prove that the unlawful act was directed against the plaintiff or was intended to harm the plaintiff. In *Associated British Ports* v *Transport and General Workers Union* [1989] 1 WLR 939 it was suggested in the Court of Appeal that the defendant union was liable for causing its members to contravene regulations, even though the breach was not actionable by the employers and the union could not be liable for inducing a breach. It was the presence of an intent to injure the plaintiff which turned a non-actionable inducement of breach into unlawful means. This is difficult to reconcile with *Lonrho* v *Shell Petroleum Co (No 2)* (above), but this tort is still a developing area.

f) *Immunity of statute*

Note that many economic tort cases have concerned industrial action, and often there is statutory immunity from action in tort.

18.3 Recent cases

Edwin Hill v *First National Finance* [1989] 3 All ER 801

Lonrho v *Fayed* [1991] 3 All ER 303

Akzo Chemie v *Commission of the European Communities* (1991) The Times 7 October (Case C–62/86)

Godwin v *Uzoigwe* (1992) The Times 18 June

Law Debenture Trust Corpn v *Ural Caspian Oil Corpn* [1994] 3 WLR 1221

Middlebrook Mushrooms Ltd v *Transport & General Workers Union* (1993) The Times 18 January

18.4 Analysis of questions

Questions on the economic torts are regularly set, but candidates should have a good overall grasp of this area and a reasonable knowledge of cases before attempting such questions. It is also vital to keep up to date as important modifications are still being made by the courts to the ingredients of these torts.

18.5 Questions

QUESTION ONE

Conrad owns and manages a private college giving instruction in art and photography. Daisy, who had dropped out of a course at the college, gave a talk to a meeting of the League of Righteous Ladies describing how students had to pose naked and indecently in some of the classes. Emma and Florence who were at this talk resolved to do something about the situation at the college.

A few days after the talk Emma was told by Gordon, who rented rooms in her house, that he had applied to enrol at Conrad's college. Emma said to him, 'If you sign up to go to that college, you'll be out in the street, bag and baggage, before the day is out.' Gordon did not want to have to look for new lodgings and telephoned the college to withdraw his application.

Florence is employed by the education department of the local authority. Her job is to process applications for student grants. When students enquire whether grants are available for courses at Conrad's college, she tells them that the authority has resolved not to make any awards for courses there, although she knows that this is untrue. As a result some students decide not to apply to the college. Two students who had previously had grants for the first year of a course applied for renewal of their grants for the second year. Florence did not put these applications before the appropriate committee, but told the students that they had been turned down. The students had to withdraw from the college.

Advise Conrad whether he had any action in tort in respect of the conduct of Emma and Florence.

University of London LLB Examination
(for External Students) Law of Tort June 1988 Q4

Skeleton Solution

Emma – intimidation – threat– unlawful means – breach of contract? – submission – damage – justification – interference with trade by unlawful means – Florence – malicious falsehood – false statement – malice – conspiracy – lawful or unlawful means? – justification.

Suggested Solution

Conrad may have a cause of action against Emma and Florence arising out of their activities. Although we are asked to advise Conrad whether he has a cause of action, in many cases it would be easier if the college were to be the plaintiff in any action because the activities of Emma and Florence were aimed against the college rather than against Conrad personally. As each incident raises different issues of legal principle we will deal with them separately.

The first issue relates to the conversation between Emma and Gordon. In threatening to throw Gordon out on the street Emma may have committed one of the economic torts against Conrad. It is unlikely to be the tort of inducing breach of contract (*Lumley* v *Gye* (1853) 2 El & Bl 216) because at the time of the conversation Gordon had only applied to go to the college and so there was no contract between Gordon and the college which Emma could seek to persuade Gordon to break. Nor is there a contract which Emma could interfere with.

Instead Conrad could argue that Emma has committed the tort of intimidation in its three party form. This tort was resurrected from obscurity in *Rookes* v *Barnard* [1964] AC 1129. This tort consists of a threat by the defendant against a third party that the defendant will use some unlawful means against the third party unless the third party does or refrains from doing some act which he is entitled to do and as a result the plaintiff suffers loss.

The first thing which must be established is that the defendant has threatened the third party. The courts formally distinguish between a threat and a warning; a threat being of an 'or else' kind. Here it seems clear that Emma has threatened Gordon. Secondly the threat must be of some unlawful act or means. Here the most likely unlawful means is breach of contract if Emma is threatening to throw Gordon out on to the street in breach of contract. In *Rookes* v *Barnard* (above) it was held by the House of Lords that breach of contract counts as unlawful means for the purposes of the tort of intimidation. Lord Devlin stated that a threat to breach a contract could be as coercive as a threat of violence and so must count as unlawful means. However if Emma is threatening to terminate Gordon's licence to occupy the premises lawfully then there will be no unlawful means and the tort will not have been committed.

Assuming the existence of unlawful means the third ingredient is submission to the threat by the third party. Again this is satisfied because Gordon has withdrawn his application. Fourthly the plaintiff must have suffered damage. Damage is the very gist of the action but the courts are generally willing to infer that the defendant's actions have caused loss to the plaintiff and do not require proof of particular damage. The problem here is that we do not know whether the college would have offered Gordon a place but in general it can be said that if people are dissuaded from applying to the college it must inevitably suffer damage.

Finally there may be a defence of justification. In *Rookes* Lord Devlin left open the question whether such a defence exists, but in *Morgan* v *Fry* [1968] 2 QB 710 Lord Denning suggested that such a defence does exist. Emma may argue that her threat was justified because of the fact that students had to pose naked and indecently in some of the classes and that she was justified in seeking to dissuade people from attending the college. In *Brimelow* v *Casson* [1924] 1 Ch 302, which was a case concerned with the tort of inducing breach of contract, it was held that the defendant union official was justified in inducing actresses to break their contracts of employment with the plaintiff because their wages were so low that they had to resort to prostitution to supplement their wages. So the court may be prepared to have regard to such moral issues and Emma may be able to succeed with the defence of justification. But it must be noted that we do not know whether these allegations are true because Emma was informed of them by a student who had dropped out of the college and who may have had a grudge against the college. If the allegations are untrue Emma will not be able to rely on the defence of justification.

Secondly Conrad could argue that Emma had committed the tort of interference with trade or business by unlawful means. Such a tort has been recognised on a number of occasions; most recently by the House of Lords in *Hadmor Productions* v *Hamilton* [1983] 1 AC 191; [1982] 2 WLR 322 and *Merkur Island Shipping Corp* v *Laughton* [1983] 2 AC 570. See also the Court of Appeal decision in *Lonrho* v *Fayed* [1989] 2 All ER 65. It is clear that there has been an interference with Conrad's business because Gordon has been persuaded to withdraw his application to attend the college. The problem is in establishing the existence of unlawful means. Once again the unlawful means could only consist of a threat by Emma to break her contract with Gordon unless he withdraws his application and again it is clear that breach of contract counts as unlawful means.

In relation to Florence it could be said that she has committed the tort of malicious falsehood in telling students that the authority has decided not to make any grant awards for courses there even though she knows that this is untrue. Malicious falsehood (sometimes referred to as injurious falsehood) consists of the making of a false statement, with malice, to a person other than the plaintiff, with the result that the plaintiff suffers damage. The false statement must be a statement of fact and this is clearly satisfied here. Conrad will have to prove that Florence made the statement maliciously; that is that she acted out of spite or a desire to injure the plaintiff. Here Florence knows that the statement is false and she has made the statement in order to inflict injury on the college and so it is submitted that Conrad will be able to prove that Florence was actuated by malice (*Greers Ltd* v *Pearman & Corder Ltd* (1922) 39 RPC 406). Finally Conrad must show that he has suffered damage as a result of Florence's statement and this should be satisfied because we are told that as a result of her information students have not applied to the college. Generally Conrad must show that he has suffered special damage but this can be satisfied by showing that he has suffered a general loss of business as a result of Florence's false statement (*Ratcliffe* v *Evans* [1892] 2 QB 524). Section 3 of the Defamation Act 1952 may apply if Florence has informed the students in writing or other permanent form. The effect of the application of s3 would be to dispense with the need to prove special damage. Alternatively Conrad may wish to use the tort of malicious falsehood as the unlawful means for the purposes of the tort of interference with trade or business by unlawful means.

In relation to the two students who have had to withdraw their applications, if the students were contractually obliged to return to the college then Conrad may have an action against Florence for inducing the students to break their contracts with the college. It could be argued that she has committed the tort by preventing performance of the contract taking place by some other direct and unlawful means (that is other than by persuasion). This is analagous to the example cited by Jenkins LJ in *DC Thomson* v *Deakin* [1952] Ch 646 of a defendant wrongfully taking the contracting party's tools so that he was unable to carry out his contractual obligations. It is essential to note that unlawful means is essential to this branch of the tort and here the unlawful means would have to consist of her failure to put the grant applications before the appropriate committee (this could be unlawful means if the students were contractually or statutorily entitled to have their applications considered).

Finally Conrad may have an action against Emma and Florence in the tort of conspiracy. We are told that they 'resolved to do something about the situation at the college'. To establish the existence of this tort it must be shown that there was a combination between Emma and Florence. This will no doubt arise because of the fact that they have resolved to do something about the situation. So although they carry out the acts separately it is likely that there will be a conspiracy because they have a common aim. The only issue is whether this is lawful means conspiracy or unlawful means conspiracy. In this connection it is important to note that it is unclear whether breach of contract constitutes unlawful means (the point was left open in *Rookes* v *Barnard* (above)), although the malicious falsehood would certainly count as unlawful means (*Sorrell* v *Smith* [1925] AC 700). The distinction is important in this connection because there is a much wider role for the defence of justification in the lawful means conspiracy then there is in unlawful means conspiracy (see *Crofter Hand Woven Harris Tweed Co Ltd* v *Veitch* [1942] AC 435). If it was held to be lawful means conspiracy they would probably be able to justify their acts but if, as is more likely, it is held to be unlawful means conspiracy then the success of the defence will depend upon the issues we considered above in relation to *Brimelow* v *Casson*.

Finally the remedies which may be open to Conrad are injunctions to restrain the commission of these torts in the future and damages for any losses sustained as a result of the torts committed by Emma and Florence.

QUESTION TWO

Catherine runs a highly successful catering business, which has attracted much custom away from older-established businesses run by Dora and Emma. Catherine made an exclusive contract with Fergus under which he was to supply fresh fruit and vegetables to her business as required. Catherine won an important order to provide the lunch for a business convention. She placed orders with Fergus, including one for papaya which the organisers had specifically requested. Dora told Fergus correctly that six South African businessmen were to be attending the lunch and was not surprised that Fergus (who is secretary of a local anti-apartheid group) refused to carry out the order. Dora and Emma also bought up all the available supplies of papaya. Catherine was obliged to make special arrangements at considerable expense to fly in papaya from Malaysia for the luncheon; she was able to procure other fruit and vegetables locally, although some was of inferior quality.

Advise Catherine whether she has any cause of action against Dora or Emma.

University of London LLB Examination
(for External Students) Law of Tort June 1987 Q5

Skeleton Solution

Catherine's initial act fair competition – direct intervention by Dora – direct – breach or interference? – justification – purchase of papaya – indirect form of tort – no unlawful means – conspiracy – justification.

Suggested Solution

Catherine has won customers from Dora and Emma by fair competition and the latter have no lawful cause of complaint arising out of the fact that they have lost customers to Catherine. Catherine has now suffered loss as a result of the refusal of Fergus to deliver the order and because of the fact that Dora and Emma have bought up all the available supplies of papaya. As these two issues raise different legal points we will deal with them separately.

Dora has 'told' Fergus correctly that six South African businessmen would be attending the lunch and as a result Fergus has refused to carry out the order. Catherine may have a cause of action against Dora for the tort of inducing breach of contract. The form of the tort which is alleged to have been committed is the direct form of the tort. The direct form of the tort is committed when a person directly persuades one of the contracting parties to break his contract with the plaintiff (see *D C Thomson & Co Ltd* v *Deakin* [1952] Ch 646). Dora may argue that she did not attempt to persuade Fergus but that she merely 'told' him correctly who would be attending the lunch. It is true that the courts do formally draw a distinction between persuasion and the mere giving of advice, but in *Square Grip Reinforcement Co Ltd* v *MacDonald* 1968 SLT 65 Lord Milligan held that where the party who conveys the information was desperately anxious to achieve a particular result then the court was likely to interpret such a suggestion as constituting persuasion. Applying this test here, Fergus was the secretary of the local anti-apartheid group and so Dora must have known that the likely effect of her telling Fred that South Africans were to be at the lunch would be that he would refuse to carry out the order with Catherine. Given that Dora seems to be intent upon securing revenge against Catherine for taking her customers away, it is likely to be the case that Dora was desperately anxious that Fergus breach his contract with Catherine. So it would appear that the persuasion element is satisfied.

Catherine must also show that Dora acted with the requisite knowledge and intention; that is that she intended that a breach of contract would ensue as a result of her information or that she was reckless as to whether or not a contract would be breached (*Emerald Construction Co* v *Lowthian* [1966] 1 WLR 691). It is likely that she would intend to breach the contract because she appeared to know that Fergus was supplying the order for the lunch.

Thirdly Catherine must show that a breach of contract ensued as a result of the persuasion by Dora. Fergus was, however, to supply fruit and vegetables 'as required'. It is therefore unclear what the nature of the relationship was between Fergus and Catherine. It may have been that there was a long term contract between them or it may have been that there was a separate contract between them each time that Catherine ordered the goods. Whatever the precise nature of their contractual relationship, it is submitted that the fact that Catherine had 'placed an order' with Fergus indicates that there was a contractual relationship between them and so there was a breach of contract induced. Had it been the case that there was no breach, but only an interference with the contract, then it would have been difficult for Catherine to succeed with her action because it is uncertain whether the tort of interference with contractual relations extends to the direct form of the tort due to the lack of unlawful means. In *Torquay Hotel Co Ltd v Cousins* [1969] 2 Ch 106 Lord Denning did appear to say that the tort of interference with contractual relations could be committed in its direct form, but in *Merkur Island Shipping Corp v Laughton* [1983] 2 AC 570 Lord Diplock interpreted Lord Denning's judgment as referring to the indirect form of the tort. It is submitted that the latter interpretation is the one which is generally accepted as being part of English law, so that if it was the case that there had been no breach then it is unlikely that Dora would have committed any tort.

Fourthly Catherine must show that she has suffered damage as a result of the breach. This she clearly has because she was unable to secure her usual supply of vegetables and so she has supplied the diners with vegetables of an inferior quality. However Dora could argue that Catherine has suffered no loss because Fergus would have been unable to perform the contract anyway because she and Emma had bought up all the available supplies of papaya. Although this may be true in relation to the papaya, there is no suggestion that the contract with Fergus was confined to the supply of papaya so that, in so far as Fergus would otherwise have delivered other fruit and vegetables to Catherine, Catherine would be able to show that she had suffered damage. Finally it must be shown that there was no justification for the action of Dora. Dora is likely to argue that her action was justified because apartheid is contrary to public policy as are dinners to which supporters of such a regime are invited. However the defence of justification is of uncertain ambit in this tort. The only case in which the defence has succeeded is *Brimelow v Casson* [1924] 1 Ch 302 where the employees' wages were so low that they were compelled to resort to prostitution to supplement their wages. It was held that this exceptional fact was sufficient to justify the defendant's action in inducing the employees to break their contracts of employment. However in *Greig v Insole* [1978] 1 WLR 302 it was held that the pursuit of altruistic goals did not constitute a justification for inducing another to breach his contract. Therefore Catherine may have a cause of action against Dora for inducing a breach of her contract with Fergus.

Catherine may also have a cause of action against Dora and Emma for buying up all the papaya so that Fergus was unable to perform his contract with her. Here two causes of actions may lie. The first is the tort of inducement of breach of contract. In this instance it would be by preventing the performance of the contract taking place by some direct means other than persuading Fergus not to perform the contract. One example given by Jenkins LJ in *Thomson v Deakin* was of a defendant taking the employee's tools so that the employee was unable to carry out his contract with his employer. In this version of the tort it must be shown that the defendants used unlawful means in preventing Fergus from performing his contractual obligations. Dora and Emma achieved their aim by buying up all the available papaya on the market and so they achieved their aim by lawful means and so no action would lie against them for the tort of inducing breach of contract.

An action may, however, lie against them in the tort of conspiracy. The tort of conspiracy consists of two distinct branches; conspiracy to commit an unlawful act and conspiracy to do an act which, if done by an individual would not be actionable, but which becomes actionable by virtue of the fact that it is done in combination. Here we are concerned with the second of these two branches. There is a combination between Emma and Dora and Catherine suffers damage as a result of their combination so these elements of the tort are satisfied. To succeed in this form of the tort it must be shown that Dora and Emma acted with the predominant purpose of inflicting damage upon Catherine, *Lonrho* v *Fayed* [1991] 3 All ER 303. In the case of *Crofter Hand Woven Harris Tweed Co Ltd* v *Veitch* [1942] AC 435 it was held that pursuit of self interest constituted a justification for this form of the tort. The difficulty here is that Dora and Emma do not appear to have acted out of self interest but out of a desire to inflict damage upon Catherine. They could, however, seek to argue that their purpose was the pursuit of self interest in that they were simply buying up products for their own businesses. Alternatively Dora and Emma could argue that their real aim was to protest against apartheid. In *Scala Ballroom (Wolverhampton) Ltd* v *Ratcliffe* [1958] 1 WLR 1057 it was held that a refusal by union members to play at a ballroom which operated a colour bar was justified. The difficulty for Dora and Emma is, however, to show that their real aim was to protest against apartheid and not to inflict damage upon Catherine. Therefore it is submitted that Dora and Emma have committed the tort of conspiracy for which they will be liable in damages to Catherine.

Therefore Catherine will be able to recover the loss which she has suffered as a result of the torts committed by Dora and Emma. She will be able to recover the expense which she incurred in flying to Malaysia to obtain the papaya because Dora and Emma had bought up all the local supplies. Catherine had been specifically asked to provide papaya for the meal and so it was reasonable for her to fly in papaya from Malaysia. Both Dora and Emma knew that Catherine needed the papaya so they could not argue that the loss was too remote. Catherine can also recover for the loss which she has suffered as a result of the provision of inferior vegetables.

QUESTION THREE

Anne, Betty, Christine, and David are members of the Blackhill Common committee, whose aim is to prevent the planned building of an American nuclear missile base at Blackhill Common. Anne, Betty and Christine are morally opposed to the use of nuclear weapons and their presence anywhere in Britain. David is a building contractor in the town of Lymeswold near to an alternative site for the base, who hopes to secure lucrative building contracts if the base cannot be built at Blackhill Common and so is sited near Lymeswold.

The committee learns that Michael has a contract with the Ministry of Defence to carry out building work at Blackhill Common and resolve to disrupt the contract by the following methods:

a) Anne informs Norman who has put in a bid to supply Michael with bricks that, if he does not withdraw the bid, the Committee will ensure that all local authorities opposed to nuclear weapons will be told of his involvement so that they will not deal with him in the future.

b) David offers Oliver, who has been engaged by Michael to survey the Blackhill Common site, a large sum of money if he does not carry out the survey.

Norman withdraws his bid and Oliver agrees not to carry out the survey. As a result Michael is not able to do work on time and the contract is terminated by the Ministry of Defence.

Advise Michael.

Written by the editor

Suggested Solution

Michael will bring actions against the various defendants with the area of economic torts.

The committee's resolution to disrupt the contract may involve a conspiracy to injure and here Michael will sue Anne, Betty and Christine and David. He must prove an agreement of two or more persons to do an unlawful act or a lawful act by unlawful means (and one conspirator alone may be found liable in tort). Where unlawful means are not used, the court must consider the motive of the conspirators in order to ascertain whether they desired to injure the plaintiff, or whether their predominant interest was, for example, to protect their business interests (*Lonrho* v *Shell Petroleum Co (No 2)* [1982] AC 173; [1981] 3 WLR 33; [1981] 2 All ER 456), *Lonrho* v *Fayed* [1991] 3 All ER 303. In *Crofter Hand Woven Harris Tweed* v *Veitch* [1942] AC 435; [1942] 1 All ER 147 there was no conspiracy where trade unionists sought to improve terms and conditions of employment in tweed mills, rather than to injure the plaintiff.

In Michael's case, the defendants may argue that their predominant purpose was a political and moral one, rather than the desire to cause injury to him. However, the object of the defendants may also be said to be the disruption of Michael's contract, so that the conspiracy becomes one of unlawful means; if injury has, as a result, been caused to Michael, then the tort has been committed. The motive or object of the defendants then becomes irrelevant. It is submitted that this is perhaps the preferable argument since the outcome of the agreement is the decision to interfere with Michael's contract and as Michael's contract is eventually terminated, he has suffered loss as a result. The four conspirators may then be jointly and severally liable to Michael for the resulting financial loss. The only defence which they could raise may be justification, but this usually only applies to the protection of business interests (*Mogul Steamship Co* v *MacGregor, Gow & Co* [1892] AC 25) or working conditions, so the defence would be unlikely to succeed.

When Anne succeeds in inducing Norman to withdraw his bid, no contract has as yet been made between Norman and Michael, so that she cannot be liable for inducing a breach of their contract. Michael must therefore rely on the tort of interference with trade by unlawful means, which has received recent support in decisions such as *Merkur Island Shipping* v *Laughton* [1983] AC 570; [1983] 2 WLR 778 and *Hadmor Productions* v *Hamilton* [1983] 1 AC 191; [1982] 2 WLR 322. In *Lonrho* v *Fayed* [1989] 3 WLR 631; [1989] 2 All ER 65 CA the Court of Appeal held that it was not an essential element of this tort that the predominant purpose was to injure the victim rather than further the tortfeasor's interest, nor was it necessary to prove a complete tort between the tortfeasor and the person against whom the tort was committed. The problem in Michael's case is in showing the existence of unlawful means; Anne has used a threat against Norman but it is a threat to pass on true information to local authorities. However, in *Square Grip Reinforcement* v *MacDonald* 1968 SLT 65, Lord Milligan held that where a person who conveys information was desperately anxious to achieve a particular result hten the court was likely to interpret the conveyancing of this information as persuasion. But even if such persuasion is proved it is merely a threat to interfere with contracts which have not yet been contemplated.

Because of the above difficulties, Michael may wish to bring an action against Anne in intimidation. This involves putting pressure on a person to do something which he would not otherwise do, and it incorporates the idea of an unpleasant sanction. Anne must also have threatened unlawful means such as a criminal or tortious act, or the breach of a contract (*Rookes* v *Barnard* [1964] AC 1129; [1964] 2 WLR 269), and there will be no intimidation if the act threatened is legal and one which the defendant has a right to do. Michael's case is one of three-party intimidation, since Anne has threatened Norman to the detriment of Michael. Again, the problem is in proving the use of unlawful means; since the threat does not involve a breach of an existing contract, and does not involve any other unlawful act, Michael would not have a good case in intimidation, and therefore would not benefit in bringing an action against Anne individually.

Oliver, on the other hand, does have a valid and existing contract with Michael, and David, by offering him money not to carry out the survey, has induced Oliver to breach his contract with Michael. A distinction was drawn by Lord Denning in *Torquay Hotel Co* v *Cousins* [1969] 2 Ch 106; [1969] 2 WLR 289 between direct and indirect interference of contractual relations, and Michael's case involves direct interference since David has induced a breach of contract (*Lumley* v *Gye* (1853) 2 El & Bl 216). In accordance with other criteria laid down by Slade J in *Greig* v *Insole* [1978] 1 WLR 302; [1978] 3 All ER 449, David must be shown to have knowledge of the contract (though not its exact terms) and the intention to interfere with it. Michael must prove that as a result he has suffered special damage and he must rebut any defence of justification put forward by the defendants; for example, they may rely on the fact that they are ultimately acting out of a moral and political aim. This defence rarely succeeds, and usually applies where the contract itself is unlawful (*De Francesco* v *Barnum* (1890)).

Michael, therefore, has a good case against David and against all four defendants as conspirators to injure him. It should be pointed out, however, that in cases where there is a conspiracy to injure by unlawful means, the plaintiff gains little benefit from pleading conspiracy and may prefer to concentrate on the substantive tort which has been committed, thus Michael may wish to bring an action against David alone.

QUESTION FOUR

The Outrageous Fellowship is a religious sect. It recruits young people into its missionary work; they are encouraged to cut themselves off from their families and careers. Emily, who is sympathetic to the Fellowship's aims, has sold to its representatives in England an option to purchase for a very low price her country estate in a quiet location as possible headquarters. Emily's nephew, Frank, a road haulier, dislikes the proposed arrangement. Giles lives nearby. His daughter joined the

Fellowship six years ago and has not been in touch with her parents since. Frank and Giles are determined that the Fellowship will not establish itself in the locality. They have learned that officials of the Fellowship will soon be visiting from the USA to inspect possible sites.

Advise Frank and Giles on the legality of these possible proposed actions:

a) Giles will visit Emily, tell her about his daughter and try to persuade her to cancel the option;

b) Frank and Giles will arrange that during the inspection they and their friends and Frank's drivers will drive their cars and lorries at high speed along the neighbouring roads, which are subject to a speed limit, in the hope that the Fellowship will have to purchase another estate at the normal market rate.

University of London LLB Examination
(for External Students) Law of Tort June 1992 Q5

Skeleton Solution

Introduction – inducing breach of contract – elements of the tort – defences – interfering with business by unlawful means – conspiracy – elements of the tort.

Suggested Solution

This problem concerns the economic torts. Emily has sold an option to purchase her country estate to the Outrageous Fellowship. Giles and Frank wish her to break that contract and they will try to dissuade the Fellowship from taking advantage of the sale.

Firstly, Giles will visit Emily and tell her about his daughter's indoctrination in the hope of persuading her to break the contract. This is the tort of inducing breach of contract, which has its origins in the case of *Lumley* v *Gye* (1853) 2 El & Bl 216. In that case the Plaintiff, a theatre owner, contracted with an opera singer, Johanna Wagner, to perform exclusively in his theatre. The Defendant, a rival theatre owner, 'enticed and persuaded' her to break the contract. The aim of the tort is to protect contractual relations.

Will Giles commit the tort? We are told he will try to persuade Emily. In *DC Thomson & Co Ltd* v *Deakin* [1952] Ch 646, it was held that a distinction may be drawn between persuasion and advice in the sense of 'a mere statement of, or drawing of the attention of the party addressed to, the state of facts as they are;' the latter not being actionable. This is a difficult distinction. In Giles's terms, it means that a revelatory statement of facts which causes Emily to recant would not be tortious. However, if the advice is intended to have persuasive effect then it is more than mere advice. Therefore, it seems likely Giles will be liable under that head.

Giles must have knowledge of the contract between Emily and the Fellowship – although he need not know of every detail: *Emerald Construction Co Ltd* v *Lowthian* [1966] 1 WLR 691. There must also be intention to break the contract. It is not a defence for Giles to say his intention is in fact to expose the Fellowship as a sham. While that may be his overriding purpose, his immediate intention is to break Emily's contract (eg *Lonrho* v *Fayed* [1989] 2 All ER 65). Giles must, for this tort, interfere with a subsisting contract. However, if Emily, under the contract, had an option to terminate which she exercised, albeit upon Giles's advice given by lawful means, then it is argued that there would be no liability. In *Torquay Hotel Co Ltd v Cousins* [1969] 2 Ch 106, Lord Denning MR talked of liability where a 'third person prevents or hinders one party from performing his contract, even though it be not a breach'. The distinction is the use of lawful means. Finally, on this tort, the Fellowship must suffer loss through the breach. Without damage, the action fails.

Giles, if sued, would wish to raise the defence of justification, saying that he was under a moral obligation: *Brimelow v Casson* [1924] 1 Ch 302. However, this is not a strong defence, despite Giles's honest intentions.

Secondly, Frank and Giles plan to drive lorries at high speed along the neighbouring roads and this may give rise to an action for interference with business by unlawful means: *Merkur Island Shipping Corp v Laughton* [1983] 2 AC 570 and *Lonrho v Fayed*. We are told of Frank and Giles's intention and also that there is a speed limit on the roads. However, this branch of the economic torts is less well-developed. While it seems logical that a proprietary right – such as the Fellowship has – should be protected, it is not clear if this is covered by this tort.

Their actions could also give rise to an action for conspiracy. A definition of this tort is provided by Willes J in *Mulcahy v R* (1868) LR 3 HL 306: 'A conspiracy consists not merely in the intention of two or more, but in the agreement of two or more to do an unlawful act, or to do a lawful act by unlawful means.' Frank and Giles's plan falls into the first category.

They satisfy the three elements of the tort: firstly, there are two of them. Secondly, there is a 'combination' between them for a common purpose. Thirdly, there must be damage to the Plaintiff – which can be measured by the additional expense the Fellowship will be put to. It is an unlawful means conspiracy, because they intend to break the law (as, for example, *Lonhro Ltd v Shell Petroleum Co (No 2)* [1982] AC 173). They may also be trespassing on the highway, and a conspiracy to commit a tort can constitute unlawful means: *Sorrell v Smith* [1925] AC 700.

It is suggested, therefore, that both proposed actions could be tortious and could result in Frank and Giles being sued by the Fellowship.

19 REMEDIES

19.1 Introduction

19.2 Key points

19.3 Recent cases

19.4 Analysis of questions

19.5 Questions

19.1 Introduction

The general remedies available are damages, injunctions and self-help. Of these damages is the most important remedy and we shall concentrate on this.

19.2 Key points

a) *Types of damages*

The general principle is to put the plaintiff in the position he would have been in had the tort not been committed, in so far as this can be done by money, ie it is to compensate the plaintiff and not to punish the defendant.

i) Nominal damages

Show that the plaintiff's rights have been infringed, but that he has suffered no loss.

ii) Contemptuous damages

Usually one penny and show that the action should not have been brought. Often the plaintiff, despite winning the case, will not get his costs and may even have to pay the defendant's costs.

iii) General damages

Damage which the law presumes to follow from the tort in question, eg pain and suffering following personal injury. Need not be quantified in the statement of claim.

iv) Special damages

Capable of being calculated exactly and must be pleaded, eg loss of earnings.

v) Special damage

This is the actual loss which must be proved if the tort is not actionable per se.

vi) Aggravated damages

Take into account the plaintiff's injured feelings, although they should be moderate: *Archer* v *Brown* [1985] QB 401 and are not usually awarded in negligence cases: *Kralj* v *McGrath* [1986] 1 All ER 54; *AB* v *South West Water Services Ltd* [1993] 1 All ER 609.

vii) Exemplary damages

According to *Rookes* v *Barnard* [1964] AC 1129 and *Cassell* v *Broome* [1972] AC 1027 they are only awarded where:

- there has been an oppressive, arbitrary or unconstitutional act by a servant of the government, eg *Holden* v *Chief Constable of Lancashire* [1987] QB 380; *Bradford Metropolitan City Council* v *Arora* [1991] 3 All ER 545.
- the defendant has calculated that he will make a profit despite paying damages: *Cassell* v *Broome* (above).
- where authorised by statute.

Even where these first two criteria are satisfied, exemplary damages are only awarded for torts for which such an award could have been made in 1964: *AB* v *South West Water Services Ltd* (above).

viii) Prospective damages

Damages must take into account future loss as well as damage already suffered, since only one action arises from the same cause of action: *Fitter* v *Veal* (1701) 12 Mod 542, and this rule also applies to claims settled out of court: *O'Boyle* v *Leiper* (1990) The Times 26 June. Successive actions will only lie for continuing torts (eg trespass to land) or where the facts do give rise to more than one cause of action: *Brunsden* v *Humphrey* (1884) 14 QBD 141.

b) *Damages for personal injury*

These damages fall into two categories – pecuniary loss and non-pecuniary loss. Dealing first with pecuniary loss:

i) Loss of earnings

The plaintiff can claim for loss of earnings to date of trial and for loss of future earnings. Calculation of the former is straightforward. For the latter the court calculates the plaintiff's net annual loss, the multiplicand, and multiplies that by a figure based on the number of years the loss is likely to last, the multiplier.

The multiplicand is found by taking gross earnings, allowing for increases in pay and promotion then deducting tax and social security contributions. The multiplier is not the duration of the disability, but a lower figure with a maximum of around 18, to take into account the 'general vicissitudes of life' and because the plaintiff has received money as a lump sum rather than over a period of years.

Note that damages cannot be awarded as periodical payments, except where both parties consent: *Burke* v *Tower Hamlets Health Authority* (1989) The Times 10 August, although s32A Supreme Court Act 1981 allows a provisional award to be made, even if there is a dispute between the parties as to the total award: *Hurditch* v *Sheffield Health Authority* [1989] 2 All ER 869. Note the restricted interpretation given to s32A in *Willson* v *Ministry of Defence* [1991] 1 All ER 638.

In *Kelly* v *Dawes* (1990) The Times 27 September a settlement was allowed in which the defendants invested part of the sum payable to the plaintiff in an annuity which provided the plaintiff with an index-linked annual sum for the rest of her life.

ii) Lost years

ie where the plaintiff has a reduced expectation of life. In *Pickett* v *British Rail Engineering* [1980] AC 136 the House of Lords allowed recovery for the lost years, although sums which the plaintiff would have spent exclusively on himself must be deducted: *Harris* v *Empress Motors* [1983] 3 All ER 561.

For very young plaintiffs no award is likely because the process is too speculative: *Croke* v *Wiseman* [1981] 3 All ER 852.

iii) Potential loss of earning capacity

The plaintiff may keep his pre-accident employment but run the risk that if he loses that job he will be at a disadvantage in the labour market: *Moeliker* v *Reyrolle* [1977] 1 All ER 9; *Smith* v *Manchester Corporation* (1974) 17 KIR 1.

iv) Loss of pension rights

May accompany future loss of earnings.

v) Loss of housekeeping, DIY, etc, capacity

In *Daly* v *General Steam Navigation* [1980] 3 All ER 696, the plaintiff was not able to perform all her housekeeping duties, and it was held that she could recover the cost of domestic help. See also *Willson* (above).

vi) Medical expenses

The plaintiff can recover private medical expenses despite the fact that treatment could be provided by the NHS: s2(4) Law Reform (Personal Injuries) Act 1948.

If the plaintiff is cared for by a member of his family, a realistic sum will be awarded in respect of that care: *Housecroft* v *Burnett* [1986] 1 All ER 332, although not where the services are rendered by the tortfeasor: *Hunt* v *Severs* [1994] 2 All ER 385.

vii) Deductions

Loss of earnings may be made up from various sources. Section 82 Social Security Administration Act 1992 provides no payment shall be made for any personal injury unless the compensator obtains a certificate from the Secretary of State giving the benefits paid or likely to be paid in the five years from the accident. The compensator deducts this sum and gives the victim a certificate of deduction; the compensator then pays this deducted amount to the Secretary of State to reimburse the State. This applies to injuries suffered after 1 January 1989 and its precursor came into force on 3 September 1990. It does not apply to payments under the Fatal Accidents Act 1976 or to payments below £2,500. For accidents prior to 1 January 1989 s2 Law Reform (Personal Injuries) Act 1948 requires one-half social security benefits to be deducted from the damages and for this deduction to cease after five years; there is no reimbursement of deductions to the State.

For other benefits, the general rule is that a benefit is deducted where it truly reduces the loss suffered: *Parry* v *Cleaver* [1970] AC 1. Thus wages or sick pay are deducted, but not insurance sums: *Bradburn* v *Great Western Railway* (1874) LR10 Ex1, nor charitable donations, nor ill-health awards nor higher pension benefits: *Smoker* v *London Fire and Civil Defence Authority* [1991] 2 All ER 449. Where the employer insures his employees, deduction of these insurance benefits depends on whether the benefits are a continuation of salary and thus in the nature of earnings: *Hussain* v *New Taplow Paper Mills* [1988] 2 WLR 266, or whether they are pure insurance benefits: *McCamley* v *Cammell Laird Shipbuilders* [1990] 1 All ER 854.

Similarly a redundancy payment will be deducted where it is unlikely that the plaintiff would have been offered redundancy but for the accident: *Colledge* v *Bass Mitchells & Butlers* [1988] 1 All ER 536.

viii) Other pecuniary loss

For example, loss of ability to carry out a profitable hobby (see also *Meah* v *McCreamer* [1985] 1 All ER 367).

Where personal injuries result in divorce it is not clear whether the financial consequences of the divorce are recoverable: *Jones* v *Jones* [1985] QB 704 allowed recovery; *Pritchard* v *Cobden* [1988] Fam 22 did not.

c) *Non-pecuniary loss*

i) Pain and suffering

Recoverable, but not if the plaintiff is in a coma: *Wise* v *Kaye* [1962] 1 QB 638. This pain and suffering does not include sorrow or grief unless it amounts to nervous shock: *Kralj* v *McGrath* (above); *AB* v *South West Water Services* (above). In *Re The Herald of Free Enterprise* (1989) The Guardian 2 May it was held that post traumatic stress disorder and pathological grief which is in excess of normal grief are recognised psychiatric illnesses for which compensation can be awarded. This head of damages may also include a sum for loss of congenial employment ie loss of job satisfaction: *Champion* v *London Fire Authority* (1990) The Times 5 July.

Note s1(1)(b) Administration of Justice Act 1982 requires the court to take into account any suffering caused to the plaintiff by his awareness that his expectation of life has been reduced.

ii) Loss of amenity

ie loss of ability to engage in pre-accident activities. May be awarded even if the plaintiff is unaware of the loss: *West* v *Shepherd* [1964] AC 326; *Lim Poh Choo* v *Camden & Islington Area Health Authority* [1980] AC 174.

iii) Loss of expectation of life

Abolished by s1(1) Administration of Justice Act 1982, and replaced by a statutory sum (£7,500 as from 1 April 1991) for bereavement for loss of spouse or child – see *Doleman* v *Deakin* (1990) The Times 30 January.

iv) Injury itself

There is a tariff for loss of limbs or faculties; awards are tabulated in Kemp and Kemp *The Quantum of Damages* which helps to bring some consistency.

v) Interest

By s35A Supreme Court Act 1981 interest must be awarded for death or personal injury. It can only be claimed for losses to date of trial.

Pecuniary loss: one-half short term interest rate from date of accident to date of trial: *Jefford* v *Gee* [1970] 2 QB 130; *Cookson* v *Knowles* [1979] AC 556.

Non-pecuniary loss: 2% from date of service of writ to date of trial: *Wright* v *British Railways Board* [1983] 2 AC 773.

In addition every judgment debt carries interest from the date of judgment until payment: s17 Judgments Act 1838 and see *Thomas* v *Bunn* [1991] 2 WLR 27.

d) *Death and tort*

Two actions arise on death:

i) By s1(1) Law Reform (Miscellaneous Provisions) Act 1934 all causes vesting in the deceased survive for the benefit of his estate, ie the estate may sue the defendant.

ii) Under the Fatal Accidents Act 1976, dependants of the deceased may sue. The dependency must be calculated ie earnings less deceased's personal and living expenses and the multiplier is calculated as above. The chance of the widow remarrying or any benefits accruing as a result of the death are to be ignored but not the chance of divorce: *Martin* v *Owen* (1992) The Times 21 May: benefits include a pension and widow's allowance from an employer's pension fund payable on the death of the husband and are thus to be disregarded: *Pidduck* v *Eastern Scottish Omnibuses* [1990] 2 All ER 69.

If a relative gives up employment to care for orphaned children, a claim may be made under the 1976 Act for the relative's loss of earnings: *Cresswell* v *Eaton* [1991] 1 All ER 484. See also *Watson* v *Willmot* [1991] 1 All ER 473 for the dependency of orphans.

e) *Damage to property*

Again the plaintiff must be put in the position as if the damage had not occurred: see *Swingcastle* v *Alastair Gibson* [1991] 2 All ER 353 for a recent example of this rule.

If goods are damaged, damages equal the loss in value: *The London Corporation* [1935] P 70. If goods are destroyed, damages equal market value at time of destruction: *Liesbosch Dredger* v *SS Edison* [1933] AC 449; *BBMB Finance (Hong Kong)* v *Eda Holdings* [1991] 2 All ER 129.

If the goods were used to generate profits, damages equal loss of profit or cost of hire of substitute: *Martindale* v *Duncan* [1973] 1 WLR 574.

If business premises and machinery are destroyed, damages equal cost of new premises and replacement of machinery (not the acquisition cost of the machinery) (see *Dominion Mosaics & Tile* v *Trafalgar Trading* [1990] 2 All ER 246).

f) *Mitigation*

The plaintiff is under a duty to act reasonably to mitigate his loss, and this mitigation will reduce his damages: *Darbishire* v *Warran* [1963] 1 WLR 1067; *Selvanayagam* v *University of the West Indies* [1983] 1 All ER 824.

g) *Injunction*

An equitable remedy only available at the discretion of the court. By s37 Supreme Court Act 1981 it must be 'just and reasonable' to grant the injunction. An injunction may be useful in (say) nuisance or trespass to land, but is not so useful in (say) negligence.

An injunction may be prohibitory; mandatory; quia timet; interlocutory.

The court may award damages in lieu of an injunction: see Chapter 12.2 for the principles involved.

h) *Self-help*

eg in abating a nuisance, ejecting a trespasser, self-defence to battery, etc.

i) *Limitation*

By s2 Limitation Act 1980 an action in tort must be brought within six years from the date on which the action accrued (three years for personal injuries – s11 1980 Act).

If the tort is actionable per se, time runs from the date of the tort; if proof of damage is required, time runs from the date of damage. See *Nitrigin Eireann Teoranta* v *Inco Alloys* [1992] 1 All ER 854. For insidious personal injuries (eg asbestosis, noise-induced deafness) s11 1980 Act provides that time runs from the date of the plaintiff's knowledge of the damage, and s33 1980 Act allows the court discretion to proceed outside the three year period. See *Stubbings* v *Webb* [1993] 2 WLR 120 and *Donovan* v *Gwentoys* [1990] 1 All ER 1018

Note the effects of the Latent Damage Act 1986 on hidden damage – six years plus three years from date damage discovered, subject to an overall period of fifteen years from the date of negligence.

19.3 Recent cases

O'Boyle v *Leiper* (1990) The Times 26 June

Smoker v *London Fire and Civil Defence Authority* [1991] 2 All ER 449

McCamley v *Cammell Laird Shipbuilders* [1990] 1 All ER 854

Doleman v *Deakin* (1990) The Times 30 January

Pidduck v *Eastern Scottish Omnibuses* [1990] 2 All ER 69

Dominion Mosaics & Tile v *Trafalgar Trading* [1990] 2 All ER 246

Champion v *London Fire Authority* (1990) The Times 5 July

Cresswell v *Eaton* [1991] 1 All ER 484

Watson v *Willmott* [1991] 1 All ER 473

Thomas v *Bunn* [1991] 2 WLR 27

Kelly v *Dawes* (1990) The Times 27 September

BBMB Finance (Hong Kong) v *Eda Holdings* [1991] 2 All ER 129

Swingcastle v *Alastair Gibson* [1991] 2 All ER 353

Donovan v *Gwentoys* [1990] 1 All ER 1018

Nitrigin Eireann Teoranta v *Inco Alloys* [1992] 1 All ER 854

AB v *South West Water Services Ltd* [1993] 1 All ER 609

Stubbings v *Webb* [1993] 2 WLR 120

Martin v *Owen* (1992) The Times 21 May

Hunt v *Severs* [1994] 2 All ER 385

19.4 Analysis of questions

Questions on damages, especially for personal injures, are popular with the examiner. Sometimes they are pure essay questions and sometimes they are set in a problem format, but in the latter case no arithmetical calculations are required and the answer expected is of the essay type. Occasionally damages appear as part of a question involving specific torts.

19.5 Questions

QUESTION ONE

John was married to Primrose by whom he had two children: Timothy aged 19 years who is a first year university undergraduate and Fiona aged 14 who attends a boarding school. John was seriously injured in a road accident in which he was driving his car. John's car was struck by one driven through a red traffic light by Stanley; John was not wearing a seat belt. John sustained severe brain damage. He never recovered consciousness but he lived for a further 18 months. At the date of the accident John was aged 48 years, he had been very fit and he had been employed as his company's chief production engineer at a gross annual salary of £25,000. His prospects for promotion had been good. What claims for damage may arise? By whom will they be brought?

University of London LLB Examination
Mid-sessional, 1989

Skeleton Solution

John – negligence of Stanley – loss of earnings – lost years – s4(2) AJA 1982 – *Wise* v *Kaye* – loss of amenity – contributory negligence – FAA – dependency – widow – children.

Suggested Solution

John was seriously injured in an accident involving Stanley and subsequently died as a result of his injuries. It seems clear that the accident was caused by the negligence of Stanley as we are told that he drove his car through a traffic light which was at red. We are not told that John brought an action against Stanley during his lifetime so the advice given here is based on the assumption that no such action was brought.

Where a tortious act results in the death of a person then there are two actions which may be brought. The first is under the Law Reform (Miscellaneous Provisions) Act 1934 (the 1934 Act) and the second is under the Fatal Accidents Act 1976 (the 1976 Act). We shall take each claim separately.

The 1934 Act provides for the survival for the benefit of the deceased's estate of any cause of action which was vested in the deceased at the time of his death. Such an action is brought by the personal representatives of the deceased's estate and any damages recovered are awarded to the estate to be distributed according to the will of the deceased or the rules of intestacy. The principles applicable to a claim under the 1934 Act are generally the same as in an ordinary personal injuries case.

Thus an action will be brought under the 1934 Act for both pecuniary loss and non-pecuniary loss. John appears to have suffered loss of earnings because we are not told that his employers continued to pay his wages. Had he brought an action before his death John could have recovered for his loss of earnings during the lost years, that is the period which he would have been alive and continued to earn had it not been for the tortious event (*Pickett* v *British Railways Engineering Ltd* [1980] AC 136). However s4(2) of the Administration of Justice Act 1982 provides that a claim for loss of earnings in the lost years can only be brought by a living plaintiff (reversing *Gammell* v *Wilson* [1982] AC 27). So the lost earnings will be confined to the 18 month period in which John was alive after the accident. In assessing John's net annual loss the court would start with John's gross annual earnings of £25,000 per annum. The court would, however, make an allowance for the possibility of an increase in pay or promotion. Here we are told that John's prospects for promotion had been good. In *Ratnasingam* v *Kow Ah Dek* [1983] 1 WLR 1235 the court made an allowance of one third for the chance that a teacher with a good academic record would pass an examination for promotion, even though he had failed the particular examination twice before and was on his last chance. Once this sum has been calculated then a deduction must be made for the tax which the plaintiff would have paid on his earnings and for social security contributions which he would have paid. A claim could also be made for any other pecuniary losses, such as medical expenses incurred and damage to property.

A claim can also be made for non-pecuniary loss. There is unlikely to be a claim for pain and suffering because in *Wise* v *Kaye* [1962] 1 QB 638 it was held that a claim could only be made for pain and suffering where the plaintiff was aware that he had suffered pain. Here we are told that John remained unconscious throughout so it is unlikely that he was aware of any pain and suffering. A claim could, however, be made for loss of amenity which is designed to compensate the plaintiff for the loss of his capacity to engage in activities which he enjoyed before his death. In *West* v *Shepherd* [1964] AC 326 it was held that the plaintiff was entitled to be compensated for his or her loss of amenities even though he or she was unaware of that loss. The case in many ways is a controversial one but it was approved recently by the House of Lords in *Lim Poh Choo v Camden and Islington AHA* [1980] AC 174. However, the damages payable under this head will be reduced because of John's shortened life span because it was held in *West* that damages must be proportionate to the duration of the loss.

John was, however, guilty of contributory negligence in failing to wear a seat belt. A failure to wear a seat belt was held to be contributory negligence in *Froom v Butcher* [1975] 3 WLR 379 and this common law rule has now been given statutory approval in s33A of the Road Traffic Act 1972 which makes the wearing of a seat belt mandatory. Thus damages would fall to be reduced by 20 per cent. Stanley may wish to argue that a failure to wear a seat belt was a novus actus interveniens as being an unreasonable act of the plaintiff, as in *McKew v Holland & Hannen & Cubitts (Scotland) Ltd* [1969] 3 All ER 1621, but such an argument is unlikely to succeed.

Secondly, a cause of action would accrue for the benefit of John's dependants under the 1976 Act. It should be noted that the defence of contributory negligence which would be available to Stanley in an action by John is also available as regards any action by the dependants. Dependants are defined in s1(2) and s1(4) of the 1976 Act as including the deceased's spouse and children and so would include Primrose, Timothy and Fiona. The dependants can bring an action for bereavement which is a statutory figure fixed at £3,500 (or £7,500 from 1 April 1991). If the dependants have in fact incurred funeral expenses in respect of John then these can be recovered from Stanley (s3(5) of the 1976 Act). In calculating the pecuniary loss which can be claimed by the dependants the court will calculate the deceased's earnings and then deduct a sum to represent the deceased's personal and living expenses. Only sums which would have been spent by the deceased exclusively upon himself fall to be deducted (*Harris v Empress Motors Ltd* [1983] 3 All ER 561). Once this has been done the court will assess the likely duration of the dependency. The duration of the dependency of the children is likely to be short as the dependency does not generally extend beyond the length of their full-time education and Timothy is already aged 19 and at university and Fiona is aged 14. The court will have to calculate how long the deceased would have continued to live had it not been for the accident with Stanley. In assessing the length of the dependency and damages the prospects of Primrose remarrying are to be ignored (s3(3) of the 1976 Act). Under s4 of the 1976 Act any benefits which have accrued or will accrue or may accrue to the dependants from the estate of the deceased or otherwise as a result of the death of the deceased are to be disregarded. Thus the damages payable to the estate in respect of loss of earnings during the 18 month period which John survived after the accident, any medical expenses and damages for loss of amenity will not be set off against the damages under the 1976 Act because the new policy is that such benefits are not to be set off.

QUESTION TWO

Is the current English law relating to the assessment of damages in cases of personal injury satisfactory? If not, what reforms would you suggest?

Written by the editor

Skeleton Solution

The law in relation to damages for personal injury has recently been amended to some extent by the Administration of Justice Act 1982, but discussion should still cover case law in this area and the Pearson Commission.

Suggested Solution

In recent years there has been much discussion of the law relating to the assessment of damages for personal injuries, both in the light of particular cases which have highlighted some of the defects in the present law and of the recommendations of the Pearson Commission on Civil Liability and Compensation for Personal Injury (1978 Cmnd 7054) and the Law Commission Report on assessment of damages for personal injury (1973 Law Com. No 56).

Some of these recommendations have been incorporated into the Administration of Justice Act 1982, a statute which deals partly with damages for personal injuries but which has perhaps more far-reaching provisions in relation to damages for death and fatal accidents.

As far as damages for personal injuries are concerned, s1 of the Act abolishes the head of damages for loss of expectation of life, a claim which used to consist of an award set at £1,250 by the case of *Gammell* v *Wilson* [1982] AC 27; [1980] 3 WLR 591 and which was initiated by *Benham* v *Gambling* [1941] AC 157. The award used to be made where a plaintiff's life expectancy had been shortened by his injuries, but the Pearson Commission recommended that this nominal award was meaningless as a head of compensation since it did not vary according to the facts. Now, if life expectancy is reduced, that will be taken into account in assessing for pain and suffering if the plaintiff is aware of that reduction. This has solved one of the anomalies in the field of personal injury awards.

The remaining heads for non-pecuniary loss are those of pain and suffering, loss of amenity and often an award for the injury itself, for example, if the plaintiff has lost an eye, he will receive a greater award than if he has broken his ankle and recovered well. Assessment of quantum for the injury itself is made by reference to a 'tariff' made up of previous decisions so that a catalogue of injuries and corresponding awards has been made up over the years. Thus, a broad estimate of the damages likely to be awarded can be arrived at before the trial.

Pain and suffering awards will only be made where the plaintiff is aware of his suffering, so that where the plaintiff remains in a coma, the award will not be made. In *Lim Poh Choo* v *Camden and Islington Area Health Authority* [1980] AC 174; [1979] 3 WLR 44; [1979] 2 All ER 910, the plaintiff who suffered heart failure and irreversible brain damage after surgery had been negligently carried out, was only periodically aware of her physical condition. In this type of case, the pain and suffering award will tend to be low, but she was awarded £20,000 for loss of amenity as she had been a psychiatric registrar aged 36. Loss of amenity compensates the plaintiff's loss of enjoyment of life, after injury. Unlike the pain and suffering award, which may vary greatly from case to case and depends on the plaintiff's awareness and the amount of pain involved, loss of amenity does not depend on the plaintiff's awareness of his or her condition.

Damages for pecuniary loss in cases of personal injury may also vary from case to case depending on profession, age, period of recovery and indeed whether the plaintiff is injured in such a way that he cannot return to his previous occupation.

Pecuniary loss falls under two main heads: special damages (actually quantified by the plaintiff, eg cost of medical treatment to the date of trial, damage to clothes, taxi-fares to and from hospital etc), and general damages which cover future loss and are assessed by the court. The latter concern mainly loss of future earnings and cost of future care (or future expenses).

Loss of future earnings is quantified by multiplying the plaintiff's net annual earnings at the date of trial (not accident) by a multiplier which represents the number of years in the future during which the plaintiff will not be able to work at all or where he will have to work at a lower salary because of his physical condition. The multiplier is usually a figure of no higher than 14 or 16; this is to take account of the fact that the plaintiff will receive a lump sum and therefore will receive interest on it, and retirement age, job security and whether he will live beyond retirement age will all be taken into account by the court. On this point a criticism can be made and indeed, it was made by the Pearson Commission, and this is that the plaintiff's investment income will be taxed so that he may be in a slightly worse position than he would have been in had the tort not happened. The Commission therefore recommended the idea of periodical personal injury payments.

This has been enacted by s32A Supreme Court Act 1981, so that now, provisional damages for personal injuries may be awarded in certain cases, subject to future review. This has the added advantage of speedier litigation, since one of the great disadvantages of personal injury litigation used to be and still is the length of time between the accident or tort and the trial, which was necessary so that the plaintiff's injuries could reach a plateau so that a more accurate assessment of damages could be made. Under the provisional award scheme, the award can be adjusted in future assessments so if the plaintiff's injuries worsen a fairer system of compensation comes into play when the injuries are reviewed. Unfortunately s32A has been subject to a rather narrow interpretation in *Willson* v *Ministry of Defence* [1991] 1 All ER 638. This has reduced the potential benefit of provisional damages for a plaintiff, although it still represents an improvement over the old law.

Loss of future earnings may be reduced under s5 AJA (confirming *Lim Poh Choo*) where the plaintiff is being kept in a hospital or nursing home and this maintenance, at least in part, at public expense has saved money which he would otherwise have expended; the saving will now be set off against lost future income. The plaintiff will still be entitled to any medical expenses incurred, but relates to what he would otherwise have spent on necessities such as food, heating, etc.

The AJA has remedied some of the defects in the current law but it may be that the system needs more radical alteration. Some States such as New Zealand have adopted a 'no-fault' scheme whereby compensation to accident victims is administered by an Accident Compensation Commission, so that compensation does not rely on fault or litigation, but it is not likely that such a scheme would be introduced in this country in the foreseeable future, even though the Pearson Commission recommended the adoption of no-fault compensation for motor vehicle injuries.

As the system exists at present, the defendant's fault will still have to be proved before the plaintiff is entitled to damages and delays will still occur in many cases while the plaintiff's injuries settle or while pre-trial procedures such as discovery are carried out (there was a 10-year delay in *Whitehouse* v *Jordan* [1981] 1 WLR 246; [1981] 1 All ER 267 between the injury and the decision). The process of litigation in personal injury cases is also costly and will remain so until the system is changed completely.

QUESTION THREE

David was driving at dusk at the maximum permitted speed. A large bird flew out suddenly and struck the windscreen of his car. David temporarily lost control and struck a pedal cycle which he was overtaking. The cyclist Paul suffered severe head injuries. He was aged 24, an articled clerk with a firm of City solicitors, unmarried and childless. He is now able to do only light unskilled work at a local supermarket. His expectation of life has probably not been reduced, but the medical experts are not agreed on this.

a) Has Paul a claim in tort against David? If so, how will the damages be assessed?

b) Do you think that English law provides a satisfactory method of compensation in such circumstances?

University of London LLB Examination
(for External Students) Law of Tort June 1993 Q3

Skeleton Solution

a) The claim: negligence – heads of damages: loss of earnings; plain and suffering; loss of amenity; other special and general damages; provisional damages.

b) Discussion of compensation, including structured settlements.

Suggested Solution

a) Paul's claim against David would be in negligence. As a road user, David owes a duty of care to other road users (eg *Nettleship* v *Weston* [1971] 2 QB 691). On the facts of this case it appears he is in breach of his duty. Firstly, he is driving at the maximum permitted speed. The speed at which a vehicle should be driven must be reasonable in the circumstances (as in, for example, *McLeod* v *Receiver of Metropolitan Police* [1971] Crim LR 364. Further, the Highway Code states that one's speed limit depends upon the conditions and we are told he is driving at dusk when visibility will be less.

Secondly, he is overtaking a cyclist. Again, he should have reduced speed and under the Highway Code a cyclist being overtaken should be given at least as much room as a car. Failure to observe the Highway Code can be relied upon to establish liability (the Road Traffic Act 1988 ss38–39). Therefore we can conclude that a reasonable driver would not have driven so fast at dusk and particularly when overtaking a cyclist.

It is not David's fault that a bird struck his windscreen, but we can argue that it is his fault that he was driving at such a speed and in such circumstances that a temporary loss of control caused an accident.

David's negligence has caused the accident and we are not told of anything that might allow a partial defence of contributory negligence.

Turning to the assessment of damages: the injuries are serious and the quantum is likely to be very high. The first head of damages is loss of earnings. His net annual loss (the multiplicand) is multiplied by a figure to denote the number of years' loss (the multiplier). This latter figure is not a 'real' number; Paul would probably have worked for another 30 or 40 years, but the multiplier will only be 15/16 in this case. Further, the multiplicand does not take into account promotion and so on and his likely earnings in the supermarket will be set off against it.

The second major head of damages will be for pain and suffering and/or loss of amenity and this figure is likely to be considerable. It is a matter for the court but there are numerous guideline cases which would allow Paul's advisers to predict quite closely what this amount should be. Both of these heads of damages are termed general damages and are largely speculative.

Paul will also claim for the special damages – quantifiable losses – incurred after the accident, such as damaged clothing, damage to his bicycle. Paul has no dependants and we are not told if his parents, for example, have incurred expenses in looking after him; if so, these would be recoverable. Similarly, any expenses likely to be incurred in the future can be claimed as general damages; for example, nursing care, special equipment.

Under the clawback rules, the accident having occurred after January 1989, any related benefits Paul has received would be deducted from the damages he receives.

Finally, there is lack of agreement as to his reduced life expectation. First, Paul can claim loss of future earnings not only for the period he is likely to survive but also for the 'lost years' and this is reflected in the multiplier (*Pickett* v *British Rail Engineering Ltd* [1980] AC 136). Second, s32A of the Supreme Court Act 1981 allows payment of provisional damages against the chance of further deterioration. An award is made now with power to make a further award if the deterioration occurs. It is submitted that this is unlikely in this case, since it is not his condition that will deteriorate and therefore justify a higher sum for pain and suffering or loss of amenity, but his expectation of life.

b) 'Damages for any tort are or ought to be fixed at a sum which will compensate the plaintiff, so far as money can do it, for all the injury which he has suffered', per Lord Reid, *Cassell* v *Broome* [1972] 1 All ER 801.

There are various arguments to be made for and against the method of compensation provided for by English law in personal injury cases. It is based upon the idea that the plaintiff is given a lump sum, part of which relates exactly to expenses, both incurred and predicted. The remainder is the notional value given to the injury itself, being compensation for the pain, suffering and loss of amenity. One cannot quantify pain and suffering, so inevitably the figures are to that extent arbitrary. However, the plaintiff receives a 'once-and-for-all' payment to meet all his needs and requirements, whether it be for a broken finger or complete paralysis.

There are two obvious comments to be made. First, recovery of compensation depends upon proof of fault. Paul must prove, on the balance of probabilities, that David was negligent. That will also involve delay and expense, although legal costs will be largely recovered if the plaintiff is successful. A system of strict liability, while not necessarily altering the way quantum is apportioned, would remove that burden from the plaintiff.

Second, the current system involves, in the more serious cases, an estimate of the plaintiff's needs and life expectancy. What if the plaintiff proves long-lived and runs out of money or if his needs alter? While provisional damages meet this difficulty to a limited extent, structured settlements provide a fairer solution. Structured settlements were first approved in this country in *Kelly* v *Dawes* (1990) The Times 27 September but they are familiar within other jurisdictions, such as Canada. They involve periodic payments for life instead of a lump sum and are therefore more flexible as well as having other benefits (such as being tax-free in the plaintiff's hands).

That may go some way to solving the inequities of the more serious cases (to date, all structured settlements in this country have been in cases with a six-figure value) but the less serious cases, which form the great majority, remain as before. It is submitted that structured settlements could be appropriate for some less serious cases, those involving some lack of amenity, for example, with periodic payments for a limited time.

However, the minor cases can only be dealt with by a lump sum and it is the procedure for awarding that sum which could be eased by removing the element of fault.

20 UNIVERSITY OF LONDON LLB (EXTERNAL) 1994 QUESTIONS AND SUGGESTED SOLUTIONS

UNIVERSITY OF LONDON
LLB EXAMINATIONS 1994
for External Students
PART I EXAMINATION (Scheme A) and
SECOND AND THIRD YEAR EXAMINATIONS (Scheme B)

LAW OF TORT

Tuesday, 7 June: 10am to 1pm

Answer *FOUR* of the following EIGHT questions

1   'I incline to the opinion that, as a general rule, it is more appropriate for strict liability in respect of operations of high risk to be imposed by Parliament, than by the courts. If such liability is imposed by statute, the relevant activities can be identified, and those concerned can know where they stand.' (*Cambridge Water Co Ltd* v *Eastern Counties Leather plc* (1994), per Lord Goff of Chieveley)

   a)   What is the significance of this case?

   b)   Do you agree with Lord Goff's view about the respective roles of the courts and Parliament?

2   Foulfoods Ltd held an 'open-day' at their factory when members of the public were allowed to visit. Dudley took his ten-year-old son Evan. Notices at the entrance to the factory read: 'Members of the public enter this factory at their own risk. The machinery is dangerous. Visitors should keep to the gangways.'

   Evan climbed on to a railing to get a better view. He lost his balance and slipped into a vat of soup. Geoffrey, an employee of Foulfoods, who was supervising visitors in that area of the factory, reached down with a long pole, but Evan's hands were covered in soup and slipped down the pole. Hugh, another visitor, jumped into the vat and held Evan up so that he could be rescued. Evan was seriously ill for some time as the result of swallowing large quantities of soup. Hugh died.

   Advise Evan and Hugh's widow as to any potential claims in tort.

3   In January Agnes was aged 85 and living in her own home which she owned. Her daughter Brenda thought that she was becoming too frail and forgetful to continue living on her own and wanted her to get a place in sheltered accommodation run by the local council. The council said that Agnes's condition would have to be independently assessed by the two doctors, one appointed by Brenda and one chosen by the council. The two doctors, Cyril (Brenda's nominee) and Daniel, visited Agnes. She was lively during the visit and the doctors reported

that she was a fit and robust lady, in good condition for her age and well able to live on her own. She was refused a place in the sheltered housing.

Brenda immediately had expensive work done to adapt her own home so that her mother could come and live with her. However in April before she was able to move Agnes wandered out one night, could not find her way home and fell over in the darkness breaking both hips. She has been in hospital ever since and is unlikely to be well enough to go to live with Brenda.

Advise Agnes and Brenda.

4   Provincial TV, a local television channel, presented a series of programmes in 1994 under the general title of 'Police Probe'. Before the series started, publicity material stated that it would focus on arousing public concern about inconclusive local police investigations which had not led to convictions.

In the first two programmes it was suggested that the police might have been improperly induced not to press charges. The third programme concerned investigations into sexual offences. It included a reconstruction of a police interview with a man described as 'the only suspect questioned' in connection with a particular rape in 1988, for which no-one had ever been charged. He was described as having 'a previous criminal record'. Fictitious names were used and the programme made clear that the parts were played by actors. The actual man questioned in 1988 was Thomas Smith who had had one conviction, when a student, of dishonestly travelling on a train without paying the fare. The actor portraying the detective very closely resembled John Robinson, an officer who joined the local police in 1990.

Advise Thomas Smith and John Robinson whether either has a cause of action in defamation.

5   'The maxim *res ipsa loquitur* makes it easier for a plaintiff to prove negligence; justice requires the creation of a similar rule for proof of causation.'

Discuss.

6   a)   What can amount to 'unlawful means' for the purposes of torts involving intentional infliction of economic loss? In what circumstances do unlawful means have to be established?

    b)   The League for Decency usually arranges to hire the hall of Barsetshire Technical College for its meetings and social functions. Mrs Proudy, the secretary of the League, heard recently that the college is to allow a pop group (the Hirams) to give a concert at the hall at which some of the musicians will appear in the nude. She telephoned the college and said, 'I am aghast. Unless you cancel these arrangements, I cannot believe that the League will ever want to use the college for its functions.'

    Advise the Hirams.

7   Statutory regulations impose upon employers and employees in the chemical manufacturing industry an obligation to ensure that prescribed protective equipment (including special gloves) are worn when workers are handling chemicals. The regulations apply to the premises of Stinks Ltd. George, Hamish and John, who are all employed there, were engaged in loading chemicals on to a

lorry and were all wearing the prescribed clothing. George and Hamish were passing casks containing chemicals up to John who was standing on the back of the lorry. A fly went into John's eye suddenly and he removed his glove to wipe it away. George did not notice and passed a cask up to him. John was unable to hold it. Some of the chemical spilled over his hand. He screamed in agony and clung on to Hamish in desperation.

John suffered serious burns to his hand. He will be permanently disfigured and will not be able to obtain manual employment. Hamish has suffered from severe depression since the incident and has not been able to return to work.

8   Luke is unemployed but has enrolled on a government training scheme. He is sent three days each week for work experience to the offices of Newfield Industries plc. The office manager Matilda was sent to a conference one day in a town forty miles away and was told to take the company car. She asked Luke to go with her as part of his work experience. She also thought that she might be drinking and that Luke could then drive the car, but did not tell Luke this. Both Luke and Matilda knew that he was not allowed to drive the company car. On the way back Matilda stopped for a drink at a pub and asked Luke to take over the driving. Luke drove out of the pub car park without looking and caused Neil, a passing motor cyclist, to swerve. Neil struck a tree and was seriously injured.

Advise Neil as to any rights of action in tort.

QUESTION ONE

'I incline to the opinion that, as a general rule, it is more appropriate for strict liability in respect of operations of high risk to be imposed by Parliament, than by the courts. If such liability is imposed by statute, the relevant activities can be identified, and those concerned can know where they stand.' (*Cambridge Water Co Ltd* v *Eastern Counties Leather plc* (1994), per Lord Goff of Chieveley)

a) What is the significance of this case?

b) Do you agree with Lord Goff's view about the respective roles of the courts and Parliament?

University of London LLB Examination
(for External Students) Law of Tort June 1994 Q1

General Comment

This involves discussing a quotation from a judgment in relation to both its context in that judgment, and on a wider, more practical basis. The scope for moving outside the confines of the question is great, but should obviously be avoided.

Skeleton Solution

a) Nuisance – *Rylands* v *Fletcher* – damage/harm – foreseeability – natural v non-natural use.

b) Strict liability – statute v common law – parliamentary supremacy/separation of powers – rule of law.

Suggested Solution

a) The most significant aspect of the *Cambridge Water* [1994] 2 AC 264 decision appears to relate both to nuisance and to the rule under *Rylands* v *Fletcher* (1866) LR 1 Ex 265, and to a consideration of whether foreseeability of a particular type of harm was necessary in determining an award of damages. The case also involved an attempt to clarify the issue regarding the assessment of the use of land as either natural or non-natural. The latter, subsidiary point was only considered briefly as the main decision of the court rendered fuller discussion irrelevant. The House of Lords appears to have concluded that foreseeability of harm of the relevant type by the defendant was a prerequisite for the recovery of damages, in both nuisance and under *Rylands* v *Fletcher*.

The *Cambridge Water* case revolved around an almost typical nuisance/*Rylands* v *Fletcher* scenario. The defendant was using and storing a chlorinated solvent, a mile from a borehole belonging to and used by the plaintiff for the abstraction of water for domestic use. The solvent, over a period of time, seeped into the water supply and, as a result of a European Commission ruling, the water was classed as being unfit for human consumption. As a result, the plaintiff claimed damages in, alternatively, negligence, nuisance and under the rule in *Rylands* v *Fletcher*. The case made a steady progression through the court hierarchy, until it fell for the House of Lords to decide upon the issues raised. The Court of Appeal had declined to determine the case on the basis of the rule in *Rylands* v *Fletcher*, but instead held that there was a parallel rule of strict liability in nuisance. The House of Lords felt unable to agree with the stand taken by the inferior court and considered that this was not a case in which extending the bounds of nuisance was proper and appropriate. In reviewing this whole area, their Lordships turned firstly to the question of foreseeability of damage in nuisance. Although the appearance of the liability is strict, in that the fact that the defendant has taken all reasonable care will not exonerate him from liability, the principle of 'reasonable user' acts as a form of control mechanism. Within this area of law no suggestion is made, however, that the defendant should be held liable for damage of a type which he could not reasonably foresee. This appears to have been the view of the Privy Council in *Overseas Tankship (UK) Ltd* v *Miller Steamship Co Pty (The Wagon Mound (No 2))* [1967] 1 AC 617. In that case, Lord Reid felt unable to discriminate 'between different cases of nuisance, so as to make foreseeability a necessary element in determining liability' (p460).

It was against this general background that Lord Goff turned to the rule in *Rylands* v *Fletcher* and, in particular, the judgment of Blackburn J. It was possible to discern a view that foreseeability of the risk was a prerequisite to the recovery of damages. His Lordship considered some of the authorities that had been presented as offering an opposite perception. However, it was felt that the undeniable connection between the rule in *Rylands* v *Fletcher* and nuisance meant that it was merely a logical step to afford the same test for both types of claim. This was not to say that the rule in *Rylands* v *Fletcher* was, as the examination of the point by the House of Lords in *Read* v *Lyons* [1947] AC 156 revealed, to be the development of a test of strict liability. It appeared that the House of Lords was concerned to have the *Rylands* v *Fletcher* rule considered as an extension of the law of nuisance to cases of isolated escapes from land. As the quotation suggests, Lord Goff did not consider that is was for the judiciary to take the law down that particular path.

The second point, that was mentioned only for the sake of completeness, related to the discussion of whether storing of solvent on land was a natural or non-natural use of land. In the original action, the trial judge had attempted to label it a natural use and thereby allow the exception to come into play. However, the House of Lords felt bound to decide that the storing of such chemicals was a non-natural use.

b) Looking at the respective roles of the courts and Parliament involves considering their places within the constitution of this country. At its most basic, Parliament makes the law, and it is left to the courts to interpret that law, in accordance with general presumptions and both internal and external aids to construction. There is a whole wealth of issues pertaining to the separation of powers within constitutional law, to which this question could relate. However, it is the extent to which the courts should take their role of interpreters of the law which appears to have been behind Lord Goff's consideration, and correct assessment, of these issues.

In general, it seems that those producing legislation are doing so in a way that is both carefully structured and well-informed. This being so, it means that the need for the courts to try and achieve the same ends via the use of the common law is reduced. This can only be of benefit as the common law is, and can only be, of general application. The 'system' is called upon to operate in so many differing environments that it cannot be too specific. Therefore, it would be unfair to expect the common law to accommodate areas of law that are overly technical. It must be left to the agency that can afford to meet those technical challenges head on and, as Lord Goff goes on to say, '... statute can where appropriate lay down precise criteria establishing the incidence and scope of such [strict] liability'.

The inherent dangers in allowing the courts to take a more active role in the defining of such controversial issues are a price too high to pay just to answer the courts' fears of a reluctant legislature. There may well come a time, and probably a judiciary, when the failure of Parliament to meet the challenges set by areas such as environmental pollution will lead to the redefining of roles. This would be a great shame and could lead to the judiciary's 'floodgate' fears acting in their favour, but against the general rule of law.

The imposition of liability in a haphazard and general way on the basis of 'no fault' may have quite a dramatic effect on the commercial ability of some businesses to survive. If, in relation to 'strict liability', Parliament is reluctant to create such a duty, it cannot really be for the courts to do it on Parliament's behalf. It seems that until the legislature can develop a fair and sophisticated system of compensation, then the courts' hands will be, and must remain, tied.

QUESTION TWO

Foulfoods Ltd held an 'open-day' at their factory when members of the public were allowed to visit. Dudley took his ten-year-old son Evan. Notices at the entrance to the factory read: 'Members of the public enter this factory at their own risk. The machinery is dangerous. Visitors should keep to the gangways.'

Evan climbed on to a railing to get a better view. He lost his balance and slipped into a vat of soup. Geoffrey, an employee of Foulfoods, who was supervising visitors in that area of the factory, reached down with a long pole, but Evan's hands were covered in soup and slipped down the pole. Hugh, another visitor, jumped into the vat and held Evan up so that he could be rescued. Evan was seriously ill for some time as the result of swallowing large quantities of soup. Hugh died.

Advise Evan and Hugh's widow as to any potential claims in tort.

University of London LLB Examination
(for External Students) Law of Tort June 1994 Q2

General Comment

This is a fairly straightforward question on occupiers' liability. Plan your answer to it carefully. In your opening paragraph explain what the question is about, then give a brief summary of the relevant facts and issues. Finally, remember to reach a conclusion.

Skeleton Solution

Introduction – occupiers' liability – contributory negligence – notices – volenti non fit injuria – remedies – conclusion.

Suggested Solution

This question concerns the liability of Foulfoods Ltd for the death of Hugh, a rescuer, and for the pain and suffering Evan was made to endure as a result of swallowing large quantities of soup when he accidentally fell off a railing into an open vat situated on their premises.

The main issues raised by this question are first, the liability, contributory of each of the individual parties; second, the effect of the notice which was placed at the entrance to the factory; third, contributory negligence; and fourth, the application of the maxim volentia non fit injuria to rescuer situations.

I turn first to deal with the liability of Foulfoods to Evan. From the facts as stated it appears that Foulfoods Ltd are prima facie in breach of the common duty of care owed to Evan under s2(1) of the Occupiers' Liability Act 1957. This duty is defined under s2(2) as being:

'... a duty to take such care as in all the circumstances of the case is reasonable to see that the visitor will be reasonably safe in using the premises for the purpose for which he is invited or permitted by the occupier.'

It is quite clear from the facts that the factory in which the incident occurred belonged to Foulfoods Ltd and that Evan was ostensibly invited onto the premises for the purpose of attending the open day. It follows, therefore, that Foulfoods Ltd are occupiers of premises within the meaning of the Act and that Evan is their lawful visitor to whom a duty of care is owed under the Act. See *Wheat* v *E Lacon & Co Ltd* [1966] AC 522. Section 2(3) of the Act also provides that:

'... an occupier must be prepared for children to be less careful than adults.'

Given that it was reasonably foreseeable that some parents might bring their children with them to the open day, it is arguable that Foulfoods Ltd ought to have taken further precautions, such as providing a lid for the vat. However, Foulfoods Ltd may seek to argue that Dudley, Evan's father, should not have permitted his son to climb onto the railing in the first place, and that they are therefore not liable for his injuries. It was stated in *Phipps* v *Rochester Corporation* [1955] 1 QB 450 that one of the circumstances which must be taken into account in measuring the occupier's obligation is the degree of care for their children's safety which the occupier may assume will be exercised by the parents. See also *O'Connor* v *British Transport Commission* [1958] 1 WLR 356. However, we shall have to argue that, notwithstanding Dudley's parental responsibilities regarding Evan's safety, Foulfoods Ltd ought to have realised that an open vat of that nature was likely to constitute a potential source of danger to children, and that by failing to cover it they failed in their duty towards Evan and are therefore liable to him in damages. A finding that Dudley himself acted negligently towards Evan would make him liable to pay a contribution towards the damages to Foulfoods in proportion to the extent of his own contributory negligence, pursuant to the Civil Liability Contribution Act 1978. However, it is doubtful whether Evan himself could be said to have acted negligently, in view of his tender years and, perhaps, inability to appreciate the danger of climbing up onto the railings. If, however, the court takes this view then the damages recoverable by him may be reduced by the court pursuant to the Law Reform (Contributory Negligence) Act 1945.

I turn next to consider the effect of the notice on Foulfoods Ltd's liability. Section 2(1) of the Act provides that:

'An occupier of premises owes the same duty of care to all his visitors, except insofar as he is free to do and does extend, restrict or exclude his duty to any visitor or visitors by agreement or otherwise.'

However, Foulfoods Ltd cannot successfully rely on the notice to escape liability because the factory constitutes business premises for the purpose of the operation of s2(1) of the Unfair Contract Terms Act 1977 which provides that:

'... a person cannot by reference to any contract term or to a notice exclude or restrict his liability for death or personal injury resulting from negligence.'

Furthermore, even if, which is doubtful, the factory does not constitute business premises for the purpose of s2(1) of Unfair Contract Terms Act 1977, s2(4) of the 1957 Act provides that:

'... a warning shall not be treated without more as absolving the occupier from liability unless in all circumstances it was enough to enable the visitor to be reasonably safe.'

We can argue on the facts that since the notice did not make any specific reference to the danger in question it was inadequate and could not have enabled Evan to be reasonably safe without further steps being taken. Furthermore, it should have been quite clear to Foulfoods Ltd that children do not normally pay much attention to such notices; therefore it was not only necessary but imperative that any dangers on their premises be brought to the children's attention. On that basis I would submit that the notice should not absolve Foulfoods Ltd from liability to Evan.

I turn next to consider the liability of Foulfoods Ltd in relation to Hugh's death. The above conclusions in relation to the notice and the duty of Foulfoods Ltd to their visitors apply equally to Hugh's case. Nevertheless, Foulfoods Ltd may seek to escape liability for Hugh's death by arguing that Hugh voluntarily accepted the risk of rescuing Evan and that there was in fact no need for him to jump into the vat as one of their supervisors, Geoffrey, was already in the process of rescuing him. We can overcome both these arguments. It is true that s2(5) of the 1957 Act provides that:

'The common duty of care does not impose upon an occupier any obligation in respect of risks willingly accepted by the visitor.'

and that, if it is shown that Hugh's death was as a result of his own foolhardiness, Foulfoods Ltd may be able to escape liability. However, from the facts, there is evidence that at the time of Geoffrey's purported rescue, Evan was still slipping down the pole and was still in danger. It is therefore arguable that Hugh acted quite reasonably in his brave attempt to rescue Evan. On the facts it can also be argued that it was foreseeable that if Foulfoods Ltd put a member of the public in danger, a brave person might step in to rescue them. See *Hayes* v *Harwood* [1935] KB 146 and *Videan* v *British Transport Commission* [1963] 2 QB 650. Therefore my conclusion on this point is that Foulfoods Ltd may not be able to escape liability because Hugh's death was their fault and not his. His wife therefore has an action against Foulfoods Ltd for damages in tort.

Before proceedings are issued it will be necessary to obtain evidence of the cause of Hugh's death in order to establish a link between his death and the events of that day.

I also advise that a sample of the soup in the vat be taken and sent for analysis in a laboratory. If it is found to contain poisonous substances then both Evan's and Hugh's case will be strengthened, in that it could be further evidence of Foulfood Ltd's negligence.

To conclude, I advise that Evan's father be asked to bring an action against Foulfoods Ltd on Evan's behalf alleging breach of the common law duty of care under s2 of the Occupiers' Liability Act 1957 and asking for damages to compensate Evan for the pain and suffering he endured during his illness. I also advise Hugh's widow that she may be entitled to damages to compensate her for her bereavement, funeral expenses, and husband's loss of earnings during his lost years. She has two rights of action, both statutory: these are a claim on behalf of her husband's estate under the Law Reform (Miscellaneous Provisions) Act 1934 and a claim on behalf of their children, if any, under the Fatal Accidents Act 1976. The two rights of action are entirely separate, though they would be founded on the same cause of action. She should, therefore, bring an action against Foulfoods Ltd whilst bearing in mind that if the court considers Hugh to have been negligent regarding his own safety, a deduction may be made from the sum of damages recoverable by her under the Law Reform (Contributory Negligence) Act 1945. This shall be in proportion to the extent to which he is assessed to have brought about his own death.

QUESTION THREE

In January Agnes was aged 85 and living in her own home which she owned. Her daughter Brenda thought that she was becoming too frail and forgetful to continue living on her own and wanted her to get a place in sheltered accommodation run by the local council. Ths council said that Agnes's condition would have to be independently assessed by the two doctors, one appointed by Brenda and one chosen by the council. The two doctors, Cyril (Brenda's nominee) and Daniel, visited Agnes. She was lively during the visit and the doctors reported that she was a fit and robust lady, in good condition for her age and well able to live on her own. She was refused a place in the sheltered housing.

Brenda immediately had expensive work done to adapt her own home so that her mother could come and live with her. However in April before she was able to move Agnes wandered out one night, could not find her way home and fell over in the darkness breaking both hips. She has been in hospital ever since and is unlikely to be well enough to go to live with Brenda.

Advise Agnes and Brenda.

University of London LLB Examination
(for External Students) Law of Tort June 1994 Q3

General Comment

At first glance, this question may appear to be a professional negligence question. However, in reality it requires the student to address all the elements of the tort of negligence, namely duty, breach, causation and loss. It is framed in such a way as to raise doubts under each of these heads.

Skeleton Solution

Duty: Did the council owe a duty of care? If so, what is the extent of that duty and to what extent did the council fulfil its duty? Did the doctors owe a similar duty of care?

Breach: Did the council breach its duty? Did the doctors breach theirs?

Causation: Agnes wandered out alone, could not find her way home and fell over in the darkness breaking her hips. Was this series of events caused by any breach of duty by the council and/or the doctors?

Loss: Agnes suffered physical injury. Brenda carried out expensive work on her home in preparation for her mother's arrival. That expense appears to have been wasted. Was the injury to Agnes and/or the financial loss to Brenda foreseeable?

Suggested Solution

Agnes and her daughter Brenda first approached the council with a view to moving Agnes into council-run sheltered accommodation in January. Before the council would provide a place, they required an independent medical assessment of Agnes by two doctors, one appointed by Brenda, and one appointed by the council.

Following the assessment by the two doctors, opining that Agnes was fit and capable of living alone, the council refused to provide sheltered housing. Brenda immediately had expensive work done to adapt her home so that her mother could move in. Before Agnes could move in, however, she wandered out one night in April, could not find her way home, and fell over in the darkness, breaking her hips. It is now unlikely that Agnes will move into Brenda's house.

The facts outlined in the question suggest a possible claim in negligence against the council and/or the doctors. The tort of negligence has been defined by Winfield and Jolowicz (*The Law of Torts*, 13th edn, p72) in the following terms:

'Negligence as a tort is the breach of a legal duty to take care which results in damage, undesired by the defendant, to the plaintiff.'

At this stage of my advice to Agnes and Brenda, it is necessary to consider whether the council, and/or the doctors owed any duty of care to either Agnes, and/or Brenda.

A duty of care is imposed on a party in the following terms, set out by Lord Atkin in the seminal case of *Donoghue* v *Stevenson* [1932] AC 562:

'You must take reasonable care to avoid acts or omissions which you can reasonably foresee would be likely to injure your neighbour. Who, then, in law is my neighbour? The answer seems to be – persons who are closely and directly affected by my act that I ought reasonably to have them in contemplation as being so affected when I am directing my mind to the acts or omissions which are called in question.'

If a duty exists, it is necessary to define the extent of that duty. According to Lord Keith in the decision of the House of Lords in *Governors of the Peabody Donation Fund* v *Sir Lindsay Parkinson & Co Ltd* [1984] 3 WLR 953:

'The true question in each case is whether the particular defendant owed to the particular plaintiff a duty of care having the scope which is contended for, and whether he was in breach of that duty with consequent loss to the plaintiff.'

Brenda was obviously concerned about Agnes, and as a result she went to the council. In those circumstances, it would appear that the council was aware of Brenda's concerns, and owed a duty of care to both Agnes and Brenda, such duty being of the nature of ensuring that Agnes was offered sheltered accommodation if she needed it.

The council, in my opinion, discharged that duty by providing a system whereby two independent doctors, including one nominated by Brenda, were appointed to assess the need, if any, of Agnes. It is difficult to argue that the council could have done any more for Agnes and/or Brenda.

Having been appointed, the two doctors also owed a duty of care to Agnes and/or Brenda, to assess Agnes for the purpose of recommending whether or not she needed sheltered accommodation. The level of that duty was laid down by McNair J in *Bolam* v *Friern Hospital Management Committee* [1957] 1 WLR 582 as follows:

'Where you get a situation which involves the use of some special skill or competence, then the test as to whether there has been negligence or not is not the test of the man on the top of the Clapham omnibus, because he has not got this special skill. The test is the standard of the ordinary skilled man exercising and professing to have that special skill ... he is not guilty of negligence if he has acted in accordance with a practice accepted as proper by a responsible body of medical men skilled in that particular act.'

Thus, in order to determine whether or not Cyril and Daniel (the doctors) breached their respective duties, it would be necessary to consider precisely what they did in purporting to assess Agnes, and whether or not their assessment technique complied with 'a practice accepted as proper by a responsible body of medical men'.

Even if it could be shown that the doctors, and either or both of them, acted negligently in assessing that Agnes was able to live alone, it would still be necessary to show that their breach of duty caused the loss and injury suffered by Agnes and Brenda.

Agnes wandered out of her home and fell over. These events took place only three months after Brenda first approached the council. It is not evident from the facts given in the question how quickly Agnes would have been re-housed if the assessment had recommended her move. If she would not have been moved in that short period of time in any event, the doctors' breach, if found, would not have caused her injury.

This is the 'but for' test as stated by Lord Denning in *Cork* v *Kirby MacLean Ltd* [1952] 2 All ER 402 as follows:

'... if the damage would not have happened but for a particular fault, then the fault is the cause of the damage; if it would have happened just the same, fault or no fault, the fault is not the cause of the damage.'

Equally, the doctors could argue that their acts or omissions caused Agnes to remain at home, but did not cause her to go out and get lost and/or injured. The level of Agnes' disability at the time of the assessment and the foreseeability of such an occurrence would determine whether or not the doctors' acts or omissions were causative of the injury.

Brenda's loss was immediate, in that she acted on the report of the doctors by adapting her home. If the doctors were negligent, they caused her loss. However, Brenda cannot be said to have relied upon the expertise of the doctors, in that her actions indicate that she did not agree with their assessment. Thus her expenditure does not fall into the *Hedley Byrne & Co Ltd* v *Heller & Partners Ltd* ([1964] AC 465) category of cases.

Brenda may still be able to claim for the expenditure by relying on *Ross* v *Caunters* ([1980] Ch 297) pure economic loss. That case could not be accommodated within the Hedley Byrne doctrine because the plaintiff had not relied upon the skill of the defendant. But the plaintiff did suffer pure economic loss (as has Brenda) and in finding for the plaintiff Megarry VC relied upon the judgments of Mason and Gibbs JJ in *Caltex Oil (Australia) Pty Ltd* v *The Dredge 'Willemstad'* (1976) 11 ALR 227.

The test which they posited was that the defendant should be held liable for economic loss caused by his negligent conduct when he can reasonably foresee that the specific plaintiff, as opposed to a general class of persons, will suffer financial loss as a result of his negligence.

Whether or not Brenda's financial expenditure could have been foreseen by the doctors will depend on their degree of knowledge of her relationship with Agnes, and her plans in the event of a refusal to re-house by the council.

The doctors might argue that even if the expenditure could be foreseen, the fact that it was wasted was not caused by their negligence. So, if Agnes' injuries were not caused by the doctor's negligence, nor could the fact of the wasted costs be caused by the doctors' negligence.

This brings the whole question of foreseeability into issue. A defendant is only liable for losses which directly result from his negligence in circumstances where some loss is foreseeable.

In Agnes' case the distinction between the tests laid down in *Re Polemis and Furness, Withy & Co* [1921] 3 KB 560 (directness of loss) and *Overseas Tankship (UK) Ltd* v *Morts Dock & Engineering Co, The Wagon Mound (No 1)* [1961] AC 388 (reasonably foreseeable loss) is of importance.

The essential question is whether it could be foreseen that Agnes would suffer any physical damage if she was not placed in sheltered accommodation. If so, according to the Polemis test, if the doctors were negligent, they would be liable for her injuries if it was a direct result of their negligent assessment.

The *Wagon Mound (No 1)* test requires that the risk of loss suffered must be reasonably foreseeable to the reasonable man, and not a risk that the reasonable man would dismiss as being far-fetched.

Again, the question of foreseeability of physical injury caused by Agnes wandering out of her house is a question of fact, and would depend on the level of knowledge of the doctors regarding Agnes' tendency to wander and to get lost, and the likelihood of her falling down and becoming injured.

In conclusion, it is apparent that both Agnes and Brenda face a number of obstacles if they are to prove that the doctors in this case have been negligent. Even if negligence is established, they face similar difficulties in proving causation and foreseeability of the loss and damage they have suffered.

QUESTION FOUR

Provincial TV, a local television channel, presented a series of programmes in 1994 under the general title of 'Police Probe'. Before the series started, publicity material stated that it would focus on arousing public concern about inconclusive local police investigations which had not led to convictions.

In the first two programmes it was suggested that the police might have been improperly induced not to press charges. The third programme concerned investigations into sexual offences. It included a reconstruction of a police interview with a man described as 'the only suspect questioned' in connection with a particular rape in 1988, for which no-one had ever been charged. He was described as having 'a previous criminal record'. Fictitious names were used and the programme made clear that the parts were played by actors. The actual man questioned in 1988 was Thomas Smith who had had one conviction, when a student, of dishonestly travelling on a train without paying the fare. The actor portraying the detective very closely resembled John Robinson, an officer who joined the local police in 1990.

Advise Thomas Smith and John Robinson whether either has a cause of action in defamation.

University of London LLB Examination
(for External Students) Law of Tort June 1994 Q4

General Comment

This is a question on the tort of defamation, in particular, libel. The general principles of defamation should first of all be addressed by way of introduction, followed by an analysis of the law as it applies to the facts of the problem. The next stage is to deal with any potential defences that may be raised by the defendant even if, in the final analysis, a court may find that they do not in fact apply. The final paragraph should conclude the essay, by advising Thomas and John.

Skeleton Solution

Introduction – distinguish libel and slander – apply relevant law to facts of problem – plaintiff must prove that statement was defamatory and that he was the subject of it – plaintiff must prove that statement was published – defence of justification – defence of fair comment – conclusion.

Suggested Solution

This question raises issues in the tort of defamation. Defamation is the publication of a statement which reflects on a person's reputation and tends to lower him in the estimation of right-thinking members of society generally or tends to make them shun or avoid him: *Sim* v *Stretch* [1936] 2 All ER 1237.

It is first of all necessary to distinguish the two forms of defamation, libel and slander. Libel is a statement or representation in permanent form such as a book or newspaper. Slander is a statement or representation which is conveyed in a non-permanent form, such as by spoken words or gestures. Under the Defamation Act 1952, radio and television broadcasts are treated as a publication in a permanent form. Therefore, in the present case, if the Provincial TV material is held to be defamatory, it will be a libel rather than a slander. The advantage to a plaintiff in suing for libel as against slander is that libel is actionable per se, which means that proof of special damage (ie temporal or material damage) is not required.

In order to succeed in an action for defamation, the plaintiff must first of all prove that the statement was defamatory in accordance with the description given by Lord Atkin in *Sim* v *Stretch*. It is a question of law for the judge to decide whether or not the words used are capable of bearing a defamatory meaning and, if so, it is then for the jury to decide as a matter of fact whether they are defamatory. In the present case, if the TV programmes were found to lower the reputation of Thomas Smith or John Robinson then, prima facie, each would be free to pursue a claim for defamation.

The next thing a plaintiff must prove is that he is the subject of the defamatory statement. In the present case this presents problems for both Thomas Smith and John Robinson as neither of them is actually named in the programmes.

However, in the case of *Morgan* v *Odhams Press Ltd* [1971] 1 WLR 1239 it was held that the plaintiff need not be named, nor does it matter if there is no 'key or pointer' indicating that it refers to him, provided that people might reasonably draw such an inference. If Thomas or John can adduce evidence to satisfy this test, then it will probably be found that there was a defamatory statement made against them.

Another aspect of whether or not there is a reference to the plaintiff, according to *Knupffer* v *London Express Newspaper Ltd* [1944] AC 116, is if the defamatory statement is directed at a class of persons (in the present case the police). If this is the case no individual member of that class may sue unless there is some indication that a particular plaintiff is implicated, such as in John's case by using an actor who very closely resembles him.

It must also be proved by the plaintiff that the statement was published to at least one person other than the plaintiff or the defendant's spouse. This test is easily satisfied in the present case as the programmes were presented on television.

If these three tests can be satisfied by either Thomas or John, then they have established a claim in defamation. However, this does not necessarily mean that they will succeed as there are a number of defences to defamation. In particular, there are two defences that may assist Provincial TV to successfully defend an action, namely, justification and fair comment.

If the defendant raises the defence of justification (truth) then he bears the burden of proof and, if he succeeds, it is an absolute defence. He need only show that the statement is substantially true. An interesting point raised here is the fact of Thomas' previous conviction, the potential defamation. Section 13 of the Civil Evidence Act 1968 says that proof of conviction is conclusive evidence that the plaintiff committed the crime. The fact that the plaintiff's conviction is spent under the Rehabilitation of Offenders Act 1974 does not defeat the defence of justification. However, if it is a spent conviction, the defence can be defeated by proof of malice. Applying this to the present case, it is unlikely that Thomas would be able to prove malice in what essentially is a piece of investigative journalism and therefore there is a high likelihood that the defence will succeed.

The other defence, which may possibly assist Provincial TV, is that of 'fair comment'. It is a defence that the statement is a fair comment on a matter of public interest. This defence has its basis in the principle of free speech which has long been recognised by our courts (see for example *Slim* v *Daily Telegraph Ltd* [1968] 2 QB 157. It is a question of law for the judge to decide whether or not the matter is one of public interest: *South Hetton Coal Co Ltd* v *North-Eastern News Association Ltd* [1894] 1 QB 133, although it is highly probable that the subject matter of the present case would be held to be so. Indeed, it was held in *Kelly* v *Sherlock* (1866) LR 1 QB 686 that it includes the conduct of every public man and every public institution. The comment must be an expression of opinion and not an assertion of fact, and must be fair. In *Slim* v *Daily Telegraph* it was said that the test was that of 'an honest man expressing his genuine opinion'. Therefore, this defence will succeed against Thomas and John if the TV programmes were presented as opinion rather than as fact (if they were presented as fact then the defence of justification is the appropriate defence).

In conclusion, I would advise both Thomas and John not to pursue a claim for defamation against Provincial TV as, even if they can establish their claim, there is a more than reasonable prospect of Provincial TV raising a successful defence. When this is allied to the fact that legal aid is not available to plaintiffs in defamation actions and the fact that any damages awarded are assessed by the jury, and may only be nominal, it is my opinion that the litigation risk is too great.

QUESTION FIVE

'The maxim res ipsa loquitur makes it easier for a plaintiff to prove negligence; justice requires the creation of a similar rule for proof of causation.'

Discuss.

University of London LLB Examination
(for External Students) Law of Tort June 1994 Q5

General Comment

This is a question that involves discussing the basis for proving a charge of negligence and assessing, in particular, whether two aspects of the negligence equation require, or should require, different standards of proof.

Skeleton Solution

Res ipsa loquitur – causation – negligence – proof – reform.

Suggested Solution

It is generally understood that in negligence actions it is for the plaintiff to prove that the defendant owed him a legal duty, which by reason of an act or omission on the part of the defendant has not been effected. The question of proving that failure to discharge the duty owed is at the heart of discussing res ipsa loquitur and causation. The question boldly asserts that the former makes it easier to prove negligence. As the law stands res ipsa loquitur does not affect the burden of proving negligence; that remains at all times on the plaintiff. The presumption that is encapsulated within the maxim is a presumption of fact, rather than it being one of law. The question of the relative easiness of proving negligence must therefore depend on the factual circumstances that lie behind the substantive allegation. This being the position, it seems difficult to use res ipsa loquitur as a justification for changing a central plank of the burden of proof.

The essence of the phrase res ipsa loquitur is that the thing speaks for itself. At the most basic level, the court requires no proof of the negligence other than the incident at the heart of the action and does not concern itself with the specifics of what the defendant did or did not do. This indicates that rather than being a rule of substantive law, it is actually an evidential issue for the court. The maxim has three central components:

a) the defendant must be in control of the thing that causes the damage;

b) the accident must be such as would not ordinarily occur without the intervention of negligence;

c) there must be an absence of explanation for the accident.

If the circumstances arise in which these conditions are satisfied, it is then necessary to deal with the most important aspect of res ipsa loquitur: the consideration of what effect the maxim has on a particular situation. These considerations have given rise to considerable judicial discussion. There are, in fact, two schools of thought on this matter. One of these takes a broad view of the maxim that coincides with the interpretation placed on it in the question. If the plaintiff is able to show a prima facie case in negligence, it then falls on the defendant to prove that he was not negligent. This means that the burden of proof must shift, invoking a completely different basis for determining liability in negligence. In the case of *Henderson* v *Henry E Jenkins & Sons* [1970] AC 282, the House of Lords considered, in response to the prima facie case of negligence raised by the plaintiff, the defendants had not managed to rebut that prima facie case. If this represented the true position in law, it would be possible to say that in having res ipsa loquitur at his disposal a plaintiff would have an easier task in proving negligence.

However, in *Ng Chun Pui* v *Lee Chuen Tat* [1988] RTR 298, the Privy Council looked again at the issue. It was Lord Griffiths, who said that:

'It is misleading to talk of the burden of proof shifting to the defendant in a res ipsa loquitur situation. The burden of proving negligence rests throughout the case on the plaintiff.'

This, then, represents not only the second school of thought, but also the current state of the law. If the defendant is in a position which enables him to rebut any inference that res ipsa loquitur raises, then the plaintiff has failed to prove that the defendant was negligent. This helps to put the maxim firmly in an understandable context. It shows that to consider that the maxim makes the plaintiff's task easier is to miss the point of it, and perhaps to give it an importance that it does not deserve.

This leaves the examination of the second part of the question in a state of crux. There is, in reality, no real difference between causation and res ipsa loquitur, insofar as they relate to what the plaintiff has to show in order to prove negligence. In both situations, the plaintiff has to show that his loss has been caused by the negligence of the defendant. In the circumstances that were present in the case of *Hotson* v *East Berkshire Area Health Authority* [1987] AC 50, it was for the plaintiff to prove that the injury to his hip was caused by the negligence of the defendant. The House of Lords held that it was for the proof to be on the balance of probabilities, and in that case, on that standard, the injury was caused by the plaintiff falling out of a tree, rather than by any subsequent failures in medical treatment. The case is a prime example of the more restrictive test that is now in place in this area. At one point, it did seem that a liberal interpretation, which allowed an increase in the risk of damage to permit a successful claim, without proving actual damage (*McGhee* v *National Coal Board* [1973] 1 WLR 1), was to be followed. The retreat from this position was not very long in coming and reflects the widely held view, that it is not for the courts to dramatically alter the basis of tort liability. The desire is for certainty in this area, for a plaintiff to know that it is for him to prove, that on the balance of probabilities, the defendant's breach of duty was the cause of any subsequent loss. It is possible to consider more and more situations in which the plaintiff has a harder job proving causation. As technology increases and medical boundaries are broken, so the plaintiff has to deal with uncertainties that make the job of proving causation nigh on impossible. If Parliament was to decide that the causation aspect of considering negligence claims should evolve, it may, then, be appropriate to do away with it. However, it is difficult to imagine a set of circumstances where this would be feasible. Justice requires certainty and also that a case can be proved on the evidence before the court. To take causation out of the negligence equation, therefore, would probably necessitate a complete overhaul of the standards and burdens of proof.

It seems that the court has to tread a very fine line when it comes to consideration of both aspects under discussion. It further seems that it is the evidence before the court that will hold sway and it is hard to draw strict academic principles from what remains a subjective assessment of what is offered by both sides. The case of proving the causative link in negligence is a difficult one but there are certain solid foundations, in terms of burden and standard of proof, that all plaintiffs and defendants must work from.

QUESTION SIX

a) What can amount to 'unlawful means' for the purposes of torts involving intentional infliction of economic loss? In what circumstances do unlawful means have to be established?

b) The League for Decency usually arranges to hire the hall of Barsetshire Technical College for its meetings and social functions. Mrs Proudy, the secretary of the League, heard recently that the college is to allow a pop group (the Hirams) to give a concert at the hall at which some of the musicians will appear in the nude. She telephoned the college and said, 'I am aghast. Unless you cancel these arrangements, I cannot believe that the League will ever want to use the college for its functions.

Advise the Hirams.

University of London LLB Examination (for External Students) Law of Tort June 1994 Q6

221

General Comment

The first part demands fairly brief discussion of a very difficult concept. There is no clear-cut answer and the best approach is to consider the requirement of unlawful means in the various economic torts. The second part looks at a fairly standard problem which is a variant of *Lumley* v *Gye*.

Skeleton Solution

a) Interference with a subsisting contract – intimidation – conspiracy.

b) Tort of interference with a subsisting contract (not intimidation): lawful means – direct persuasion – causing breach of contract.

Suggested Solution

a) The economic torts aim to protect business interests from unlawful interference. The means used to cause that interference will very often themselves be unlawful. It is also the case that at times unlawful means must be established for the interference to be deemed tortious.

Interference with a subsisting contract is perhaps the broadest of the economic torts. In the well-known case of *Lumley* v *Gye* (1853) 2 El & Bl 216, the defendant persuaded a famous operatic singer to refuse to perform at the plaintiff's theatre, in breach of her contract. This action was tortious, but – although the intention was to inflict economic loss – it is arguable whether such direct persuasion amounted to unlawful means.

However, preventing a contract from being performed by a trespass to the goods forming the subject matter of the contract (*GWK Ltd* v *Dunlop Rubber Co Ltd* (1926) 42 TLR 375), for example, would clearly amount to direct intervention by unlawful means. Between these two cases, there are many different examples of conduct which may or may not amount to unlawful conduct.

While direct persuasion aimed at interference with a subsisting contract does not require unlawful means to be tortious (as held by the Court of Appeal in *DC Thomson & Co Ltd* v *Deakin* [1952] Ch 646), direct and indirect intervention with a subsisting contract do require unlawful conduct. An example of the latter would be where A brings about a breach of the contract between B and C by causing X to take unlawful industrial action (*JT Stratford & Sons Ltd* v *Lindley* [1965] AC 269). However, it might be said that such a rule is somewhat arbitrary; it means that A's liability to C turns on what may be no more than a purely technical contravention of the law.

The economic tort of intimidation requires a threat to B which A has made in order to cause B to act to his financial detriment or to the detriment of C. The threat is of an unlawful act and, of course, the unlawful act may never occur. Further, what B does as a result of the threat need not itself be unlawful. In *Rookes* v *Barnard* [1964] AC 1129, the House of Lords held that the tort also extends to A threatening to break his contract with B unless B acts to the detriment of C.

Conspiracy as a tort was established in *Crofter Hand Woven Harris Tweed Co Ltd v Veitch* [1942] AC 435. In *Crofter*, their Lordships held that, if the predominant purpose of the combination is to injure another in his trade or business, then – if damage occurs – the tort is made out. In other words, the means themselves may not be unlawful. On the other hand, in the recent case of *Lonrho plc v Fayed* [1992] 1 AC 448, the House of Lords reaffirmed that a conspiracy involving unlawful means would be tortious, notwithstanding that the predominant purpose was not to injure the plaintiff. There must be an intention to injure, but – as Lord Denning MR put it in *Lonrho v Shell Petroleum Co (No 2)* [1982] AC 173 – it may be mixed with other motives.

It may be that there is a general principle which underlies at least parts of the economic torts: it is a tort intentionally to inflict economic harm by using unlawful means. What constitutes unlawful means will cover crimes, conduct that is itself tortious or amounts to a breach of contract, though even these examples are arguable. However, a single definition is impossible to formulate and that perhaps reflects the range of the economic torts themselves.

b) The League for Decency (LD) wants to interfere with the contract Barsetshire Technical College (BTC) has entered into with the Hirams (H). It appears that LD habitually hires BTC's hall but is not under any contract to do so. Therefore LD's actions would not involve any breach by them.

LD is attempting to interfere with this contract by persuading BTC to cancel the arranged concert. This is a form of the tort of interference with a subsisting contract (*Lumley v Gye*). The persuasion is direct and, although the means used are not themselves unlawful, the intention is to cause BTC to break its contract with H, and the interference is therefore actionable by H. However, LD might try to raise the defence of justification by reason of its moral obligation to prevent nudity on stage, applying *Brimelow v Casson* [1924] 1 Ch 302.

Although LD is making a threat, it is the threat of something LD may lawfully do, in that LD is not bound to continue to hire BTC's hall in the future. Therefore, this does not amount to intimidation.

Consequently, I would advise H that, if they can show they have suffered damage, they may sue LD in the tort of interference with a subsisting contract, even though LD's means are themselves lawful.

QUESTION SEVEN

Statutory regulations impose upon employers and employees in the chemical manufacturing industry an obligation to ensure that prescribed protective equipment (including special gloves) are worn when workers are handling chemicals. The regulations apply to the premises of Stinks Ltd. George, Hamish and John, who are all employed there, were engaged in loading chemicals on to a lorry and were all wearing the prescribed clothing. George and Hamish were passing casks containing chemicals up to John who was standing on the back of the lorry. A fly went into John's eye suddenly and he removed his glove to wipe it away. George did not notice and passed a cask up to him. John was unable to hold it. Some of the chemical spilled over his hand. He screamed in agony and clung on to Hamish in desperation.

John suffered serious burns to his hand. He will be permanently disfigured and will not be able to obtain manual employment. Hamish has suffered from severe depression since the incident and has not been able to return to work.

University of London LLB Examination
(for External Students) Law of Tort June 1994 Q7

General Comment

This question is specifically addressed as a possible breach of statutory duty, although it could be argued that the employer owed a like duty in the tort of negligence. The importance of the dual heads of liability is that the statutory duty could be pitched at a higher level than the duty of care in negligence. The question does not indicate the level of duty imposed by the regulations, but suggests that the duty is one of 'strict liability'. Similarly, the question does not actually specify what is required of the student, and this answer is based on the presumption that John and Hamish require advice on liability and assessment of damages.

Skeleton Solution

The concept of employers' liability – statutory duty and strict liability – distinction between strict liability and liability for negligent acts or omissions – method of assessment of damages in personal injuries cases.

Suggested Solution

If John and Hamish are to rely on the tort of negligence as the basis of their claim against their employer, they face an onerous task.

An employer owes certain duties to his employees. Those duties are derived from both common law and statutory sources. For many years an employer was not liable for injury negligently inflicted by another employee on the ground that the employee had consented to the risks involved in his employment: *Bartonshill Coal Co* v *Reid* (1858) 3 Macq 266. This doctrine was finally abolished by s1 of the Law Reform (Personal Injuries) Act 1948.

The employer may now be vicariously liable for the negligence of his employee committed in the course of his employment or for breach of his own non-delegable duty.

In the question set, any negligence appears to be limited to (a) John removing his glove; (b) George failing to notice and passing him a cask; and (c) John clinging on to Hamish in desperation. The question does not specifically ask, but it must be presumed that John wishes to claim damages for his burns injury, and Hamish for his depression and loss of earnings.

I will first address John's potential claim. As against his employer, a claim would lie for the negligence, if any, of George, for which the employer would be vicariously liable, and for the primary negligence of the employer for failing to provide a safe system of work (see *General Cleaning Contractors* v *Christmas* [1953] AC 180).

John will be in great difficulty if he is to claim negligence in respect of either of these heads of allegedly negligent acts. There is nothing to suggest that George was negligent in passing the cask up in circumstances where he and Hamish were engaged in an ongoing process of 'passing casks' to John. That is a matter open to argument on the facts.

Similarly, the employer appears to have discharged his duty to provide a safe system of work by providing gloves.

However, John may have a claim for breach of statutory duty, namely the regulations cited in the question. The duty imposed was an 'obligation to ensure that prescribed protective clothing (including special gloves) are worn when workers are handling chemicals'. If that duty is strict, it matters not that the act of a fly causing John to suddenly remove his glove to wipe his eye was in no way the fault of the employer.

It will be left to the court to determine whether these regulations afford a remedy to an individual employee who suffers injury as a result of breach: *Cutler* v *Wandsworth Stadium Ltd* [1949] AC 398. The court will look to see if the regulations specifically provide for a remedy, and if not, will determine whether the regulations are directed at protecting a class of persons as opposed to society as a whole.

In this case, the effect of the regulation is to provide protection to employees in John's position, and it is highly likely that the court would find that he is entitled to a personal remedy, namely compensation, if the employer breached the duty: *John Summers & Sons Ltd* v *Frost* [1955] AC 740.

Volenti is not a defence to breach of an employer's statutory duty. However, the defence that the employer did all that was reasonably practicable is often provided in regulations (see *Larner* v *British Steel plc* [1933] 1 All ER 102).

There is no information in the question as to whether such a defence is provided in the regulations in issue. If not, it will be assumed that the liability is strict. In view of the unexpected way in which John came to remove his gloves, nothing short of strict liability will assist him. I do not think he has a claim in negligence, nor for breach of statutory duty if the employer's liability is limited to doing what is reasonably practicable.

It should be noted that a person who is the subject of a statutory duty cannot generally discharge that duty by entrusting it to someone else.

Presuming that the duty is strict, it is clear that the breach of duty (ie not ensuring that the gloves were worn for that short period during which John suffered the injury) caused John's injury, and he would therefore be able to claim damages.

The issue of contributory negligence arises, and would go to reduce the employer's liability in a negligence claim, and arguably a breach of statutory duty claim. Although the courts are very reluctant to find contributory negligence in employer/employee cases, as the regulations are designed to protect the employees (see *Caswell* v *Powell Duffryn Associated Collieries Ltd* [1940] AC 152), they will do so if the employee has himself been very foolish or fails himself to comply with the regulations, as in *Bux* v *Slough Metals Ltd* [1974] 1 All ER 262 where an employee removed protective goggles which were misted up.

John's reason for removing his gloves is apparently more legitimate, and verging as it does on an 'emergency' or instinctive situation (see eg *Jones* v *Boyce* (1816) 1 Stark 493), it is unlikely that there would be any finding of contributory negligence.

Hamish's claim is in some respects similar to John's, in that he will only have a claim if the duty is a strict one. He has an added difficulty in that he has to prove that the breach of statutory duty regarding John wearing gloves caused his loss, and that the loss suffered is a recoverable loss.

In terms of causation, the employer will perhaps argue that John's act of grabbing Hamish was a 'novus actus', breaking the chain of causation instituted by the initial breach. The court may well take the view that injury by chemicals, and specifically, by shock brought about by seeing the effects of a chemicals-related injury, was foreseeable, so not too remote. Lord Reid in *Hughes* v *Lord Advocate* [1963] AC 837 said:

'... a defendant is liable, although the damage may be a good deal greater in extent that was foreseeable. He can only escape liability if the damage can be regarded as differing in kind from what was foreseeable.'

Finally, for Hamish to succeed his 'depression' must fall into the recognised category of 'nervous shock', in that it must be more than simply grief and sorrow and must be a pathological nervous injury (see *Brice* v *Brown* [1984] 1 All ER 997).

If the extent of his depression is of a clinical nature, he will be able to recover if he falls into the category of persons whose relationship to the primary injured person is sufficiently close to justify the imposition of liability on the tortfeasor. The test of proximity has been recognised in several cases, and it is submitted that a worker whose co-employee grabs hold of him whilst the two are engaged in a joint task is sufficiently proximate for his nervous shock to be foreseeable.

In conclusion, the cases of John and Hamish hinge on the degree of liability attaching to the regulations. If strict, their claims have a good chance of success. If there is a statutory defence within the particular regulations of 'reasonable practicability', I feel that their respective claims will fail.

QUESTION EIGHT

Luke is unemployed but has enrolled on a government training scheme. He is sent three days each week for work experience to the offices of Newfield Industries plc. The office manager Matilda was sent to a conference one day in a town forty miles away and was told to take the company car. She asked Luke to go with her as part of his work experience. She also thought that she might be drinking and that Luke could then drive the car, but did not tell Luke this. Both Luke and Matilda knew that he was not allowed to drive the company car. On the way back Matilda stopped for a drink at a pub and asked Luke to take over the driving. Luke drove out of the pub car park without looking and caused Neil, a passing motor cyclist, to swerve. Neil struck a tree and was seriously injured.

Advise Neil as to any rights of action in tort.

University of London LLB Examination
(for External Students) Law of Tort June 1994 Q8

General Comment

This is a question that involves a consideration of the relationship between employer and employee, and the way in which tortious acts fit into that relationship.

Skeleton Solution

Negligence – vicarious liability – employer/employee – course of employment.

Suggested Solution

It is possible from a consideration of the parties mentioned in the question to discern a number of people who, on face value, could be considered responsible for Neil's accident. These range from Luke, the obvious cause of the accident, through to Newfield Industries, the party most likely to be able to bear any costs, and even to an external body, like the Motor Insurance Bureau.

It seems appropriate to begin with Luke, as the driver of the car that caused the accident. The central difficulty with Neil initiating proceedings against any individual defendant is that they will either be impecunious or certainly not in a financial position to meet any claim. So, the issue of culpability becomes submerged in the reality of the economic situation and highlights that this problem involves discussion of practicalities as well as academic points. In the light of Luke's unemployed status, it seems unlikely that he will be able to compensate Neil. It seems probable that the same will apply to Matilda who, although she is in employment, is not likely to be in a position to pay the sorts of sums that can be involved in serious personal injury actions.

It then falls to consider Newfield Industries plc, who would be in a much better position to meet the claim, if not through any insurance they may have, then certainly through their position to pass on any losses. This, in essence, is the heart of the problem, namely whether Newfield Industries can be held vicariously liable for the actions of Luke and of Matilda. In order for the courts to find in favour of Neil, there are certain hurdles that such a claim must surmount. First, Newfield Industries will only be held responsible if a wrongful act has been committed by another person. There must have been a tortious act. It is difficult to see that there is any other interpretation to place on the incident in the light of the facts given in the question.

Second, Newfield Industries will only be responsible if it is possible to show a special relationship existing between them and the wrongdoer. This relationship has to be one recognised by law, and in reality this limb of liability only relates to the relationship between employer and employee. Matilda would obviously fall into the category of employee on the factual situation under discussion. There are, however, problems in relation to Luke and whether he is an employee of Newfield Industries. It seems probable that they would try to argue that any responsibility for Luke does not lie with them because he is on work experience as part of his government training scheme. In general terms, where an employer (A) 'lends' an employee to another employer (B), if that employee then commits a tortious act, it is difficult for A to shift any responsibility onto the temporary employer (B). It remains, however, a question of fact and it appears that the circumstances in this case would not allow Newfield Industries to deny that they controlled Luke. This being the case it seems undeniable that Luke would be seen as operating within the necessary special relationship.

The final hurdle will, in this case, prove the most difficult for Neil to establish, namely that Newfield Industries should be held vicariously liable for the actions of Luke. Neil needs to establish that Luke was acting in the course of his employment and so found a connection between Luke's act and his special relationship with

Newfield Industries. This involves considering a mixed question of law and of fact and considering whether, at the time of the accident, Luke and Matilda were undertaking unauthorised deviations from their work. It was in *Joel* v *Morrisson* (1834) 6 C & P 501 that the courts considered that a 'master' will not be liable for a 'servant's' actions, if the servant is on a frolic of his own. It is therefore for the courts to establish what is meant by a 'frolic of his own'. There is a suggestion in *Williams* v *A & W Hemphill Ltd* 1966 SLT 259, a Scottish case, that the actions must be solely for the selfish purposes of the employee. It therefore seems that stopping for a drink at the pub could not be seen as incidental to the journey and doing so takes the detour outside the course of their employment. It would also appear that the intentionally wrongful act by both Luke and Matilda, in allowing Luke to drive while knowing he was not permitted to do so, would take their actions outside the course of employment. Therefore, Neil appears not to have any recourse against Newfield Industries plc. However, mention should be made of *Ilkiw* v *Samuels* [1963] 1 WLR 991, where a lorry driver allowed a third party to move his lorry without ensuring that he was able and insured to do it. The employers were vicariously liable because the lorry driver was employed not only to drive the lorry but to be in charge of it. Likewise, it might be possible to argue that Matilda was in a similar position. The potential scope of an action against Newfield Industries would be limited but in advising Neil on a purely practical basis, it may be worth, at the very least, initiating proceedings.

Finally, for the sake of completeness and bearing in mind the difficulties that Neil would face in tackling Newfield Industries plc, mention must be made of the Motor Insurers' Bureau (MIB). Neil may find that in the event of his failing to succeed in levelling the blame for his accident at Newfield Industries, the MIB may meet the unsatisfied judgment, if Luke was not insured to drive the car that caused the accident.

APPENDIX

ANALYSIS OF PAST LONDON UNIVERSITY LLB TORT PAPERS (JUNE)

	1986	1987	1988	1989	1990	1991	1992	1993	1994
General liability in tort					•			•	
General defences		•							
Vicarious liability	•	•	•			•	•	•	•
Negligence: duty of care	•	•			•	•	•		•
Negligence: breach	•	•			•			•	
Negligence: causation & remoteness		•	•		•	•		•	•
Economic loss	•				•	•			
Negligent misstatement		•	•	•	•	•			
Nervous shock				•			•	•	•
Contributory negligence		•	•						
Statutory duty		•		•		•	•		•
Employers' liability		•				•	•		
Product liability			•	•				•	
Occupiers' liability	•	•		•	•	•	•		•
Nuisance, private & public	•	•	•	•	•	•	•	•	
Rylands & Fletcher	•		•	•		•		•	•
Animals		•	•		•				
Defamation	•	•	•	•	•	•	•	•	•
Trespass to the person	•		•	•	•	•	•		
Trespass to land	•						•		
Deceit, malicious falsehood, passing off									
Economic torts	•	•	•	•		•	•		•
Damages & other remedies	•		•				•	•	

HLT Publications

HLT books are specially planned and written to help you in every stage of your studies. Each of the wide range of textbooks is brought up-to-date annually, and the companion volumes of our Law Series are all designed to work together.

You can buy HLT books from your local bookshop, or in case of difficulty, order direct using this form,

The Law Series covers the following modules:

Administrative Law

Commercial Law

Company Law

Conflict of Laws

Constitutional Law

Contract Law

Criminal Law

Criminology

English Legal System

Equity and Trusts

European Union Law

Evidence

Family Law

Jurisprudence

Land Law

Law of International Trade

Legal Skills and System

Public International Law

Revenue Law

Succession

Tort

The HLT Law Series:

A comprehensive range of books for your law course, and the legal aspects of business and commercial studies.

Each module is covered by a comprehensive six-part set of books

● Textbook

● Casebook

● Revision Workbook

● Suggested Solutions, for:
  ● 1985-90
  ● 1991-94
  ● 1995

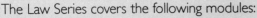

Module	Books required	Cost
To complete your order, please fill in the form overleaf	Postage	
	TOTAL	

Prices (including postage and packing in the UK): Textbooks £19.00; Casebooks £19.00; Revision Workbooks £10.00; Suggested Solutions (1985-90) £9.00, Suggested Solutions (1991-94) £6.00, Suggested Solutions (1995) £3.00.

For Europe, add 15% postage and packing (£20 maximum). For the rest of the world, add 40% for airmail (£35 maximum).

ORDERING

By telephone to 01892 724371, with your credit card to hand

By fax to 01892 724206 (giving your credit card details).

By post to:

HLT Publications,
The Gatehouse, Ruck Lane, Horsmonden, Tonbridge, Kent TN12 8EA

When ordering by post, please enclose full payment by cheque or banker's draft, or complete the credit card details below.

We aim to dispatch your books within 3 working days of receiving your order.

Name

Address

Postcode

Telephone

Total value of order, including postage: **£**

I enclose a cheque/banker's draft for the above sum, or

charge my ☐ Access/Mastercard ☐ Visa ☐ American Express

Card number

Expiry date

Signature

Date

Publications from **The Old Bailey Press**

Cracknell's Statutes

A full understanding of statute law is vital for any student, and this series presents the original wording of legislation, together with any amendments and substitutions and the sources of these changes.

Cracknell's Companions

Recognised as invaluable study aids since their introduction in 1961, this series summarises all the most important court decisions and acts, and features a glossary of Latin words, as well as full indexing.

Please telephone our Order Hotline on 01892 724371, or write to our order department, for full details of these series.